WHAT IS A CRIMINAL?

Bringing together a collection of essays by writers with diverse knowledge of the US criminal justice system, from those with personal experience in prison and on patrol to scholarly researchers, *What Is a Criminal?* explores the category of "criminal" through the human stories of those who bear and administer that label.

This book performs a rare feat in bringing together the perspectives of justice-impacted people, those who work in law enforcement and social services, and scholarly researchers. Each chapter is a compelling narrative sharing the experience and perspective of a unique person with knowledge of the justice system. The first section, "Incarceration, Reentry, and Rebuilding," gives a glimpse into the "black box" of prison, with firsthand accounts of daily life on the inside and the struggle to begin a new life after prison. Section 2, "Journeys in Law Enforcement," presents perspectives from police officers, school resource officers, and corrections officers who are working to better their communities. The third section, "Ripple Effects," addresses some of the broader impacts of the justice system, showing what it is like to be the child of an incarcerated parent, to be profiled, to be an undocumented immigrant, and to make art about the justice system. The final section, "Scholarly Perspectives," is comprised of accessible articles by academics who study law and crime. Each chapter stands alone as an individual story, but taken together they provide a uniquely nuanced view of the US justice system.

This book will be of interest to anyone who wants to know more about criminality, the US justice system, and the people involved in it. It is designed for a general audience, with accessible, compelling stories that will appeal to a variety of readers. It is an effective text for college and high school courses about crime and criminality, and provides excellent fodder for discussion in law enforcement and social services training programs or professional development workshops.

Katherine S. Gaudet is Associate Director of the University Honors Program and Faculty in Humanities at the University of New Hampshire. She holds a PhD in literature from the University of Chicago. Her scholarly interests revolve around the history of reading and how narratives shape social understandings of complex and difficult topics. She is currently working on a project about narratives of addiction.

"The best way to improve the criminal justice system and reduce incarceration is to keep people out of the justice system in the first place. Having worked as a career police officer and as a voice for reform, I believe *What Is a Criminal?* provides critical perspectives from those with lived experience on both sides of the law, academics, and reformers in understanding how to do so."

Lieutenant Diane M. Goldstein (Ret.), *Executive Director, Law Enforcement Action Partnership*

"Such a powerful combination of stories, narratives, and perspectives from scholars studying these issues. It was incredible to read the definition of what a criminal is before they walked us through their compelling story. Sharing the journeys of those in Law Enforcement is a great way to help change the narrative and humanize the work that is done in these fields. To end the book with the scholars is so wonderful. In legislative work, I tell people the only way we will ever get anything done is by combining the personal stories with the data. This book does that masterfully, and I can't wait for others to read this and then have a desire to get involved in criminal justice reform work."

David Garlock, *Criminal Justice Reform Leader*

WHAT IS A CRIMINAL?

Answers From Inside the US Justice System

Edited by Katherine S. Gaudet

Routledge
Taylor & Francis Group
LONDON AND NEW YORK

Designed cover image: David Wall / © Getty Images

First published 2023
by Routledge
4 Park Square, Milton Park, Abingdon, Oxon OX14 4RN

and by Routledge
605 Third Avenue, New York, NY 10158

Routledge is an imprint of the Taylor & Francis Group, an informa business

British Library Cataloguing-in-Publication Data
A catalogue record for this book is available from the British Library

Library of Congress Cataloging-in-Publication Data
Names: Gaudet, Katherine S., editor.
Title: What is a criminal? : answers from inside the US justice system / edited by: Katherine S. Gaudet.
Description: Milton Park, Abingdon, Oxon ; New York, NY : Routledge, 2022. | Includes bibliographical references and index.
Identifiers: LCCN 2022037008 (print) | LCCN 2022037009 (ebook) | ISBN 9780367770297 (hardback) | ISBN 9780367770273 (paperback) | ISBN 9781003169468 (ebook)
Subjects: LCSH: Criminal justice, Administration of—United States. | Criminal psychology—United States. | Crime—Sociological aspects. | Criminal anthropology.
Classification: LCC HV9950 .W53 2022 (print) | LCC HV9950 (ebook) | DDC 364.973—dc23/eng/20220823
LC record available at https://lccn.loc.gov/2022037008
LC ebook record available at https://lccn.loc.gov/2022037009

ISBN: 978-0-367-77029-7 (hbk)
ISBN: 978-0-367-77027-3 (pbk)
ISBN: 978-1-003-16946-8 (ebk)

DOI: 10.4324/9781003169468

Typeset in Bembo
by Apex CoVantage, LLC

CONTENTS

ACKNOWLEDGEMENTS

This book exists because of the generosity of those people who agreed to share their stories within it. For many of them, it was a struggle to delve into dark parts of their past and find ways to put the unimaginable onto the page. These writers and storytellers spent many hours and much effort on their contributions simply because they believed in the importance of putting these experiences and ideas into the world. My deepest thanks go to Alex, Anna, Blair, Bobby, Brendan, Christian, Diane, Lawan, McKenzie, Michelle, Jamel, Jasmine, Jennifer, Jessica, "John," Joseph, Justin, Patrick, Ra'Shaun, Seren, and Valena.

I could not have completed this work without the support of many colleagues at the University of New Hampshire. Catherine Peebles has been a steady supporter of me and of this project for many years, and I am deeply grateful for her encouragement and friendship. Alex Holznienkemper and Donna Perkins offered up their knowledge and passion to create a "What Is a Criminal?" lecture series, which became a series of remarkable conversations that is at the foundation of this book. The series was funded by the Saul O Sidore Memorial Foundation, and it was supported logistically and morally by Sandy Coit, and by Katie Umans and Steven Trzaskoma of the Center for the Humanities at UNH. I am grateful to Melissa Sprague for her careful and thoughtful assistance in preparing the manuscript, and to the Global Racial and Social Inequality Lab for funding Melissa's work. My Honors Program colleagues Kristen Butterfield-Ferrell, Emily Schoonmaker, and Andrew Ferris have supported this work through their interest and ideas, and by letting me slide at the office while I finished it. The National Endowment for the Humanities provided the initial funding for this project in the form of an "Enduring Questions" course development grant in 2015. The UNH students who have taken that course have been contributors to this book since before it was imagined, and I owe special thanks to the Fall 2021 class for their readings of some early drafts.

My husband, Jeff Gnecco, got me thinking about the law in the first place, and has done all he could to give me the space and time to make this book a reality. Thank you for always helping me think, learn, and grow.

INTRODUCTION

Katherine S. Gaudet

In 399 BCE, a 75-year-old man was sentenced to death. In his city, people accused of a crime had the right to a trial, and their fate was decided by a jury of their fellow citizens. It happened that this man, who was a philosopher, had a student who liked to write down his teacher's wise discourses. So today, we can read what Socrates said when he was accused of corrupting the youth of Athens (or, as Socrates sees it, helping them learn to think). Socrates's trial, recorded by his student Plato, is an example of a long-ago argument about what it means to be a criminal. Socrates was forced to drink poison hemlock because his peers decided his continued life would pose a grave threat to their community. In the modern United States, a justice system with roots in ancient Athenian principles metes out the same verdict (with varying sentences) to staggering numbers of people. More than 2400 years after Socrates's death, what it means to be a "criminal" remains a crucially important question.

Several years ago, I began teaching a college class called "What Is a Criminal?" I'm not a criminologist; my background is in literature. But I'm an American citizen, and it was becoming clear to me that the ways we think about criminality are of central importance to our society. As I've learned more about the topic, I've become convinced that it's important for anyone who cares about justice to learn about the criminal system and the people involved in it. Furthermore, I think it's essential to hear from people with firsthand knowledge, as well as those who have done sophisticated academic research. Criminality is such a complex, important topic that any single perspective will miss a great deal. The individual stories of people involved in the justice system often run counter to popular narratives, and in all cases offer context and depth.

While there are a lot of people who have deep knowledge of the justice system, many of them never talk to one another. People working in law enforcement, for example, may not be sharing their experiences with academics who are studying particular aspects of law and justice. Others may be passionate about reforming

DOI: 10.4324/9781003169468-1

the justice system, but have little idea what it's like to live and work inside it. This book is one attempt to bring these diverse kinds of knowledge together. It includes personal stories from people who have been incarcerated or treated as criminals, people who work in law enforcement, and people who strive to improve their local systems, as well as essays by academic researchers that provide historical and philosophical context. By reading these essays together, I hope readers will find that their perspective on the justice system becomes more open and nuanced.

"What Is a criminal?" is a deceptively simple question. At the beginning of each course, I ask students for their answers. At first, here's what they say:

- Someone who breaks the law

It's easy to see that you'd have to have an extremely strict definition of "criminal" to apply the first suggestion. Most of us have broken the law; we've speeded, jaywalked, downloaded content illegally, lied on forms. It quickly becomes clear that there needs to be an "and." A criminal who is someone who breaks the law . . .

- And is convicted of a crime

(What if a murderer never gets caught? Aren't they still a criminal?)

- And harms someone

(As humans, we are all destined to harm other people, so the kind of harm has to be specified. And what if you harm someone accidentally? Also, what about crimes like drug use, in which the harm to others is unclear? What if I try to harm someone and fail?)

- And intends to seriously harm someone

(If I drive drunk, or fall asleep at the wheel, and hit someone, I had no intention of doing harm. Am I a criminal? What if I lack the cognitive ability to understand that my actions will create harm?)

We could go on. Most people believe that criminality has something to do with harm; that it requires some degree of intent, but that even unintentional harm is criminal if it could have been foreseen or avoided; that a "criminal" needs to be mentally competent and of an age to be responsible for their actions; and that the law needs to be just in the first place. There's also a lot of disagreement about where these lines should be drawn—and who should be trusted to draw them. In short, though most of us think we know what it means to be a criminal, it turns out to be quite tricky to settle on a definition.

This is why societies throughout history have had complex criminal codes, standards, and norms. There's no evidence of a civilized society *without* criminality—that is, without a system for identifying and punishing people who act in certain ways. From ancient Sumer to the present, these codes discuss questions of intention, ability, harm, and social status. Criminality is complex.

Why it important to explore what *criminal* means? For one thing, in the US, a vast number of people are affected by that label. About 3% of American adults have served or are serving time in prison—7.3 million people. People who have been convicted of felonies (which are crimes that can carry prison sentences of more than a year) make up 8% of the adult population; alternative sentences, like probation, mean that many with felony convictions do not go to prison.[1] Those numbers, large in themselves, form just the narrow top of the "criminal" pyramid. About 80% of all arrests are for misdemeanors, which range from petty offenses, like not wearing a seatbelt, to crimes that carry up to a year of jail time.[2] The enormous number of misdemeanor arrests in the US means that a full third of American adults carry an arrest record—about the same proportion as those who hold a college diploma.[3] Even without a conviction, arrest records can show up on background checks—and arrests can be costly and even traumatizing in themselves. Furthermore, arrests and convictions are concentrated in certain places and among certain groups of people.[4] While you're almost certain to come into contact with people with criminal records in any social circle, criminalization has a far greater effect on some communities, contributing to inequality and undermining community structures.

On a more abstract level, digging into what it means to be a "criminal" can tell us a lot about the society in which we live. One way to think about a criminal justice system is as a summary of the behaviors a society wants to prevent. Criminal codes can specify not only that you can't murder or steal, but what you can't wear, where you can't go, what you can't sell, and with whom you can't have sex. These rules differ between cultures and change over time. In the US, for example, within the past generation interracial and same-sex marriage were illegal, while it was legal to assault one's spouse or child. It seems likely that within the next few years we will see changes in the criminal status of abortion and drug use. Criminality is not a fixed, universal category but one constructed within a particular culture and power structure.

In the United States, the societal stakes of criminality are apparent in the fact that under criminal law, it is not the victim who is the plaintiff, but "the People" or "the State."[5] This structure suggests that the injured party is less the person who was directly harmed than the nation itself. Criminal law encompasses all cases that can carry prison time or capital punishment; only the government can seek and impose these penalties. (If non-governmental parties were to incarcerate or kill someone, those would be crimes in themselves.) It stands to reason that this power must be carefully limited, and these limits were a priority for the writers of the Constitution. Even for the crime of making war against the United States—treason—they specified that "no person shall be convicted of treason unless on the testimony of two witnesses to the same overt act, or on confession in open court."[6]

Of the ten amendments that form the Bill of Rights, half (Amendments 4, 5, 6, 7, and 8) concern the rights of people accused of crimes. Crime, as a concept, is intrinsically bound up with the State, its power, and its values; a "criminal" is someone who has crossed a line set by the State.

A person convicted of a crime loses, to a remarkable extent, the rights of a US citizen. Most dramatically, when the 13th Amendment abolished slavery, it specified an exception: slavery can still be used as a punishment for people convicted of crimes. People convicted of felonies can lose what many Americans think of as inalienable rights: life, liberty, and the pursuit of happiness. Importantly, once a person is convicted, their status may be forever changed, even after they have, as the phrase goes, paid their debt to society. People who have felony convictions may continue to be ineligible for many governmental benefits and types of employment for the rest of their lives. While many people do rebuild productive, happy lives after being convicted of a crime, the label of "criminal" often continues to dog them socially and professionally.

Should we be using the word "criminal" to describe people at all? Some believe it is a slur, and should be avoided in the same way we avoid offensive words about race and disability (see Jessica S. Henry's contribution to this volume for a discussion of this idea; Patrick Schmucker also discusses the problems with labeling). Similar concerns apply to words like "felon," "inmate," "convict," and so on.[7] In this book, each writer has used the terms they felt comfortable with. Whatever words one employs, the reality is that for many people, a criminal conviction signals a loss of humanity. In addition to the loss of citizenship rights discussed above, people with criminal convictions face the knowledge that others may see them as undeserving of basic human needs, like comfort, connection, and the ability to improve their lives. Criminality carries a stigma like nothing else in our society, and that stigma can obscure the uniqueness of the people who carry it.

This book aims to share the human stories of people involved in the criminal justice system. As I gathered these stories, it became clear that every one could be a book in itself. Each of the first-person essays allows a glimpse of a unique person—where they came from, why they made the choices they did, what happened to them, where they might go in the future. They are stories of journeys, of learning, and of change.

The first section, **Incarceration, Reentry, and Rebuilding,** includes first-person stories of people who have served time in prison. These are all success stories, to some extent. All but one of the writers have left prison and reintegrated into society. (The other, Bobby Bostic, was serving a life sentence when he wrote the essay, and has since been granted parole.) Joseph Lascaze and Jamel Muhammad served long sentences before leaving prison to work for social change. Writer Diane Gottlieb interviewed three men who are working to rebuild their lives after release. In telling their stories, these writers dug deep into their pasts to relate how they ended up in prison and how they left criminal behavior behind, and they share the struggles of living with a criminal conviction.

Section two, **Journeys in Law Enforcement,** gives the perspectives of people employed within the justice system. Like people with criminal convictions, those who work in law enforcement can be subject to dehumanizing stereotypes. They, too, are people on their own journeys, and the stories here show how members of the law enforcement community have learned, changed, and worked to better their communities. This section shows what it is like to be a corrections officer (Blair Rowlett), a police officer (Brendan Cox, Lawan Cancer), and a school resource officer (Patrick Schmucker and Cancer). Rowlett and Cox also discuss the programs they now lead, which provide alternatives to sentencing and arrest.

The third section, **Ripple Effects,** is about people whose lives have been affected by the justice system in somewhat less direct ways. It includes stories of the children of incarcerated parents (Seren Sensei and Anna Roberge), a filmmaker deeply affected by making a film about solitary confinement (Jennifer Fischer), and an asylum seeker who risks detainment and deportation because of his immigrant status (Alex Masias). Each of these stories shows how criminalization ripples outward.

The final section, **Scholarly Perspectives**, presents four pieces of academic work that put individual stories into broader contexts. McKenzie Wood presents an overview of research into what makes people more likely to commit crimes. Valena Elizabeth Beety examines how pseudoscientific forensics and bias against queer people resulted in the wrongful conviction of two Mississippi women. Jessica S. Henry, too, discusses a wrongful conviction—which occurred in a case that involved no crime at all. Michelle C. Sermon shows how one family in Washington, DC has been affected by the criminalization of one of its members, and how their experience is linked with broader social issues. Jasmine E. Harris discusses the problematic role of disability in the criminal justice system, and argues that bias against people with disabilities is rooted in how we perceive other people.

These stories are not meant to provide a thorough overview of the criminal justice system, but rather to dive deeply into particular experiences. Nor does this book advocate for specific changes to the justice system, though several of the essayists offer up models of transformation. Nevertheless, this book does make an argument. It attempts to show that creating a more fair and successful justice system requires listening: to the individual people who live and work within it, as well as to the research of scholars who dedicate themselves to careful, in-depth research.

During Socrates's trial, in explaining how he came to have a reputation as a sage, he recounts how the oracle at Delphi named him the wisest of men. Thinking this must be false, Socrates sought out people who seemed wiser. Each, he decided, was not really wise. Because those people knew a lot about something—politics, poetry, or craft—they assumed they understood everything, and so became foolish. His own wisdom, Socrates concludes, is in knowing how little he knows.

Making fools out of powerful people didn't win Socrates many friends, and the Athenian jury voted to put him to death. But his message of intellectual humility remains a valuable one; too many of us, secure in what we know, forget what we don't know. My hope in presenting these 17 accounts of our justice system is that each reader will encounter new knowledge and new perspectives around the question "What Is a criminal?"—and will close the book with a desire to learn more.

Notes

1 There is no comprehensive, centralized data on arrest, conviction, and incarceration in the US, so scholars have used available data to produce estimates. The estimates that 8% of adults in the US have felony convictions and 3% have served time in prison are from Sarah K. S. Shannon et al., "The Growth, Scope, and Spatial Distribution of People with Felony Records in the United States, 1948–2010," *Demography* 54 (2017): 1795–818. For a discussion of the lack of available data about the US justice system, see John Pfaff, *Locked In: The True Causes of Mass Incarceration and How to Achieve Real Reform* (New York: Basic Books, 2017), 16–17.

2 On misdemeanor arrests and their effects, see Alexandra Natapoff, *Punishment without Crime: How Our Massive Misdemeanor System Traps the Innocent and Makes America More Unequal* (New York: Basic Books, 2018).

3 Matthew Friedman, "Just Fact: As Many Americans Have Criminal Records as College Diplomas," Brennan Center for Justice, November 17, 2015, www.brennancenter.org/our-work/analysis-opinion/just-facts-many-americans-have-criminal-records-college-diplomas.

4 Black men in particular are extremely overrepresented in the criminal justice system; 33% have felony convictions and 15% have been to prison. See Shannon et al. for analysis and discussion.

5 Victims may personally sue those who injure them under civil law. If a person is convicted in a civil case, they may have to pay damages to the person injured or penalties to the government, but will not be sentenced to prison. Civil defendants do not have the same constitutional protections as criminal defendants, and the standard for conviction is easier to meet.

6 US Constitution, article 3, section 3.

7 The Marshall Project website has a helpful section called "The Language Project," which presents multiple perspectives on the use of contentious terms, as well as a style guide. www.themarshallproject.org/2021/04/12/the-language-project

I

Incarceration, Reentry, and Rebuilding

1

LIVING THROUGH A LIFE SENTENCE

An Insider's View of Crime, Punishment, and How to End Mass Incarceration

Bobby Bostic

Criminals are not born, they are made. I know this because I lived it. I was among criminals during my childhood as well during my adulthood. I have spent over a quarter of a century and three-quarters of my life in prison. I write these words from a prison cell now. I have listened to my fellow prisoners' life stories. Based on what I learn about them, they were raised in normal households just like I was. The common thread running through most of these stories is that we all grew up in poverty.

There you have it: the answer. It was ultimately poverty that led us to crime.

How I Got Locked Up for Life at 16

My foray into the life of crime started off early. As with most criminals, I was initiated into this life through petty shoplifting. I was raised in extreme poverty, and I committed these early crimes because I was hungry. I stole from stores because we did not have food at home. Then there were other delinquent activities, such as truancy. Crime was everywhere I looked in the ghettos where I grew up. There was no escaping it. I saw it when I walked down the streets going to school every morning. I saw it in the school bathroom at my elementary school. I even saw crime when I played softball in my backyard, because drug dealers sold drugs on the gangway alongside my house.

My mother told me to stay away from crime and not to mingle with the dope boys who hung out next door to our house. Nevertheless, these guys became my role models. I wanted what they had. I was tired of being poor and hungry while waiting for my mother's welfare check and food stamps every first of the month. (That check was never enough to pay the rent and bills, so we always went without heat, gas, lights, water, or some utility. Sometimes we went without all at once.) I desired the cars, the clothes, and the girls. The drug dealers in my neighborhood

DOI: 10.4324/9781003169468-3

had it all. They were proof of success, as far as my young eyes could see. I was determined to get what they had. I didn't see doctors or lawyers in my neighborhood. Everyone was living in poverty, below poverty, or lower middle class. Living from one check to the next, the people around me were just struggling to survive.

As kids, we did not play organized sports. We couldn't afford protective gear or equipment, so we played street sports with no helmets or pads. We played tackle football on the concrete, as well as baseball. We were too unkempt to go to the local gym. For gymnastics, we did flips on old mattresses we found in alleys. We could not afford uniforms at the local Boys and Girls Clubs, so we formed our own underground sports clubs. We didn't know of anyone who made it to college or a career by playing sports. Since I understood that sports were not a way to leave the ghetto or escape my poverty, I chose the more immediate option in front of me. I became a student of crime.

I grew up a lot faster than many peers my age, and I began to congregate with older adolescents. Hanging with guys five years older than me, I ventured into petty crime—like joyriding in stolen cars. Broke, hungry, and desperate, we snatched purses. We stole loose change out of parked cars. We became criminals. However, my criminal ventures were still more of an extracurricular activity at this early age. My life at home was consumed with school, homework, and church. As a preteen, I mainly mowed lawns for money. I pumped gas at the gas station for loose change. I collected aluminum cans, shoveled neighbors' snow for five dollars, or washed cars.

As I grew older, that money did not come fast enough. Other guys my age were making hundreds of dollars a day selling drugs. At 12 years old, I decided to join them, and started hanging out with neighborhood drug dealers. I began smoking marijuana and drinking alcohol regularly. By the age of 13, I was selling drugs all day and night after school. School became a fashion show to display the money and stylish clothes I had. The drug dealers at middle school dressed more fashionably than the teachers. In our young minds, we had arrived. All my life I never had anything, so when I started selling drugs and got something, I showed it off to the world. From my drug proceeds, I purchased two front gold teeth and a pager so customers could reach me. My crown possession was my first vehicle, bought when I was 13 years old. School no longer interested me, so I quit when I was 14 and began working full-time selling drugs in the streets.

Guns were everywhere in my neighborhood. I was no stranger to guns. I never thought I would live to be 18 years old. All around me, my peers were getting killed, so I thought it was just a matter of time before I would be next. Gangs were also everywhere. You ran with them or got run over. During drug droughts, drug dealers would commit robberies. I was robbed at gunpoint three times. No matter how careful you were, you could still be a victim of robbery in the ghetto. Robbery was not my thing, but when I was 16 years old, I committed two robberies that would land me in prison for the rest of my life. Thus, my life of crime was short-lived.

However, crime doesn't stop when criminals go to prison. In fact, prison has been called the "University of Crime." Crime is everywhere in prison. Drugs, knives, murders, assaults, and extortion are all here in these cell blocks. I have seen it all during my 26 years in prison. I am not a model prisoner, because prison does not model me. I grew up in this place and I had to survive here. Therefore, I had to fight. I've been in my share of trouble here.

I changed my life for the better in prison because I was tired of the lifestyle. It is a dead-end road. I no longer carry myself like a criminal. I chose to rehabilitate myself. I vowed to feed my mind with books and become a contributing member of society. Prison does not rehabilitate the man; the man must rehabilitate himself, and that is exactly what I have done. Some of the world's greatest minds are in prison, and some of the greatest words ever written have originated from within a dungeon cell. We must not allow our talents to go to waste.

As an 18-year-old teenager sent to a maximum security prison in Missouri, I knew that I wanted a better life for myself. But with no guidance or direction, I had no idea how to find such a better life. As a result, when I first went to prison, I followed the footsteps of the blind prison masses and continued in my life of crime. I learned how to make prison knives, how to make prison wine, how to smuggle drugs into prison, and everything else that comes with the crime life inside of prison. The judge told me that I would die in prison, so in my young mind there was no incentive to change. In fact, I was about to get worse.

As a small-time criminal in prison, I participated in prison riots, got into several fights, disobeyed orders, flirted with female staff members, and broke all the prison rules. This is what my prison peers did. I just joined the party. We tried to carry on by acting like we were still on the streets. Every day in prison, I smoked marijuana from the time I woke up until the time I went to sleep. There was so much gang warfare that we had to carry knives in our possession or keep them hidden somewhere close. It was a do-or-die lifestyle. If someone stared at you too long, you had to address it. You had to be ready to kill or become a victim. Predators stalked the prison yard day and night. It was common to see stabbings, to see robberies, to see guards assaulted, and all other kinds of violence. A majority of us in maximum security had life sentences. Everything was serious, and problems were addressed with violence. Diplomacy was put on the back burner. Prison was wild. I adjusted to my environment and became wild, too. Crime was the order of the day.

But even a young, wild prisoner like myself could get tired of the criminal lifestyle. For me, it didn't happen overnight. But when my change did come, it was certain and swift. Two life-changing events took place when I was 21 years old that put me on a path of change. The first event that propelled me to change my lifestyle was my religious conversion. I learned about God. I knew I needed a relationship with a Higher Power. My second life-changing event was when my mother died of lung cancer at the age of 42. I had been incarcerated for five years when she died. Losing her felt like losing my entire world. This caused me to change.

My Education

I started reading hundreds of books. There is power in words. The books I read opened up much larger worlds to me that I did not even know existed. Books and reading made me free, even while inside of prison—allowing me to go anywhere I wanted in the entire universe. The more books I read, the more I found myself. Then I applied what I read. I studied everything: oceanography, astronomy, politics, philosophy, self-help, business, memoirs of world leaders and entrepreneurs, history, social movements, sociology. I wanted to learn. For years I wanted to go to college, but I didn't have the money. Contrary to popular belief, college was not free in Missouri prisons. I didn't even have funds in my prison account to get the everyday essentials, much less money for college. Nevertheless, my appetite for a college education would not go away. It took me many years to obtain money for college. In fact, it took over a decade after I got my GED to get money for just one college course.

Finally, I began taking college correspondence courses through the mail. It was extremely hard to get my college degree in prison. I had no teacher, no tutor, and no one to help me. I hadn't done math problems in 20 years. I failed college algebra four times. I had to figure everything out by trial and error. I studied in my cell with the constant, deafening noise of prisoners hollering, screaming, playing music, arguing, and laughing. All around me, the prison violence, gangs, and drugs were the normal order. I kept my head in the books while tuning out all the madness. It cost me over $24,000 out of pocket (including textbooks, postage, paper, calculators, and other materials). Finally, through sheer effort and determination, I earned my Associate of Science degree from Adams State University.

I am now a few classes away from earning my Bachelor of Arts in sociology with an emphasis in criminology. When taking criminology courses, I base my papers on my true-life experiences. Having been a criminal and being surrounded by the worst criminals in a maximum security prison, I truly know what a criminal is. In this regard, my prior experience gives me an advantage over my college peers, who only know about crime from what they read in books, see on television, or hear in lectures. Academics do not always prepare us for everything that we will encounter in life or in our chosen careers. When it comes to crime, I understand why some criminals do what they do. I have been there, so I can relate. I am not speaking for sex criminals or people that commit crimes just for thrills. I must admit that a lot of crime is senseless. But you have to actually be in that world to know why criminals do what they do.

We must ask ourselves, who was this person before they became a prisoner? Surely, this is someone's father, brother, sister, mother, aunty, uncle, or cousin. A person doesn't lose their humanity by being branded a criminal. With millions of prisoners in their custody, the state and federal governments simply don't have the capacity to address the individual needs of their prisoners. In such an overpopulated system, it is much easier to assign each human being a prison number and view them as a thing. Prison is a well-oiled machine. But just because a machine is well-oiled doesn't mean that it runs well. In fact, the prison machine is broken in many places. If you ask the majority of prisoners, they will tell you that the system treats them more like a cog on a wheel than as the human beings they consider themselves to be.

While studying criminology, I have come across a lot of theories about crime. There are too many to list here, but I will name a few. Over 250 years ago, during the Age of Enlightenment, Cesare Beccaria developed what we call classical criminology. This school of thought holds that people have free will to choose either criminal behavior or lawful means to meet their needs. However, criminal behavior seems more attractive because it promises greater pay for little work. Classical criminology purports that people will be deterred from crime if the possible punishment is more than the expected payoff.[1] This school of thought is the foundation of the "hard on crime" approach. Some argue that this approach to criminal justice has waned. I beg to differ. The "tough on crime" era is more alive now than ever.[2] I am not just theorizing this in some academic text. I am living this in the flesh by serving a 241-year sentence for robberies that I committed when I was 16 years old.

Based on my lifetime of personal experience living with and around criminals, I agree with the rational choice theory. This school of thought holds that crime follows a decision-making process where the person weighs the benefits as well as the cost of a potential crime.[3] Furthermore, this theory considers other factors, such as the personal reasons people commit crimes, as well as their environment. Finally, and most importantly, this theory considers how criminals are likely to reform themselves once they see that the risk of crime is not worth it in the long run. The current age of mass incarceration has shown that general deterrence, perceptual deterrence, and deterrence theory are not effective concepts in making crime decline in our society.[4]

Learning all of this was part of my change. Education is a ladder to freedom. It puts a prisoner back in touch with his humanity. It exposes his mind to a larger world—one in which he longs to participate as a positive, contributing member of society. College was the light that I needed in a dark place like prison. That light, along with my spiritual awakening, enlightened me and served as my impetus for change. This is how I elevated myself above the criminal mentality. I saw a future in education. I knew there could not be a successful future in crime. I underwent a metamorphosis and stopped thinking like a criminal. I chose to believe in the goodness of life, despite being surrounded by hopelessness and crime. Life is a gift and not a curse.

A Better Approach to Crime

Locking criminals up and throwing away the key will not solve the problem of crime. As I have said before: the root cause of the majority of crime is poverty. I started selling drugs because I was dirt-poor without a cent in my pocket. Since there was no food at home, I ate in the streets as a kid. A few years later, as a teenager, I was sentenced to die in prison. I am very remorseful for my crime. There is no excuse for it. I was immediately sent to a maximum security prison, where I have been for over a quarter of a century. Again, criminals don't stop being criminals when they come here.

Crime needs to be controlled, but it must be done on a rational basis. In the age of mass incarceration, prisoners are not given individual or even group treatment for the particular criminal behavior that landed them in prison. Often these people are just warehoused until they go home or die in prison. The crime problem is serious, so we must create radical solutions. I would like to share how I view a rational approach to crime control in the age of mass incarceration, which is based on my own real-life experiences and what I have learned in sociology and criminology classes.

Statistics show that incarceration rates have increased, even as crime continues to decrease. We do have a serious problem in this country that needs to be addressed. Crime presents a social harm that poses a threat to all elements of society.[5] However, those in power address crime in ways that are unequal and unfair. Street crimes are often heavily punished with stiff penalties. White-collar crimes, which cause more social harm to society, are often punished with minor penalties.[6] Such inequality in the criminal justice system has contributed to the current crisis of mass incarceration.

In order to solve crime, we must address its root causes. Poverty is at the root of most economic street crimes.[7] It starts in childhood for those most affected.[8] Entire communities become "hollowed out."[9] Social ecologists have studied such neighborhoods and have linked abject poverty to crime.[10] Thousands of studies have established a direct link between urban blight and crime.[11] The government can help to reduce crime by providing more funds for social welfare programs. This has been proven to reduce crime.[12]

Another factor in this equation is how we address the so-called war on drugs. Many crimes are drug-related. The errors associated with this war on drugs are endless. People of color are being criminalized disproportionately. Addicts should be treated and not arrested. Being addicted to drugs is a public health issue and not itself a crime, yet this is how the problem is currently being addressed in the criminal justice system. Drug arrests make people ineligible for housing, education grants, and welfare benefits. This only exacerbates the problem, pushing drug users further into a life of crime. Billions of tax dollars are wasted in this fight. Treatment is the solution. Drug courts are a better alternative to address public health problems linked to drug abuse: "Drug courts provide an ideal setting to address these problems by linking the justice system with health services and drug treatment providers while easing the burden on the already overtaxed correctional system."[13] Group therapy, outpatient programs, residential care, counseling, detoxification, mental health care, and other alternative sources of treatment must also be integrated to address drug addiction.[14]

Non-violent offenders need to be rehabilitated instead of merely being warehoused in prison. Probation and parole violators should be placed in community corrections centers instead of being sent back to prison. The Violent Crime Control and Law Enforcement Act of 1994, commonly known as the crime bill, has proven ineffective as well. There needs to be a varied approach to reducing violent crime. Making first-time violent offenders serve 85% of their sentences has not had a deterrent effect on violent crime.[15] Even three-strikes laws, which have been enacted in many states, have proven to have little or no deterrent effect upon crime.[16] Violent offenders also need rehabilitation. Pell Grants that fund college classes for prisoners can have a big effect on recidivism rates.

The only way to really reduce mass incarceration is to allow some of our life-sentence prisoners a chance for parole one day, should they prove themselves worthy. The vast majority of prisoners will be released back out into society, so it only makes sense that more money and resources should be directed toward rehabilitating them. Failing to do so will only perpetuate the problem of mass incarceration.

Furthermore, mass incarceration creates its own set of problems. It costs vast sums of money to incarcerate people. States now spend more of their budget on prisons than they do on education. The United States has over two million people in prison, with an increasing number of these prisoners over the age of 50. These older prisoners have cost the government and taxpayers billions of dollars in healthcare alone, thanks to harsh prison environments that trigger health complications. Many of these older prisoners no longer pose a threat to society, because they have aged out of crime.[17] Some prisoners serving this harsh sentence deserve a second chance. For those who no longer pose a threat, it is logical for society to reevaluate their harsh sentences, helping us to reduce the prison population. We waste billions of dollars warehousing such people in prison, when they could contribute positively to society and also add to the tax base.

Former prisoners can also make a positive impact and find meaning by using the lessons they've learned to help keep kids out of trouble. Many of us criminals were lost in the streets, and finding our life's purpose (or destiny) inside of prison has been a blessing in disguise for us. One morning, I woke up with a vision, or should I say, a dream. I saw myself mentoring a dispute between two 16-year-old youths. It appeared to be some kind of gang dispute or neighborhood beef. I made my way into the epicenter of the commotion and got between the would-be combatants, trying to reason with them. I explained to these young brothers how I ended up in jail at 16 years old and was sentenced to die in prison. At first, they were so enraged at each other that they didn't want to listen to me. They felt like they had nothing to lose and everything to gain by proving to each other who was toughest. However, as I continued to counsel these young men, the anger on their faces began to fade away. I was able to reach beyond their hard exterior and touch on their humanity. I explained to them that their anger was not so much at each other, but was really about their condition of poverty and hopelessness in their urban blight conditions. I had to talk their own language to them. It was a language that no one else there could understand but us. When I was able to break through to these young brothers in my vision (or dream), I realized right then that part of my purpose in life is to reach troubled youth and help them turn their lives around and to find their purpose in life. When I resolved the dispute between those two rivals, I felt a sense of worth in myself that I had never felt before. I looked back on my journey and realized that this is why I had to experience all of this. I had to go through these rough decades in prison so that I could teach others not to repeat my mistakes. This was the purpose of my education. I don't have all of the answers, but men like me can contribute to the solution.

Living among criminals (and former criminals) in prison for 26 years has given me a front-row seat in the field of criminology. I am not writing about what I heard or read from others. I have lived it every day. This is why I am well-qualified to answer the question, "What Is a criminal?" I must strongly implore society not to forget the humanity inside of these prisoners. People do change—even criminals. There are people in these prisons who have done horrible things, but that should not preclude some of them from getting a second chance.[18] When criminals change and age out of crime, should they still have to die in prison? With our harsh laws, society has given up on these men and women and thrown away the key. What purpose does this serve? Ultimately, we all lose with this approach. This is not just a theory. It is based on facts. I believe that humanity can be restored. I maintain that justice can also be restored in the world and for the countless people who have stopped believing in the concept of justice. If we take steps to improve our criminal justice system and our societal approaches to criminalization, we can end this saga of mass incarceration.

Editor's note: The judge who sentenced Bobby Bostic later regretted her action, and campaigned to reduce Bostic's sentence. His case inspired a change in Missouri law that allowed people sentenced as juveniles to be eligible for parole. Bostic was the first person granted parole under the new law.

At 16 years old, **Bobby Bostic** was sentenced to 241 years in prison for robbery—the longest sentence given to a juvenile for non-homicide offenses in the state of Missouri. While incarcerated, Mr. Bostic completed his GED, a Legal Assistant/Paralegal Diploma from Blackstone Career Institute, a Certificate in Basic Business Studies from Missouri State University, and an Associate of Science degree from Adams State University. Mr. Bostic is a prolific reader and writer, and a published author. His essays have been featured in various magazines, and he has published 13 books of poetry and nonfiction. While serving his sentence, Mr. Bostic founded book groups for inmates and advocated for the creation of programs to improve literacy in prison. Thanks to changing laws regarding life sentences for minors, Mr. Bostic has received significant media attention in recent years and was granted parole in 2021, with a scheduled release date in November of 2022. You can learn more about Mr. Bostic by visiting his website at freebobbybostic.com or by following him on Instagram and Twitter @FreeBobbyBostic.

Notes

1 David A. Ward, Mark C. Stafford, and Louis N. Gray, "Rational Choice, Deterrence, and Theoretical Integration," *Journal of Applied Social Psychology* 36, no. 3 (March 2006): 571–85.
2 Ronald Bayer, "Crime, Punishment, and the Decline of Liberal Optimism," *Crime and Delinquency* 27, no. 2 (April 1981): 190.
3 Hung-En Sung and Linda Richter, "Rational Choice and Environmental Deterrence in the Retention of Mandated Drug Abuse Treatment Clients," *International Journal of Offender Therapy and Comparative Criminology* 51, no. 6 (January 2008): 686–702; Neal Shover, *Aging Criminals* (Beverly Hills: Sage Publications, 1985).
4 I discuss this in more depth in my book *Life Goes on Inside Prison* (self-pub., 2021).
5 Charles H. McCaghy, *Deviant Behavior: Crime, Conflict, and Interest Groups* (New York: MacMillan, 1976).
6 Miriam D. Sealock and Sally S. Simpson, "Unraveling Bias in Arrest Decisions: The Role of Juvenile Offender Type-Scripts," *Justice Quarterly* 15 (September 1998): 427–57.
7 Oscar Lewis, "The Culture of Poverty," *Scientific American*, October 1966, 19–25.
8 Jeanne Brooks-Gunn and Greg J. Duncan, "The Effects of Poverty on Children," *The Future of Children* 7, no. 2 (1997): 55–71.
9 Rodrick Wallace, "Expanding Coupled Shock Fronts of Urban Decay and Criminal Behavior: How U.S. Cities are Becoming 'Hollowed Out,'" *Journal of Quantitative Criminology* 7, no. 4 (December 1991): 333–556.
10 Robert J. Bursik Jr., "Social Disorganization and Theories of Crime and Delinquency: Problems and Prospects," *Criminology* 26, no. 4 (November 1988): 519–52.
11 Matthew R. Lee, Michael Maume, and Graham Ousey, "Social Isolation and Lethal Violence Across the Metro/Nonmetro Divide: The Effects of Socioeconomic Disadvantage and Poverty Concentration on Homicide," *Rural Sociology* 68, no. 1 (March 2003): 107–31.
12 John L. Worrall, "Reconsidering the Relationship Between Welfare Spending and Serious Crime: A Panel Data Analysis with Implications for Social Support Theory," *Justice Quarterly* 22, no. 3 (September 2005): 365–91.
13 Larry J. Siegel, *Criminology: Theories, Patterns, and Typologies*, 12th ed. (Boston: Cengage Learning, 2016), 536.
14 "DrugFacts: Treatment Approaches for Drug Addiction," National Institute on Drug Abuse, January 17, 2019, https://nida.nih.gov/publications/drugfacts/treatment-approaches-drug-addiction
15 Steven N. Durlauf and Daniel S. Nagin, "Imprisonment and Crime: Can Both be Reduced?" *Criminology & Public Policy* 10, no. 1 (February 2011): 13–54.
16 Cheryl Marie Webster, Anthony N. Doob, and Franklin E. Zimring, "Proposition 8 and Crime Rates in California: The Case of the Disappearing Deterrent," *Criminology & Public Policy* 5, no. 3 (August 2006): 417–48.
17 James Q. Wilson and Richard J. Herrnstein, *Crime and Human Nature* (New York: Simon and Schuster, 1985), 126–47.
18 For more on this topic please see my book *Time: Endless Moments in Prison* (self-pub., 2021).

2

THREE FORMER "CRIMINALS"

Diane Gottlieb

Christian Gonzalez, Ra'Shaun Muller, and John Braga* are three men whom many might refer to as criminals. All three served long sentences in the New York State prison system. All were convicted of murder and are now back in society, working, and creating new lives for themselves.

I came to know these men as a result of a horrendous crime. Patrick Logsdon, a Catholic deacon who ran Anthony House, a transitional home for men right out of prison, was brutally murdered, allegedly by another former resident. When I learned of the deacon's murder, just a few miles from my home, I wanted to learn his story through the eyes of the men whose lives he'd touched. Chris, Ra'Shaun, and John are helping me with that project. For this essay, I interviewed each of them about their answers to the question "What Is a criminal?" The following stories have been edited for length and readability from the transcripts of those interviews.

Christian Gonzales: The Power of a Helping Hand, and the Difficulties of Starting Over

Chris is a 40-year-old man of Puerto Rican and Peruvian descent. He grew up in a rough part of Yonkers, New York. His mother, according to Chris, was addicted to crack—and to violent men. In school, Chris was placed in special education classes due to learning and emotional concerns. When he entered prison, Chris could barely read.

Chris's dream was to become a police officer or be in the military. But in February 1996, a fire killed two toddlers, and Chris was brought to the Juvenile Detention Center in Yonkers for questioning. He was incarcerated at the age of 15, 5'2" tall and weighing 104 pounds. He did not go home until 19 years and 10 months later, after spending many of his formative years behind bars at 22 different prisons,

DOI: 10.4324/9781003169468-4

including over 1000 days in solitary confinement. Chris was released from prison in 2015 and is now no longer under parole supervision. He recently started his own business in trucking. Chris maintains he did not commit the crimes for which he was convicted. He claims he was intimidated into a confession during a time when the courts were notoriously hard on juvenile defendants.

Chris's Story

A criminal is someone who lives a life of delinquency. One act of passion does not make you a criminal. What resonates with me is: he's a repeat offender. It's a lifestyle.

I didn't think of myself that way at first, but in prison I started to. In prison, you are reminded that you're an inmate, told over and over you're no good. "Don't trust him. Search him." Nonstop. After a while, you start to believe it, digest and regurgitate it. After a while, they force you to become a criminal. If you work in the commissary or get food for sick people, giving them Ensures, you take a case and sell them for a carton of cigarettes. If you want to get in shape, you want those Ensures, but you have to smuggle them out of the cafeteria and pay a staff two packs of cigarettes, so he will escort you out with a bag.

In every prison there's a black market, and the guards are involved too. Guards become criminals. It becomes their way of life too. Whoever has the most power, controls. Correctional officers, then the gangs. When there are more members in one gang—when their "weight is up"—they become more abusive, become the oppressors. When their numbers are small, they become more diplomatic. It's a power-struggle mentality.

You need to remove yourself from all that. Remain neutral. Be by yourself. Working out became my refuge.

I was tried at the age of 15 as an adult. At that time, I fell under the Juvenile Offenders Act of 1978. If I hadn't been, I would have done 18 months until I turned 18, and then been released.

When I first got locked up, I had a really hard time adjusting, being a Latino with the racial wars in prison, with my mother continuing her drug addiction in the streets, being in prison for something I didn't do. There was a tornado going on in my mind. I got into a lot of trouble at the beginning of my sentence. Eventually I found normalcy in an abnormal environment. I learned when to be quiet, when to turn the other cheek, at least with the prison staff.

It didn't take much to be put into solitary. Rack up a few tickets on small, miscellaneous infractions, like dirty urine with marijuana, being argumentative with staff. If you had enough of those, they'd write you up and put you in solitary. To the bitter end, I had a problem adjusting to it. When I was finally transferred to medium security prison, my disciplinary record followed me. They'd look at that record first. Despite the accomplishments I had—vocational trades, volunteer programs—my disciplinary record overshadowed all of that. My murder conviction was the icing on the cake.

When I was sent to Washington Correctional, I was assigned to a counselor, Mrs. D. She was my fresh air, an angel sent from God. A little White lady with curly hair. She wasn't scared of nothing. "Tell me about yourself," she said. She pointed to my file. "What's this? Are you a monster? You don't seem like a monster. Tell me the real story."

So, I told her everything, and she said, "Sounds like you really got railroaded. You know what?" She told me about another inmate she'd helped named Hunter. "You're going to be my next Hunter." Mrs. D. took the lost boys and changed their lives. "Our job in corrections is to grab you and reform and rehabilitate you." She made me into a facilitator. "You have to stay out of trouble," she told me. I agreed to. She gave me a syllabus of ART—anger replacement training. I studied it. I was nervous. Then she gave me a classroom with inmates. I didn't think I could do it. She told me not to worry.

I was able to control the environment. We got into subjects like nutrition and business in class. We read books like *Rich Man, Poor Man*. The class became a sponge for topics like real estate. We did ART with skits and role plays. I'd captivate them with topics and then bring it all back to ART.

When I went to the parole board, Mrs. D. spoke for me. It was my seventh appearance before the board. I went in with a defeated mindset. By then I had accepted prison as my life. I used to yearn for freedom. Now I was scared of it. Scared to go home.

In my 19 years in prison, I must have cried a river. When I was told that I made parole, I couldn't cry. I just couldn't believe. If I was to die and my life flashed before my eyes, Mrs. D. would be one image I would leave this earth remembering.

When I entered prison, I had a very low reading level. I couldn't write. All my life I was in special education. I know part of it was because of my behavior. I remember my mom being promiscuous and a crack addict and alcoholic. And she used to beat me—not the way you would beat a child with a belt. She hit me so hard, she once hit my head through a window. Whoever she was dating at the time would hit me as well. They never stuck around long. Who would stick around with my mom?

The first book I read in prison was called *Racehoss*. It took me a very long time to read. I'd have to read each page over and over again. I read Jackie Collins's series, and little by little raised my skills. One of my dreams was to get my GED, which I did.

Being released was incredibly scary. I didn't know whether to stand, walk, sit, look around. I brought what I learned in prison to the outside. I had to learn again, reprogram. When I first came out, I slept at my uncle's house. I didn't feel ready. My feeling was I didn't belong on the outside. In prison, when you had trouble socializing with people, you locked yourself in a cell. I did that when I came out, stayed in my room. That caused friction with my uncle's wife. That was the only thing I knew to do, and instead of her understanding, she felt offended.

I tried to fall into things as a normal 30-something-year-old man—tried to have a relationship and get a job. When you're someone who's been on hiatus for that long, you're constantly being judged. When I came out here, it was very cold. A dog-eat-dog world.

I was desperate for work. I came out and was ready to do whatever I could do. I had grand schemes. I wanted to buy a car and do Uber. I was denied. I signed up for MTA and never heard from them. I even went to a state senator's office to tell her about the problems I'd been having a getting a job. She promised me the world and never delivered.

I finally got a job in construction. My boss kept saying, "There's something's different about you, Chris." One day, we all ate lunch in his office. He said, "You like working out, right?" And everybody got quiet. He said, "Did you always work out in prison?" My heart went to my stomach. I felt like throwing up. I didn't know about employment law—thought I was going to get fired. This set the tone for my relationship with my coworkers.

They would give me the dirty assignments. My boss played Jedi mind tricks. He told me that if the main boss found out I had been in prison, I would be fired. I didn't know any better, so when they gave me the low-end jobs, I did them. While I cleaned trash, they put up sheetrock. They weren't in the cold or rain. They were inside, sipping Coronas. We were at the same pay rate, but I was always outside.

I went to ACCES-VR [New York State Adult Career and Continuing Ed Services] and was denied services. Prison isn't enough. You have to have a disability. I showed them documentation of my learning disability. I went to CDL school but couldn't pass my road test. The supervisor denied me additional schooling. He said I didn't have the mental ability to pass. But I appealed the decision and won. I took 19 more classes and aced the test.

I get discouraged every day of my life. One thing about me is that I have a burning desire—I didn't do 19 years 10 months for nothing. If I go back to prison, I fail. I have to do something with my life.

I'd like society to see me as a human being without the blemish that I carry—my incarceration. Just see me as a regular person driven to succeed. Don't judge me for the past, judge me for my heart. Get to know me.

I believe in God. I make so many mistakes, but the would-of, could-of, should-of just doesn't exist in my life. I make a mistake, it's just "go and fix it."

When I was still on parole, I got pulled over for a traffic infraction. The minute the officers ran my ID, they had me sitting in the back of a police car. "When I punch in Christian Gonzalez, the only thing that pops up is murder, parole," the officer said. He even showed me. When I got teary-eyed, he told me, "This won't last forever. One day this will be over."

Just give me back my name. I was incarcerated for something I didn't do. I didn't set the fire. You got the guy who did it, but just forget about that. Forget about my time in prison. The biggest blessing I could have would be to get my name back. Give me the option of doing what I want to do with my life. Don't segregate me.

I started my own business. I'm nervous as hell. I sacrificed every penny I have. I live in a pickup truck with a 40-foot trailer, and I go state to state hauling, chasing my dreams. My prediction is that in six months I'll be in a semi. My dream is to own three to five semis and to have a successful company. I'm making a lot of mistakes in the process. I'm learning the hard way, but I'm really pushing the envelope on this. I want to succeed.

There are some days when I am so lost. I went out with a friend who's a roofer. He was incarcerated when he was 17. I asked him, "Do you ever feel like you don't belong here?" He got quiet and then said, "All the time." "Do you feel like that around your family?" He said, "yeah." I was a little relieved that I wasn't the only one that felt that.

I sometimes feel like I was teleported to a different dimension. Was it a dream? I remember every part of that cell–vividly. I could close my eyes right now and see cell 19 in Great Meadow Correctional on F2 block. I could close my eyes and look at the S block. I remember the panels. I remember the corners, the edges. I remember the abrasive cement sand floor to prevent people from slipping, and the shower, the nozzle I hated because it didn't spritz enough water. We used to clean the toilet and put our food in to keep it cool or to preserve it. I remember that vividly. What happened out here last year, I barely remember. Prison is an experience that will forever be branded in my brain. We would be in our bunkbeds and tell each other stories all night long, but my stories were sad. Like of my mom being a crackhead, of me not eating for days, having to run and eat at a friend's house. I didn't have good childhood stories and I don't want to be the guy that just has sad stories to tell.

If I could go in spirit form into that prison cell and speak to myself back then, I think I would call myself a liar, if I told myself what I would be doing right now. (I'd also warn myself, "There's this one girl you're going to meet—stay away from her, she's going to break your heart.") I thought I would cut hair and open a beauty salon. In prison, everyone has a thousand and one ideas of what they are going to do when they get out.

If my prison self could see me now, he'd be shocked. And he would have more hope. Out here, as long as you're not dead, everything can be fixed.

Ra'Shaun Muller: Don't Write Off People Who Have Been in Prison

Ra'Shaun is a 46-year Black man who grew up in Bedford-Stuyvesant, Brooklyn, when Bed-Stuy was one of the toughest areas in New York. Like Chris, Ra'Shaun's upbringing was one of violence in the home, and he had trouble in school, constantly getting into fights. Ra'Shaun had what he describes as Coke-bottle glasses, and was brutally teased. He had little tolerance for teasing.

Ra'Shaun lived for a time, in his young teens, at Mount Loretto, a group home for troubled or orphaned kids and teens. It was there that he got his first pair of contact lenses, and where he developed a close relationship with Sister Bernadette, who took a special interest in Ra'Shaun. Sister Bernadette was the only person present at his trial for support.

When he was 18 years old, Ra'Shaun lived in an apartment with several roommates. He believed one of them had stolen a few new items of clothing that he had recently purchased. Ra'Shaun confronted the roommate and then attacked him with a hammer. The roommate died from his injuries. Ra'Shaun had no prior arrests.

Ra'Shaun's Story

On Oct 8, 1992, when I was 18, I was arrested for burglary and second-degree murder. I sat on Rikers Island for almost two years and then was sent upstate to the New York Department of Corrections. I stayed there for 24 years of an 18-to-life sentence and came home on parole on July 19, 2016.

What Is a criminal? Sometimes you'd be surprised about who a criminal turns out to be. At Woodstock, everybody was a criminal. Criminals are contrarians, as opposed to the rest of society who are conforming. A person could be a contrarian in opinion. But criminals are contrarians in both opinion and action. When I imagine a criminal, I imagine someone doing something that somebody else wrote down not to do.

I think arrests and convictions are just by-products of the behavior—the residue. Sooner or later, you'll get caught—either go to jail or the cemetery. People are criminals before conviction. The behavior makes them a criminal.

I don't believe the word relates to me because I don't have a rap sheet for people to look at. I only have one occurrence. That's not a reference point. That's a landmark.

I never used a weapon because if I carried a razor in prison, I would have been a victim of the same prison mentality that turned criminality into a career. That's what makes a criminal a criminal. It's second nature to them—fresh air. In prison, people boast about how many times they've been back and forth in prison. They don't see themselves as criminals. They see the government as criminals, and the cops can't be trusted.

When I was in prison, I felt like I was in school because I'd never been to prison before. I studied the environment. I wasn't trying to learn the deviant behavior but trying to figure out *why* the people in my environment were engaging in that behavior. How does someone continue to do what got them in trouble and convince themselves that this time they won't get caught? What goes through your mind to come up with new ways to engage in that behavior?

When I first came home, I was shocked by how everyone was always on their cell phone. Nobody was paying attention to what was going on. In prison, I observed and listened to the words—which ones they used and how they used them. I still listen for contradictions.

There's a self-imposed segregation in prison—the Whites stay here, Blacks here, Spanish here. The correctional officers said it's just like society. Right outside prison is a White bar, a Black bar. Prison reflects society.

I had a lot of fights on Rikers—90% defending myself. After the fifth year, I had a good foothold on how to discern a personality and became an expert at listening and watching people.

The guards are paid to watch. I did it for free. Watched the prisoners and watched those who got to go home.

I also taught myself how to research the law and spent my time in the law library in addition to studying my surroundings. When I first came home, I heard a lady say that she got a notice her house was going to be foreclosed on. I told her how to go to court. She listened and the judge issued a stay on the foreclosure.

I used to help so many guys with parole appeals. I don't trust parole. They say, "Our job is to help you guys transition," but they stopped me from working overtime or at night.

Curfew and reporting are the worst part of parole. Parolees have an 8:00 p.m. to 8:00 a.m. curfew. If your job is in the daytime, that's good, but if you have a night job, they will tell you to get a different job. You have to live your life for their convenience. Of course, you're expected to follow the rules of society, but parole has a lot more rules—beyond laws. For example, to visit my mom in Jersey, I need an out of state pass 30 days in advance.

If you bring any complaints to parole's attention, they make it difficult for the parolee. There's no way to protect yourself from what they do. I'm always afraid to report to parole because you can't protect yourself when you're in there.

When society writes people off, they're missing out on people who can contribute in a valuable way. That person who was in prison is coming back soon. They get out and they go right back to their neighborhoods. If you discount people, it may hurt you because you may need them in the future.

I don't like being in places where people know I've been to jail and don't know me. I want people to know me before they make a judgment. Society sees me as what they see on the TV screen when they watch a show about prison. For them that's reality, but it's far from the truth of how prison is—it's somebody's imagination of how it is.

All the ideology they believe about someone in prison—whatever ideology was instilled within them about prison and prisoners—that's what they will embrace and believe about me. They're not going to see me for me if they know where I was at. After they already know who I am, if they find out where I was, it doesn't make a difference. But if that came first, they will never get to know me.

Prison is society's basement. People put what they don't need anymore in the basement.

And people don't believe individuals with records. Even in relationships, the person is going to hear, "It's because you were away for so long." I always hear that.

I want people to see me for me. If after knowing me, they don't like me, that is something I'll have to respect, but I would rather them do that then say, "Oh, he was in jail. He's a criminal."

I don't need you to validate me. But if you write me off, you write off the chance for me to help you.

John Braga: Putting Criminality Behind

John, the youngest son of Portuguese immigrants, grew up in Carteret, a New Jersey suburb, in a middle-class family in a private home on a tree-lined street. John's adolescence and young adulthood resembles those of many other justice-involved individuals in one critical aspect: addiction. John drank heavily as a young teen and later became addicted to several other substances, including crack cocaine. He beat his girlfriend to death while in a drug-induced rage. John claims to have no recollection of the incident.

In 1996, John was incarcerated for murder in the second degree after an assault that resulted in homicide. He spent over 15 years at Greenhaven Correctional before being transferred to lower security facilities, including Clinton Correctional in Dannemora and then Fishkill Correctional. He served 21.5 years of a 20-year-to-life sentence.

John was released in 2017 and is no longer under the supervision of parole. He married on Christmas Eve 2019 and currently works for a trucking company, driving 18-wheelers across the East Coast. John's been sober and drug-free for over 20 years.

John's Story

A criminal is anybody that disobeys the law. People try to justify their actions and behavior in all sorts of ways, but it's who you are in the dark when nobody's looking that is your true measure. If you decided to do something wrong and you know it's wrong, it's criminal.

You can split up the definition. You can attach it to somebody's character. The other half is statutes and going through the system. The people who haven't gotten caught are the "nice next-door neighbors." You wouldn't know a criminal unless they're in the system or you'd witnessed them in the act.

If you're on trial for a crime, they're going to label you a criminal and say it out loud. If you're convicted, they're going to say it out loud. If you're in the system, correctional officers are going to treat you as such. Once you're outside of the system and done with supervision, nobody refers to you as that. People may call me other things, but nobody's called me a criminal or treated me like that in my current situation.

The only one who may want to say something like that is a parole officer. But they say that to the people who are screwing up because those people's actions are continuing to be criminal. The only person who is going to think of me as a criminal is a person who is working for the criminal justice system, and that is only going to come into play if I do something outside the law again.

Someone calling me a criminal just because they've been able to look at my background? I've never had that experience. Here's the perfect example. I was pulled over for a size restriction violation on a restricted road today. The officer did not come to the cab and say, "Oh, you criminal," even after he ran my license. He didn't say, "Oh, that figures."

I no longer live outside the law, so I don't see myself as a criminal. I'm an ex-felon. I committed a crime. I was convicted and I served my time, but I don't consider myself a criminal. If you bump into me in the street, you'll never know. I am still going to be the guy who will hold the door for you; I might engage you in polite conversation. I'm not going to be the one who will pull a weapon on you if you get in my way. I'm not that guy.

Being labeled a criminal while I was in prison was tough at first, but then you become desensitized to it. If you are trying to change your life and become a better person and grow, after a while it doesn't bother you. They call you a con. They call you a felon. That's just part of the system. A lot comes down to your perception. It's a matter of how you handle the information presented to you. The officers in the system are not my friends; they work there. Am I going to go back to my cell and say, "I'm going to get this guy?" No. I'm going to survive and persevere no matter what anybody says.

Society doesn't even know who I am. When I go to apply for a job and the issue of my background comes up, I've had mixed reactions, which I've also had to deal with. They try to play it off like that's not the reason. Again, I don't take that personally. I've had to move on to the person who's going to give me a chance. I have to keep hustling and moving forward because in the next few years, no one's going to be concerned with that.

When you apply for a job, they go back 10 years of work history and addresses. What happens when you only have three years? They will ask you straightforward questions like, "Are you still under active supervision?" I also have the choice not to answer those questions. And sometimes electronic applications have loaded question that I refuse to answer. "Are you currently or have you ever been on parole?" That's a double question, discourages people from applying.

You feel it out. You know if a company is going to move forward or blow you off. They might say, "I'm going to talk to my managers and get back to you." So, I might wait a day and hear nothing and send a message and hear nothing. It's my choice to wait or not. I've been able to land two pretty good contracts with companies that gave me a chance. It's not the end of the world when someone doesn't give me a chance. There's always something else out there.

If someone doesn't have the level of perseverance, they might fall into old criminal behaviors and say, "This is why I have to do what I do." But that's a lame excuse, a cop-out.

There really isn't anything in life that if you want it bad enough, you can't do it. People do carry hard feelings. But if you go around carrying resentments and are bitter, you're never going to accomplish anything remotely like being successful. Not at all.

I don't get stuck on the negativity. And like I said, I've been called worse. If you want to get my hackles up, calling me a criminal is not going to do it.

Whatever is in their head is their business. I can't control your thoughts, so I don't lose sleep over that.

Even when I was pulled over today, the only thing I was thinking was, "This is going to be a big ticket." I wasn't thinking "Oh, I'm going to be in trouble." This cop wasn't even interested in my background because I wasn't doing anything criminal where he's going to call for backup. If he did mention my record, I would have that conversation with him. He might be interested in how I changed my life around. I might be helping his nephew. You don't know. Not everything has to be negative. If someone continues to do criminal activity, even after they're off parole, then they're a criminal. If someone thinks they're going to beat the system and not get caught—doing it at the expense of innocent people—then they're a criminal. That's not who I am.

*The name John Braga is a pseudonym used for privacy protection. All other names and identifying information are real and accurate.

Diane Gottlieb is a writer and educator living in Florida. Her essays, fiction, interviews, and reviews have appeared in *About Place Journal*, *The Manifest-Station*, *The VIDA Review*, *PRISM International*, *The Rumpus*, *The Hedgehog Review Blog*, and *Hippocampus Magazine*, among others. She won the 2021 Tiferet Writing Contest in nonfiction. Ms. Gottlieb holds an MSW and an MEd. She received her MFA from Antioch University Los Angeles, where she served as lead editor of creative nonfiction for *Lunch Ticket*. She also served as lead creative nonfiction editor for the 2020 Women's National Book Award contest and is the prose and creative nonfiction editor for *Emerge Literary Journal*. Ms. Gottlieb is currently writing a hybrid nonfiction narrative/memoir about the lives of five formerly incarcerated men. You can find her at https://dianegottlieb.com and on Twitter @DianeGotAuthor.

3

LIFE SUPPORT

Organizing for Justice Inside and Outside of Prison

Jamel Muhammad, as told to Katherine S. Gaudet

I went to prison in 1992 at the age of 20 and came out in 2008 at the age of 37. Before I went to prison, I had gotten rich on the streets and had a whole organization under me. In prison, I organized against injustice. Now I spend every day working to prevent violence and give young people a chance for a better life.

I went through 14 facilities over the course of 19 years, state and federal. When they move someone around that much, it's punitive—sometimes for violence, fights, stabbing, that kind of thing. But the problem with me was on the political side. I went in very angry. A group of guys got to me and reshaped my thinking and attitude. I became more politically and socially conscious and active; I started organizing the prisons in a different way. Once they saw I had a footing, they would ship me out.

I always say that looking at prison is like looking at society through a microscope. Everything is exactly replicated, exactly the same. The same things that are happening in society, drugs and weapons and prostitution, are happening as much, if not more, in the prisons. You have corruption in the cities; there's corruption in the prison system. There are social justice issues in society and there are social justice issues in prison, with officer brutality and terrible living conditions. There are problems with education and resources. A lot of what I was organizing around was social justice. Why were we not being given the education and tools and training to keep from going back to prison when we got out?

Prison Mentors and a Turning Point

Prison definitely changed me. When I went in, I was mad at the world. I'd found out that people close to me—some of them in my family—had informed on me. Those things had me so angry and closed in and against the world. I didn't trust anybody, didn't like anybody. I had just turned 20 years old and was facing 20 years

DOI: 10.4324/9781003169468-5

in prison, in a max penitentiary with lifers. I was afraid. I had seen jail movies, heard jail stories. My attitude was about survival: fight or flight.

I'd been there four or five months and was in the law library all the time, focused on my legal work. But a group of guys had been paying attention to me more than I was paying attention to me. There was an older Muslim guy, 69 or 79 years old, Sheik Abdul.

He approached me: "Hey, young brother, how you doin'?"

My response was, "Fuck you. Get the fuck out of my face. Who the fuck you talking to?"

He just shook his head and walked off. This went on for almost a month. This dude was persistent. At one point he said to me, "You need to do the time and stop letting the time do you."

It threw me off. All I could say was "Fuck you." This old man with his slick-ass words. What the hell was he talking about? It was the first time I'd heard that piece of advice.

I went to some older guys I did know and said, "Who is this old-ass dude Sheik Abdul? He told me some bullshit about do the time, don't let the time do you."

And this guy (he grew up with my mom), he said, "Do you know who Sheik is?" He told me Sheik was one of the original members of the Black Liberation Army, one of the founding members of the Black Panther Party here in New York.

Damn. I felt like shit. This is a dude worthy of all honor.

So I went and I found him that evening down in the program area. I said, "I just want to apologize to you."

And he said, "Listen, I kept coming because I like you. I like that fire. You remind me of when I was a young revolutionary."

I heard later that after the 1971 rebellion at Attica, as a preventative measure, they took those guys who were politically and socially conscious, and stuck them all at Greenhaven. So here I am at Greenhaven, in the company of all these historical revolutionaries, and all of them had been watching me. It was primarily because I was the youngest in the population.

They said, "Here's the deal. The reality is that we're here for life. Many of us are going to die here. You have a chance; whether you get out on appeal or you serve 20 years, you will go back home. You have a chance to make a difference in society, to make sure our young Black men don't continue to fill these prisons."

By the way, there were at least four families there—grandfather, father, and sons, in the same prison.

So that was their thinking, why they pushed me to not let my mind be captured by that environment. They said, "They don't own your mind. Make sure this isn't what you're comfortable coming back to because it's the only thing you know. Keep your mind on your family and what you're going to do for them whenever you get out of here."

I still had a long way to go. Things didn't flip around until one day when I got put in a position of responsibility.

I grew up religiously, exposed to everything. My family was not going to tell me what I had to believe; I could choose when I was old enough. But they wanted to make sure I always had spirituality. In prison, I had started getting involved with the Nation of Islam, but I wasn't sure yet that I wanted to be part of it. I was already familiar with the Nation of Islam growing up, because I had family members who were involved with the Nation. My resistance initially was the fact that I was still angry and focused on retaliation against those who had violated my trust.

Practicing Islam wasn't allowed in the prison system when I got there, but in 1994 Congress passed the Religious Freedom Restoration Act. It meant that if any person could present bona fide tenets of practice, that religion had to be recognized. So at that point the state Department of Corrections had to allow the Nation of Islam to practice inside the prisons, and they were trying to get established in Greenhaven, but there was a lot of infighting and conflict.

Ministers from the mosque came into the facility one day. I organized the meeting, set up the gate clearance, but I still wanted no part of anything else. The ministers were addressing a lot of things, a lot of bickering, and one of them said, "Where's Brother Jamel at?" I was standing at the back and was ordered to the front, to face the others. He said, "Right now, as it stands, this is the representative for Minister Farrakhan inside this facility."

In my mind, I was like, how about asking me first? If you go from Christian scripture, you would say I was in a Valley of Decision. I was confused. I had never asked to lead the Nation of Islam in the prison. I didn't even openly embrace it.

I went back to my cell, and literally stayed up until the sun came up wrestling with myself, my attitude, my energy. Until that day I could not look in the mirror; I couldn't embrace the person I was seeing in that mirror. I said to myself, "Jamel, with how you were raised, how did this become you?"

I cried half that night. I tried to make sense of my journey, the people I hurt. I had a sense of so much that has happened by my hand. I was totally opposite of the person my grandmother wanted me to be. It was an intense, deep conversation with myself before I could look in a mirror and just look at myself. As I looked in my own eyes, the person I saw was not who I am. I said, "You're going to face yourself tonight." I stood there and cried.

From the tears I went into prayer, begging for forgiveness, guidance, strength. I said, "If this is what you desire of me, give it to me. If not, take my life. I don't want to stay here as this person." I sat on my bed and processed and cried that entire night, forcing myself to look into that mirror. Then I pulled myself together. I stood up. I said, "I'm not going to give in. I owe it to my mother. I owe it to my family." I looked in my mirror and said, "Jamel, you're back." And from that moment I never looked back.

That was in February or March of 1994, two years into my sentence.

Becoming an Organizer

I committed myself to working things from a different angle. I was already helping younger inmates in the population, but once I was designated as a prison representative for the Nation of Islam, more responsibility and accountability came. I had already established a relationship, or rather, a reputation with the administration. They knew I was level-headed but also very firm. They were also kind of uncomfortable, because even though I was level-headed I was very quiet. They didn't know much about what to expect from me in that position. I was also chairman of the NAACP Criminal Justice Committee and got involved with the Inmate Liaison Committee (ILC), which was a buffer between the prisoners and the administration. I would carry prisoner concerns up, and if administration wanted to inform us of changes, I would carry those back down. Both of those committees were established as a result of the Attica rebellion of '71.

There were a lot of hats I wore and a lot of duties that I carried. I had to make sure I carried them responsibly. There were a lot of things going on in the system that needed addressing: direct abuses of authority, assaults on inmates. There was one group of officers that were some of the most racist and prejudiced people you can find on the globe, probably. It went right up into the administration. They did a lot of psychological manipulation and abuse.

One morning there was an incident with a young Puerto Rican inmate. He was diabetic and was going up to the infirmary early in the morning. In the infirmary holding cell, you don't touch the keys, don't touch the gates, don't touch the radios. That's something you know. This young man, though, was very young. He didn't know the environment. And they had this game they would play. What's supposed to happen is the officer pops the gate with one hand and reaches over to open the door with the other. But once this officer popped the gate, he told the kid to open the gate and come out. So another officer starts yelling at him—"Why are you touching the gate?" They put him up against the wall, claimed he moved his hand. They beat this kid very bad. You could hear him yelling and crying. It doesn't deserve to happen to anybody, but this kid was so young and naïve. It touched everybody.

I'm supposed to be the responsible guy, but I can't be so levelheaded that abuses go unchecked. So I said, "Shut it down." When they came around after lunch to ask whether we wanted to go to programs, everyone said no. The administration can't have that. Part of the prison population is industry population, called Corcraft. They make things that are sold to state agencies. Without that operating, a lot of things shut down. Also, the prison is obligated by law and standards to give us three meals a day, and at least two have to be hot. If we're not going out, they have to come in and feed us. Demonstrating control like that lets them know they don't have control of their facilities. They don't know what can come next.

I got called up front to talk to the superintendent, deputy superintendent for programs, and deputy superintendent for security, and demanded that my ILC team be with me. I said the only way they were going to have their jail open back up was to get those officers out of their position by the hospital. For the administration it was, "Do we get rid of Jamel and risk someone popping up who's less levelheaded, more aggressive? Or keep him in place, keep him satisfied enough to keep him from flipping this facility upside down?" The officers were moved from that post. From that point it was a whole other level as far as my ability to get reform.

That let me see what I had thought up to that point was not possible: that you could get people to come together as a common cause if you had the right message and the right timing. It didn't make me arrogant. It actually humbled me, had me doing a lot more self-reflection. Why me? Why do I qualify as this special element, this person, that God, Allah, Jehovah, whatever you see as that higher entity, had selected to fight against the oppression that was going on in the system? It changed a lot of my energy and my attitude going forward. I was a voice for the voiceless. And I started to look at the prison population to study recidivism. Why are so many people gone and coming back before you can make it to your next meal?

One of the things that I thank God for: I don't know any other person who was in as long as I was without a vice or an escape—drugs, gambling, sex, or psychotic medications. By the grace of God I avoided every one of them.

It's funny—one of the things that helped me get there was very early in my sentence watching a movie that had Sylvester Stallone in it. At some point he ends up incarcerated. There was another individual in the population who was muscling other inmates and saying, "This is my TV, this is this, the environment belongs to me." Sylvester Stallone told him, "Once you claim this environment, they own you." So my thing was always to detach myself from the environment.

Another thing was an interview with Mike Tyson. I had known him personally; we were part of the original Team Tyson, when he was fighting Golden Gloves. In the interview he was asked how he gets through his days, and he said he does a lot of reading. That was true for me too; I was an avid reader. He said he had read a book from a philosopher that said, "Blessed is the man or woman who is too busy to think during the day, and too tired to think at night." And that worked for me. I didn't have time to stress. I was so busy during the daytime dealing with issues, that by the time 9:00 lockdown came, my head hit the pillow, and I'd wake up the next day and I was on the next grind.

Those are the two things I now give back to individuals: don't claim the environment, and keep yourself occupied.

Everywhere I went it was the same agenda: educate, advocate, empower. I would do what I could while on the inside to fight against institutionalization and break recidivism.

Federal Time and Preparing for Release

The state commissioner pushed me in front of the early parole board to be released, but it was only because I still had 12 and a half years of federal time to do. Federal was much more professional, I'll give them that. They still had issues that could be better, but did not have blatant abuse. It was a completely different environment. It wasn't cells, it was dorm rooms. You had to keep things polished; there was a white-glove inspection every morning. Officers had to be able to see their reflection on your floor or you'd get a sanction. The people in the state system were lower educated, in there for street crimes. The people in the federal system were there for more sophisticated crimes. There were members of the mafia, political people who were tied into different schemes or bribes, Fortune 500 company owners. We called it Club Fed. You could go to a facility where one of the activities was polo. When I got there in 1998 it was starting a transformation. There were large-scale drug raids, and individuals who normally would have had state offenses were now in the federal system. As more inmates of color with street-level crimes came in, all of those things were taken away. Danbury, Connecticut had a lake on the campus; they filled it up with dirt. They got rid of all the activities.

But for me, federal time was easy going until my last leg of it. I was transferred to a prison camp in Manchester, Kentucky. The village had so much poverty, you had houses that still had dirt floors. The education and literacy rates were below any standard you could imagine. It was a town of Caucasian citizens who literally had zero contact with people of color. We did a program during the holiday season where inmates would collect money and the counselors would take it to buy toys for the local kids, who were invited to the facility visiting room to get their presents. I had a kid that came over to me, no more than 5 years old, and started rubbing my hand.

I asked him, "What do you want, what do you need? You want a cookie?"

The mother turned beet red and started apologizing. She said, "He's never seen a colored person before. And I tell you honestly, this is my first experience also."

This lady was 30 or 32 years old and had never had contact with a person of color. And that's who made up the population at that camp. Out of 112 or 115, probably 100 were locals.

By then I had been 15 years in the system. It was my job to clean the administrative offices. It was all women up there. Until that facility, I would never, never, ever communicate with female staff in the prison unless I was answering a question.

That was part of the trauma from my state time. There was a guard who was a very small, well-shaped White female. They made sure that her uniforms were two sizes smaller than what she could get into. In the state they have a charge called "reckless eyeballing." So any time some of the guards wanted a victim to beat up, they would bring that female officer into general population during program movement, or chow movement. The rule is, keep your eyes in front of you. You're going to smell her perfume (we're around funky dudes all day). You always get that one who looks to the side, or makes a "Mmmm" sound—that one gets snatched out. Me, I'm not going to see anything. I'm going to stay clear of all females.

It's something I still wrestle with. I get frustrated. It stirs a little anger. I thought I withstood institutionalization, but it made me handicapped with females, even 13 years post-incarceration.

So when I cleaned the offices I would go in and be out faster than the bird on Roadrunner. But Miss Barrett, the secretary for the camp administrator, picked up on this. One day she locked the main door, so I had to come to her to get out of the office. She asked me "Where are you from? Why are you always running? You can't stand around for two seconds? Why don't you talk to us?"

I was nervous as hell, and she was getting a kick out of it. Finally, I broke down and explained to her. I'm grateful for her. She told her colleagues about the situation, and they did everything they could to make me as comfortable as possible around the opposite gender.

When it was time for me to transfer out, she wanted me to have a furlough transfer. That means you get a bus pass and a time period that's designated to get from one facility to the other, instead of being tackled and shackled. She said, "You can't go out there like that. You're not going to make it if you don't start adjusting now."

But I denied the furlough transfer; I wouldn't sign the papers. Just the thought of it alone gave me so many different feelings it's not even explainable. I was scared, nervous, angry—every emotion within 90 seconds. I could not see myself functioning in the community without that control and structure of prison. That's what made me angry. I realized, "I can't make it outside of this."

It wasn't until that case manager came to me with that information that I understood those individuals who were returning to prison. That's when I started seeing and understanding all that apprehension and fear. How do you handle it? How do you deal with it? For some guys, it was easy. Go snort some coke, use heroin, weed, or alcohol. I didn't have those vices. I had a family, I had community support. But most of those guys have nothing.

Anyway, Miss Barrett insisted that Jamel is going to go on a Greyhound. I argued and fought. She said, "At the end of the day I'm the one with a pen in my hand, and you're going. You're going to be fine." She made me come down and spend some time with her and her colleague every day, so I could try to adjust. But it's something you can't prepare for.

The day came, and I had to jump in the car with another inmate who was taking me into town, to the bus station in Manchester, Kentucky, to get on a bus by myself. That was like an out-of-body experience. It was different, it was interesting, it was hard, it was scary. It was everything.

I got on the bus, nervous as hell. I was in a gray sweatsuit, with nothing to show I was an inmate. But in my mind, everybody knew. As I looked down the aisle, everybody was putting stuff in the seat next to them, looking out the window, to make sure I didn't have anywhere to sit. As I got to the back, there was a Black guy sitting there with a duffel bag, and as he saw me getting closer, he slid the bag off his lap onto the seat. I said "Excuse me, I need to sit down. Can you move your bag so I can have a seat." I was giving plenty of attitude. "Is it a problem?" He grabbed his bag and put it on his lap.

I was flared up, mad at Miss Barrett because I told her to let me go regular transportation. The irony is, me and this guy became buddies before the end of this trip. We split in Ohio. Talking to him, keeping my mind off everything, kept my anxiety and stress down. By the time we split I was better, but I was sad, too, to realize how much society had changed.

I had two hours in a bus depot with nothing to do, so I thought I'd get some fresh air. I stepped up to the entryway, and the door opened on its own. It scared me. I couldn't step past the threshold. I turned around. I started getting angry. The tears were coming down. I was so angry at the fact that I was afraid to go out that door. That was the beginning of seeing how hard it would be to go from prison back into society.

Building a Life of Service

In July 2008 I was released and ended up under home confinement at my mother's house in Albany. I couldn't leave the house unless I was going to work. You get one hour a week for religious service worship, and one hour a day for recreation. We had to fill out a request for the week that said what every day was going to be, so there was no running out to the grocery store unless it was planned in advance. Jobs got me out of the house. I worked at BJ's and a cleaning agency.

I also started getting involved with what was going on in the legislature. I have a godmother who was a county legislator at the time I was released. She was the mother of my cousin who got murdered. After that happened, and I got locked up, she decided to run for public office and try to change some of the laws and local ordinances. We stayed in contact through my incarceration. The last six or seven years, she was getting me more and more involved in the things she was interested in. At first it was kind of a head-butt. She's a firecracker.

At one point while I was incarcerated she wanted to bring a gun buyback program to Albany. She told me about it on a phone call, and I listened to her because it was difficult to say what I thought. She had pride and hope in this idea. But I said, "Honestly Mom, you want my honest thoughts, it would never work."

She went off. She had put three years into this idea, and I had just put a pin in her balloon. I was down to 90 seconds on my phone call. We had 12-minute times, and you couldn't call right back; you had to wait 25 minutes. Maybe it's a good thing we had to wait, because she was livid. When she got back on the phone the first thing she said was, "I'm listening."

I told her that we carried those guns because they were our sense of security. There's no way a person in that predicament is going to say, "Let me go turn my guns in." If I'm one of the people carrying guns on the street, I'm not going to make myself unsafe for $250, and be walking around knowing that I made myself vulnerable. What I would do is take a dirty gun, a gun that had a crime on it, and turn it in for $250. Then I would take $100 of that and get a new gun that's clean. The only thing she'd be doing is helping me to dodge the cases that would take me off the streets.

She understood, but it made her frustrated. Her golden egg just got crushed. She said, "So, what do we do? How do we take guns off the streets?" That helped her realize that she needed the perspective of someone like me.

When I came home, she was working on a reentry task force, part of the Second Chance Act in New York. She asked me to come down and sit in on the Albany County Reentry Task Force meetings. I'd be a listening ear and would sit with her afterwards, and tell her what I was hearing. Up to that point, formerly incarcerated individuals had not been part of the reentry task force. But at that time it did include one gentleman who had been released in 1981. When he spoke in a meeting, everyone's pens went down and attention went up. People got uneasy in the room. One person said, "We had a rule of thumb that those guys would not be in here, because of the things we're talking about." There was a conflict; the group was divided about whether he should stay or not. My godmother's decision was the one that mattered. She knew how important it was to have that voice there, and he stayed. At one point, she asked me if I would speak to the county legislature on reentry: what it is, what it looks like, what it needs to look like. The press was there, and after I left, people were asking her for my business card, wanted to know who I was working for. They felt I should be more involved.

I started working as a case manager for a community organization called Trinity Alliance that worked with juveniles. Then I got pulled over to be a street outreach supervisor for a gun violence program. I was responsible for hiring my team: two violence interrupters and three outreach workers. When shots were fired, the violence interrupters went in to try to contain the situation and mediate conflicts. The outreach workers were the long-term engagement part of the program. They identified who were at highest risk for shooting or being shot and tried to recruit them into the program, tried to move them into the non-risk category. The state legislature named the program SNUG—guns spelled backwards.

It was not a cakewalk. There was major opposition, lots of racism and prejudice. But my team, we were very effective. That turned out to be a double-edged sword for me. SNUG became known as "Jamel's program," and there was some tension with Trinity. My supervisor, who also was the executive director, told me I intimidated him, and I was difficult to control. That did not sit right with me. Wrong words, wrong person. I was two years out from 17.5 years of people controlling me; now he was talking about controlling me.

I had a mentor named Lloyd Stuart that I would sit with every Saturday at 1:00. I had met him one day when I was out campaigning with my godmother. He was 67 years old and had come up through the civil rights movement. For him it was impressive, intriguing, and hopeful to see a young Black man out doing campaigning. He invited me to go sit with him, and the chemistry was perfect. I was comfortable with him, and he was comfortable with me. After one or two times it became a standard lock-in on our schedules. He helped me decompress from my trauma after incarceration. He would get me to talk about things I didn't realize I needed to be talking about. He made me realize I'm not fine.

When things went downhill at Trinity, he said, "We've got to get you out of there." He had a team of elders, individuals who were retired from different positions at nonprofits, government, and faith organizations. He ultimately came to me with a conversation about setting up a nonprofit that would focus on preventing gun violence and retaliation. His team would do the administrative stuff, and I would be the face of the organization. That became Youth L.I.F.E. Support Network, Inc., which was recognized by the state charities bureau in November of 2012.

We first got a foothold in Schenectady with the implementation of a spin-off of the SNUG program I set up in Albany. It was modified to fit the culture of

Schenectady and called 1Life2Live. Later I would set up programs in Albany that focused on youth.

At first there was pushback from law enforcement leaders. They said, "You have information on homicides, and you don't give us the information. It flies in the face of everything we've been taught about policing."

I explained it this way: "Jamel's job is not to solve a crime. Jamel's job is to prevent the next trigger from being pulled." We could show that it worked, that retaliation rates went down. The city police chief and county sheriff, Chief Chaires and Sheriff Dagostino, got on board and have been great partners ever since, primarily because we have established respect for boundaries and mutual understanding.

We've grown as an organization, including having been called upon to assist in setting up programming as far away as the Bronx, New York. We also have a contract with the Albany County Department for Children, Youth, and Family Services, to work with children who are removed from their homes due to a parent's petition or juvenile delinquency charges. We work with them and their families to stabilize the situation at home.

One of the things we are able to do is when youth are in court-ordered placement, we can take them off campus and work with them in the community. Our whole thing is not making them adjust to the facility, but adjust to coming home, to society. If they're having a hard day at the facility, trying to deescalate them in the environment that has triggered them in the first place is counterproductive. If Tequan is ripping phones off the wall, I'm not going to have the conversation there. I'll take him to McDonald's or Dave and Buster's, then have the conversation. The idea is life support. From your placement back into society, we want to help you get your life together—to make it a life, not just existence.

Now we're working with adults as well. We oversee inmate services at the Schenectady County Jail. We created a network of services to wrap around every inmate who's at the jail, to make sure their barriers are dismantled as much as they can be. That includes mental health, substance use, making sure they are connected with insurance, housing, clothes, employment. We have a Discharge Coordinator and Community Transition Coach who work with them before release, so they walk out of the facility toward their plan.

That's where things are. I have an 11-year-old; he is the balance of my life. Every parent is going to say their child is amazing, but I stand firm on that. I'm very spiritually rooted and grounded. I'm not saying I'm perfect, but I'm concerned that what I do is pleasing to God, and when it's not, I beg for forgiveness. I was given the opportunity to show that even in today's world, you can bring a great child into it. I want him to find whatever spirituality can water him and make sure he gets his cup full. I don't want him to be some monk, but have some groundedness, to act in his day-to-day life, dealing with people, treating people in a way that makes a difference. I want him to know that if he has the spirituality and the groundedness of knowing how to please God, and not those around you, he can be a community leader. That's what I hope to achieve in my life.

Jamel Muhammad is the proud father of two sons, Isa Muhammad and Ali Sharah. Mr. Muhammad was born in Albany, NY, the middle child of two brothers, and was raised predominantly by his mother. She taught him the importance of respect, self-worth, and a well-rounded religious background. As Mr. Muhammad grew into his teens and early manhood, he strayed from his home teachings and became involved in "street life," which caused him to become incarcerated with a 20-year prison sentence. Mr. Muhammad served 17 years in the state and federal prison system. Although he was locked up physically, he never allowed his circumstances to imprison him mentally or emotionally, but used his imprisonment as an opportunity to re-evaluate his past and present and to plan for his future. Today, Mr. Muhammad is President and CEO of Youth L.I.F.E. Support Network, Inc., a community-based nonprofit organization with a focus on public safety. Under the nonprofit, Mr. Muhammad operates programs that work with high-risk youth as well as individuals involved with gun and gang violence—those at the highest risk of either shooting or being shot. Mr. Muhammad has a great appreciation for his partnerships with both the community and the law enforcement/criminal justice departments, as well as a host of colleges and universities in the Capital Region. You can reach him through his email at j.muhammad@ylsninc.org.

4

RACISM, ABUSE, AND RESTORATIVE JUSTICE

What's Wrong with Our Criminal Justice System, and How to Change It

Joseph Lascaze

I would like to share with you some of my personal experiences with the criminal justice system. I would not consider this a full version of my experience of incarceration, as there are many aspects of my journey I'm still unpacking to this day. However, I'm hoping that by sharing some of my experiences, you will gain a transformational understanding of our current justice system, the challenges and barriers incarcerated people face, and the changes desperately needed within our current system. While I've had numerous bad experiences with law enforcement, I can't say all my experiences have been negative. The positive experiences all have the same thing in common: I was treated with respect and as a human above all else.

Valley Street

I entered Valley Street County Jail for the first time when I was 19 and spent more than 21 months there over four different rounds of pretrial detention. When I think back over the months, days, and countless minutes I spent housed in that facility, I see that the majority of my life's worst experiences occurred there. I did learn quite a lot about life, people, and human nature while locked up in jail. One of most valuable lessons I learned was about the effect on human character when control and power are left unchecked, with no oversight.

While I was there the facility used, and still uses, a behavioral modification "instrument" (I call it a torture device) called "the chair." Correctional officers forcefully place an inmate on a solid plastic chair that sits on wheels. They proceed to place Velcro straps around the inmate, securing the person to the chair at eight different points. You cannot physically move when placed in the chair. Your limbs fall asleep due to lack of movement and compression from the straps. The only thing you can do is try to ignore the overwhelming feeling of helplessness over the

DOI: 10.4324/9781003169468-6

two to four hours you're confined. During rounds, correctional officers will walk by and taunt you, often laughing in your face and saying something like, "I bet you wish you could stand up."

I was placed in the chair once. I was in it for four hours, and I can tell you that I felt every minute of those hours pass by. Not only was I painfully restrained in the chair, I was also covered in OC spray that the correctional guards had used on me during my cell extraction. As my skin burned from the pepper spray and my limbs became numb from poor circulation, a different burning sensation started to take place inside me that would change me forever. I will admit, tears freely flowed down my face as I struggled with the emotional rollercoaster I was on for those 240 minutes.

In my experience, it was routine for correctional officers to assault residents in the Restricted Housing Unit during their rounds. Even with cameras on the pod, there were no cameras in the cells, and this is where they would cause the most harm to residents. The culture was one that encouraged correctional officers to make the facility as uncomfortable as possible, so it would be seen as a deterrent to committing crime. To me it seemed that most of the correctional officers, specifically the ones who worked the "hole" unit, embraced this philosophy by administering their own form of punishment on residents. Young males, the majority being Black or Hispanic, were punched in their ribs, OC sprayed in their face, dragged around their cells while handcuffed, and regularly strapped into "the chair." This approach to "corrections and rehabilitation" only did one thing—it created survivors of deep traumatic experiences with an extreme distrust of the system and the image of a badge and uniform.

The abuse of power and lack of oversight that led to devices like "the chair" cause real harm to people. This kind of punishment doesn't help anyone take positive steps towards rehabilitating their life. The only thing it does is condition you to survive being treated like an animal in a cage.

Welcome to the State Prison

After jail comes prison. When I entered the state prison for the first time, at the age of 19, it was like stepping into a different world. When you're transported to the prison, you pass through a double security gate and into Reception and Diagnostics (R&D). R&D is the oldest part of the prison system, first constructed in the 1800s. It feels like a castle dungeon (and yes, I have been in a castle dungeon). The officer who was doing my intake said to me, "I see this is your first time here, and you're going to be here for a while. Let me give you some advice. Do exactly what we tell you, when we tell you do it, and you won't have any problems. Otherwise, saddle up for the ride!"

I don't know how the guard expected me to interpret his welcome speech, but it is an example of the one-sided power dynamic between correctional officers and prisoners. That's when it started to sink in that I was not viewed as a human, a community member, or a person who made poor choices but could still be redeemed. This notion would be reinforced time and again over the 13 years I spent incarcerated.

Since I was no longer at the steering wheel of my life—that privilege had been handed over to the New Hampshire Department of Corrections—the only thing I could do was prepare for where I was told I would be headed: Gladiator School. Anyone who has ever served time in the state's prison for men knows about Gladiator School. This was a name given to a specific housing unit located inside the prison. It was an initiation and rite of passage among residents to survive living on this pod.

Fighting was a daily occurrence, and not just among the residents. Correctional guards could get into it too. It was the concept of the unit itself that created gladiators. You were supposed to fight when you lived on this pod. When there weren't real fights occurring, play-fighting was a top pastime, trying to sharpen our techniques, because the number-one rule was to stay sharp. Gambling, tattooing, selling drugs, and drug abuse are the realities of the prison environment. There was not a single thing about F-pod that was designed to rehabilitate you.

An institution that is supposed to rehabilitate you needs to create a safe and educational environment, where you learn better ways of acting in the world. But life in jail or prison is not what average community members experience. Residents witness and experience everything from assaults to rapes to overdoses to violence that ends in murder, and are conditioned to see that as normal. It finally hit me recently: that was the environment where I and others like me grew up, where we learned everything about how to evaluate risk and make decisions. When violence is a common experience or even a possibility, how do we expect to people to get ready to go home?

Fast Track

The lieutenant at the time was an older White biker lady who could do a one-handed pull-up. We called her Mama Whitten. She came up with an idea as a last-ditch effort to break the cycle of Gladiator School. She decided to remove young, first-time offenders from Gladiator School and instead house them together on a pod that was designed to offer programs like anger management, victim impact, and financial literacy as well as life skills. All of it was taught by the "old-timers" living in the prison.

Lt. Whitten didn't take shit from anyone, and residents in the prison respected her. So, when she proposed the idea, the old-timers volunteered to help create a mentor program for the young kids training on F-pod. They choose the name Fast Track for the program. So, after I'd lived through Gladiator School for six months, 47 other people and I were slowly moved downstairs to A-pod to participate in the first run of Fast Track. I was going from an 8-man room to a double. Instead of 96 people living on the pod, there would be 48. It was a small step up.

Fast Track was a brilliant program, in my opinion, because it utilized mentors who had real lived experiences. It put their knowledge and their personal steps to rehabilitation in a central location for young residents to tap into. These mentors weren't random people. The knowledge and experience in Fast Track were coming from people who were living prison life 24/7, individuals who had made the exact same poor choices as we had—or worse. Since they had now put their lives on a positive course within the walls, they were a mine of priceless advice for choices and situations we would inevitably face during our prison bids. The initial mentors had decades of prison time under their belt, and most of them were or are going to die in prison. They had nothing to gain by volunteering. The mentors were respected as "OGs," and all they wanted was a chance to help young individuals avoid making the same life mistakes they did. Their reward was the satisfaction of knowing they used their experiences to help someone make better choices in life and become more than a statistic.

When a person is sentenced to serve prison time, the state court system or the Department of Corrections will require or recommend (respectively) that the person complete certain "rehabilitative" programs offered by the Department of Corrections. The theory behind these programs is that they will teach a resident the skills needed to make a better choice when faced with a decision similar to the one that led to their incarceration. But the downside is that once a program becomes a requirement, a resident cannot go home unless he completes the program. This strict barrier often causes a backup in the parole system. People will go months over their minimum sentence solely because they didn't complete a program—whether it's their fault (because they got disciplinary tickets) or not (because there isn't a staff member to facilitate the program).

Lt. Whitten recognized this was a problem with the system. In Fast Track, every program that participants were required or recommended to complete would be facilitated on the pod within a year—along with additional voluntary life skill programs. The graduates would be on a Fast Track to returning home, equipped with new life skills and hopefully a more mature mentality. Completing Fast Track meant the graduates wouldn't be denied their new security status when they became eligible—minimum security when you're within 24 months of your sentence's end, and eventually halfway-house and parole. Barring getting a disciplinary ticket, this pretty much guaranteed you would go home on the day you became eligible. That's big for someone in prison. I read somewhere a person describing the value of time by comparing it to different life circumstances. They said, "If you want to understand the value of a year, ask a person in prison waiting to go home." I don't know who they were, but I would agree with them. When you're sentenced to multiple years of prison time, especially at a young age, when that time is completed, getting out is the only thought your brain can process.

Fast Track worked for many of the members of the first graduating class: they didn't go back to prison once they eventually paroled. For me, Fast Track was a positive experience—but uncompleted. On New Year's Eve, I broke the rules by smoking weed, and coincidentally was selected for a random drug urinalysis test two days later. Back then a dirty urine was an A-level offense, along with things like assault, murder, and planning an escape. So when the urine results came back, I was booted from Fast Track and "disciplined" accordingly. (Today, dirty urine is only a B-level offense, and you can get multiple ones before any serious disciplinary action is taken.)

I'm responsible for the choice I made and shouldn't have done it. But the sanctions I received were not focused on rehabilitation or teaching me to evaluate my decisions through a mature lens. To correct behavior, it's critical that sanctions are proportional to the offense. For smoking weed, I was sanctioned to 5 days in solitary confinement, and when that was done I spent an additional two weeks in the Secure Housing Unit under 23-hour lockdown while I waited for a bed to open in a different unit. I received a six-month security classification upgrade to the Close Custody Unit—a disciplinary unit one step down from the hole, where you're locked in your cell more than 20 hours a day. I lost contact visits with my family and friends for a year, phone use for 25 days, and the privilege to buy food items off the canteen list for 25 days. I also had to pay a $65.00 restitution fee for a failed urinalysis test.

That one decision set the course of the rest of my prison sentence. I was sent to the hole for the first time ever for smoking weed.

After catching my A-ticket, I started on a downward spiral that would last several years. Some of that had to do with a particular correctional guard we referred to as Shower Shark, or Sharkie for short. Shower Shark was part of the Special Emergency Response Team—those correctional guards you see on TV that look like Ninja Turtles, in black uniforms with vests, helmets, and riot shields. Their job is to perform cell extractions, entire-unit searches, and whatever other "emergency" situations they get called for. Shower Shark got his nickname because he made a habit of ripping open the shower curtain, exposing the person inside to the rest of the people on pod. It was degrading, frustrating to the person trying to shower, and a complete invasion of privacy. A couple of months before I got the A-ticket for dirty urine I got into my first incident with him, which had to do with him making negative comments about my skin color.

Racism Behind the Walls

It's worth mentioning that growing up as part of a Black family in a northern New England state, I could count on one hand the number of people we interacted with who looked like us. In 1990, less than **one percent** of the entire state identified as Black, and over the course of the last three decades, this percentage has only grown to 1.8%. It would be later in life when I would come to fully understand the relationship between lack of diversity—both in race and perspective—and some of the more painful experiences I've had.

When Sharkie made those comments to me, I was young, angry, and humiliated. My mentor encouraged me to file a grievance to inform higher-ups of Sharkie's actions. I went through the grievance process until a judgment was made that my grievance had no merit. Sharkie claimed he never made those comments to me. It was a guard's word versus an inmate's. As my Fast Track mentor once told me, "You can't win from this side of the walls."

Jail and prison environments are not immune from the ugliness of racism, elitism, criminal profiling, and every other form of discrimination. It exists on all levels: between residents, staff, and even systemically. When I was there, racist gangs were obsessed with carving their opinions of non-Whites on the walls, mirrors, and windows of the cells they lived in, so that whenever the next person moved in, it was clear what the previous person thought. Staff members discriminate against residents for a host of different things. At the administrative level, discrimination and racism take on a more complex form. They manifest in which prison a person lives in, what unit, who can be approved to visit them, and so on.

During my first trip to the Secure Housing Unit, I was placed in a single-man cell where a swastika took up the entire back wall. I asked the guard to place me in a different cell and told him why. There was no response, but I'll never forget the look on his face. It's what I'd imagine it would be had I asked him to let me go home for the weekend. I don't know if the guard was a Nazi or not. But the way he dismissed my perspective was a reinforcement of the racist culture that corrupted many individuals inside the walls.

Most Blacks in the prison were social with each other and would meet up at the ball field, gym, or other common places. We are a minority in the state and the prison. At one point, I was labeled a gang member simply for being Black and associating with other Black men deemed to be gang members, when what we were doing was working out, going to chow hall together, and playing basketball. Since the time of the Nixon administration and J. Edgar Hoover, Black spiritual groups like the Five Percenters have been labeled and prosecuted as gangs. To me, that's a demonstration of systemic racism.

Segregation

There are two disciplinary housing units in the prison: the Secure Housing Unit (SHU) and the Close Custody Unit (CCU). I spent several years combined in both units over the span of my prison bid. The only thing I've come to understand about them is that they're simply containment warehouses where humans learn how to adapt to the most extreme trauma—both physical and mental.

Early on in my prison sentence, I had an experience that exemplifies the dehumanization that's at the root of what's wrong with the prison system. I had filled out a request slip to ask if I could have some of my personal belongings delivered to my cell. I placed the request slip outside my cell like I was supposed to, and waited for it to be picked up during that evening's mail call. The next day, I got the request slip back, but there was no response or even an acknowledgement that the slip had been seen. I called to the correctional guard that was handing the mail out and asked him why there wasn't a response. He asked to look at it, and after a few seconds he said, "Your ID number isn't on the request slip. We don't know who you are without the number there."

I said, "If you didn't know who I was, how did I get this slip back?"

"Kid, put your number on your slip. That's who you are."

I was only a number to them. Even with my full government name hand-printed on the request slip, that was not who I was to them. I was #40070. This is how individuals lose their connection to humanity. They become a number. They see themselves as a number. A number just exists. A number just survives. A number doesn't relate to the outside world. A number isn't a human being.

When you're treated as a non-human day in and day out, it eventually becomes easy to start behaving that way. Those that have support from family, friends, and the community have the highest chance of maintaining their connection to humanity. I was one of the fortunate and blessed people; I had family and friends to support me mentally throughout my incarceration. It would take upwards of a decade for me to start my road to redemption. When I finally did, it was only possible because of the support I had in my life. For the ones that don't have this level of support, well, it's just a law of the universe: for every action there is an equal and opposite reaction. So when correctional guards do monstrous things to people, what are they creating?

To be blunt with you, I don't wish to redescribe the inside of those cages. In 2020, my testimony was included in a report that was submitted to the US Civil Rights Commission, outlining changes that needed to be made to the practices and policies governing solitary confinement in New Hampshire. If you would like a more detailed description of segregation, I would highly recommend reading the report.[1]

Let's call it like it is. Prison is not a place that naturally promotes positive behavior or self-growth. It's a negative space that tests your limits and ability to adapt to trauma. Events and experiences that would traumatize the average community member become routine life in prison. I don't remember when, but at some point I just came to accept it. Everyone does in one way or the other. It wasn't the physical violence that had the most impact on me. Bones heal and bruises fade. But I still haven't figured out how to describe or articulate the type of psychological wound that's inflicted through the blatant abuse of power and position by corrupt correctional guards.

Turning a Corner

SHU and CCU are pressure cookers where it's easy for people to become overwhelmed and succumb to destructive patterns. My first CCU trip, I ended up spending 13 months total in the unit. During that time, I was still making bad choices and getting involved in situations I shouldn't have. But I did make one good choice that kept me connected to humanity and started the life course shift I would eventually undertake: to pursue an education. This choice gained the support of pivotal people in my life, including a prison high school teacher named Laura Hardwick.

Laura taught a class in CCU, and I enrolled only because it would get me out of my cage for an extra hour twice a week. I didn't believe there was actual value to the class. Why would I, when the environment I was living in conditioned all of us to believe we didn't hold value as humans?

But Laura was one of the few prison employees who genuinely believed in human redemption. She saw her students as humans, not just prison uniforms or CORIS numbers.[2] She held me accountable and started helping me gain the mindset I needed to transform myself into something more than just a negative prison statistic. Laura demonstrated that faith in the redemptive aspects of humans is more powerful than the belief that people are only the summation of their single worst moments.

Another program that helped me a lot was the woodshop. I worked in it for two years and learned to be a craftsman. It was a positive and educational program, teaching skills that I could utilize when I got out. It meant that when I returned home I had a job right away, building furniture. The woodshop manager also helped me become certified as an office administrative assistant; I learned to use Microsoft and QuickBooks. I was managing the inventory of the shop, ordering inventory, getting people hired. I started an initiative to teach people Computer Aided Design. Since we needed to design furniture and make blueprints, I wrote the software company a long email and got a response. They gave us a discount of 80% on the software, plus licenses and add-ons. There happened to be someone locked up who was a mechanical engineer, and he'd only been in prison a year, so his knowledge was fresh. He started teaching people how to design.

Well, eventually the prison shut the woodshop down, along with the auto shop, the farm, small engine repair, and other extremely beneficial, educational programs. They said the closings were temporary but as of this writing, all those shops are still closed. Keeping your mind focused and engaged is crucial to maintaining a positive course while incarcerated, and I knew I had to find another job. I knew if I stopped the momentum, it would be easy to be swept back into the ocean of negativity that flows throughout the carceral system. I chose to reach out to Laura Hardwick, who had become the director of the education department. She agreed to hire me as a worker in the prison library. I started off managing the small library network with the help of other residents. I went from that to learning some coding and the ins and outs of LexisNexis. Working in the library was my largest exposure to the law itself. It's where I learned the most about gaps in the law and the reality of how carceral settings actually function. I would just pick a manual off the shelf and read whenever I could. It still amazes me how individuals that seemingly have little to no actual knowledge about how jails and prisons actually work can create laws that have the opposite effect of what the system was designed to do in the first place.

Restorative Justice and Second Chances

In my second year of working in the library, the last thing I ever expected to happen actually did. One day while I was checking books out (part of my library responsibilities), a resident gave me his ID number to enter into my computer to assign the book to him. When his name came up on my computer I froze. The name on my computer screen was the name of my former victim, from the case that had sent me to prison. I couldn't believe it. He was here, in front of me in the prison, standing in the library. He had never seen my face during the altercation over almost a decade and a half before, and there was nothing in the library that would identify me to him. Anxiety immediately set in. I didn't know what to do or what would happen. I finished checking his books out. Seeing him in the library each week taught me about remorse and the desire to pay it forward more than any program or class the DOC could offer. We got to know each other for who we were in life at that moment, not for the worst mistakes we had made previously. We got to know what common interests we had, not the things that set us apart or made us different. One day I asked to speak to him outside the library in the education hall. I told him my name. I told him how sorry I was to have caused pain and trauma to him and his family. After a few quiet and awkward moments, he chose forgiveness as his response.

There's no way to describe the liberation and healing that entered our lives after that point. I fully understand and recognize that not every victim is able to get to that place. But for those who can, restorative justice can make the biggest impact. It bridges the gap and heals the rift that occurs when people cause harm by losing sight of treating other humans as they would want to be treated.

In 2019, I filed a 651:20 motion to suspend the remainder of my prison sentence, which would allow me to return to the community on parole. The suspension is considered a privilege, and can only be granted by a judge, at their sole discretion. The judge encouraged me to continue the path I was on, and said he had faith I would do so. That had a profound impact on me. The judge was one of a series of gatekeepers in the criminal justice system who chose to see my humanity, and give me a chance.

After I got out, I was working at the woodworking shop of one of my friends, building custom pieces of furniture. The lawyer who represented me in my 651:20 motion introduced me to a friend of hers who was the political director for the ACLU-NH. I told her my story, and she said, "We would love to have you volunteer to advocate for issues with us." It sounded great but it wasn't a paid job, and I needed to work. But 31 days from when I came home, my friend's woodworking business folded. The very next day, the ACLU director called me back, and said they were getting grant funding for a position, and I could apply. Since then, I've been working for the ACLU, advocating to change our justice system.

Laura reached out to me recently and asked me to come and speak at the prison high school graduation ceremony. I know that support, encouragement, and second chances are motivations to drive positive behavior, and I want to offer what I can to those still behind the walls.

How Do We Make Things Better?

I'm proud to be part of NH-ACLU's Smart Justice campaign. The work I do allows me to advocate for and pass critical reforms to the justice system. At its core, the criminal justice system is made up of humans, and every human is imperfect. If humans are controlling a system, there will always be abuses of power and position. I don't say this to discourage people from working to fix or change the current system. I'm not suggesting there aren't impactful solutions we can use. I say this to wake people up to the reality that, due to human nature, there *is* a need to fix it. I've heard too many people say there's nothing wrong with the current criminal justice system.

So, what are some of the solutions we can enact now to combat mass incarceration and racial inequities in the current system? This is what I'm thinking.

Reduce the number of people who needlessly enter prison in the first place

Incarceration should not be used as a penalty for certain classes of low-level, non-violent offenses—especially when those offenses are the result of mental illness or drug addiction, or are first-time offenses.

Become serious about investing in alternative solutions to incarceration that are more effective than the tough-on-crime, super-lengthy prison sentences

Drug courts, mental health courts, and diversion programs WORK. While we all learn differently, mentorship by people with lived experience has proven to be effective. Support programs that provide this mentorship.

Increase the use of early-release avenues for incarcerated individuals who have demonstrated they are ready to re-enter our society. Give them an opportunity to transition out of confinement and back to the community

Once a person has shifted their thinking from a "criminal" mindset to a "healthy" one, there is no further benefit in keeping them locked up in cages. There needs to be a process of reviewing those currently in prison to determine who continue to pose threats to safety, and those who are ready to re-enter society.

Require regular in-depth evaluations of our criminal justice system

The criminal justice system, like any effective system, must be evidence-based, have measures of performance, and be able to quickly address concerns raised through fiscal, cost-benefit, and racial impact analysis.

Prioritize the voices and knowledge of those with lived experience when it comes to reforming the justice system

It's those who have gone through the system who know it best. Bringing formerly incarcerated people to the decision-making table to make policies at both local and federal levels will help ensure equitable and effective solutions are being employed.

As one of those people, I am dedicating my life to using my knowledge to make our justice system, and my community, better. I hope that reading part of my story has helped you see the need for reform. And more than that, I hope it's a reminder that the people locked up in prison are people, humans, like everyone else.

Joseph Lascaze is a prison reform activist whose personal experience with the incarceration system gives him an invaluable perspective about the barriers and challenges within the current system. In his role as the NH ACLU's Smart Justice Campaign Manager, Mr. Lascaze advocates for meaningful changes to the NH criminal justice system by lobbying for justice-oriented legislation at both the state and federal level, serving on state commissions, and building community partnerships with other key stakeholders in the criminal justice movement. He has worked on policy changes including banning the use of chokeholds by law enforcement; requiring law enforcement officials to report witnessed instances of misconduct; expanding earned time credit opportunities for residents of the NH Department of Corrections; defending the prison education department from being eliminated from the state budget; and ending the shackling of pregnant incarcerated women during labor, childbirth, and postpartum. His work has resulted in the passage of a law that creates an oversight committee, to include community members, to review all instances of law enforcement misconduct in the state, and specifies that correctional officers will wear body cameras and are held accountable to the state's definition of misconduct. He is currently working on repealing Truth in Sentencing in New Hampshire. Mr. Lascaze is also an educator who believes that continuous learning is essential to community and personal growth. He is a frequent visitor and guest lecturer at various institutions across the state, where he advances knowledge of the varying complexities and possible solutions to mass incarceration. Mr. Lascaze is deeply passionate about changing the narrative for youths involved in the court system. For him, the most rewarding part of doing this work is helping these young people avoid the incarceration system by providing mentorship through a court diversion program. Mr. Lascaze has recently been named the New Hampshire Changemaker of the Year, which honors a young Granite Stater who, through their actions, has effected positive change in New Hampshire or their corner of it.

Notes

1 "Solitary Confinement in New Hampshire: A Report of the New Hampshire Advisory Committee to the US Commission on Civil Rights," April 2021, www.usccr.gov/files/2021/04-26-New-Hampshire-Advisory-Committee-Report-Solitary-Confinement.pdf

2 CORIS stands for criminal offender record information system. It is the prison computer management system that contains every resident's offender record.

II

Journeys in Law Enforcement

5

NOT AN EASY JOB

A Police Officer Works to Better His Community in a Difficult Time

Lawan Cancer, as told to Katherine S. Gaudet

I was born and raised in Albany, and I've been a police officer for the past 14-plus years. I grew up an area called Arbor Hill. It's the more urban community in the city of Albany. I've been through it. And with police it was always taught to us that it was us against them. It's really not. You'd be amazed. There's more people in our community who really want the police. The people who don't want them are the ones that shout louder. If you ask kids in the community why they have a bad interpretation of police officers, it's never from their own experience. They talk about other people's experiences—especially now, with social media. Look, this is a big country. There are a lot of police officers. People are going to make mistakes. I say, understand what I do. If I start to fail, judge that. I understand the bad history. I grew up in this neighborhood. But if we were getting talked to by police, it was because we were doing something we shouldn't be doing.

I became a police officer when I was 34 years old, after doing all kinds of other jobs. In the academy, I was one of the oldest guys. I already had a kid, I was married. It kind of made it easier. I think to become a police officer you should have a little more life experience. When you get put out there, you're hit with a lot of stuff. I kind of hate to say it, but I was immune to some of it. I've dealt with a lot in my life. I don't know if that's always a good thing. But certain things don't affect me the way they do other people.

Don't get me wrong. This job is tough for somebody from the community. I could go from seeing one of the kids I work with at a Little League game, and then get a call and go to a scene where I see a little kid shot and killed. My little brother was murdered at 19, and my first cousin was murdered in 2018. To be a police officer in the community you've got to have a tough skin, and you have to understand what your job is.

People forget that police officers are human. I remember an EMS call my partner and I went on. There was a young lady and she'd rolled over on her 4-month-old

DOI: 10.4324/9781003169468-8

baby. Something like that—we both had kids—we were hurt by that. We had to try to resuscitate the baby; we had to be professional and do our job. But we immediately sat down with our EAP guys, and they gave us some time off. [Employee Assistance Programs provide confidential services to help address personal struggles and difficulties.] Some guys don't seek the help they need. I'm human. I have kids at home. You just walk in and see a beautiful baby, gone. That stays with you.

After two years of midnight patrols, I was detailed out to a pilot program called TRAC—To Reach and Connect. We work with kids from age 12 to 15 and get them and their families connected to services they need. My partner, Nate Pendleton, and I ran the program for six months, and we blew it out of the park. At the end of the pilot, they wanted to make it a permanent unit, but that took two or three years.

After the TRAC pilot, I was a School Resource Officer at Albany High School for two years. I loved doing SRO. I'd worked in the schools before, so I already knew a lot about it, but being SRO gave me a better relationship with the kids. I'd sit down and eat lunch with them in the cafeteria. I walked the halls, I went to classes, went to a lot of their games, PTA meetings, award events. You don't want someone in there just to work eight to four and walk away. It's your opportunity to open up, to explain to them, and a lot of kids respect that. That way if there's something going on they aren't reluctant to talk to you.

The SRO is there in case of someone doing harm to kids. Thank god I never had to protect them from a shooter. I loved doing the scenarios of potential things that could happen in the school. At this point when kids are being shot in schools, we should be practicing active shooter drills as much as we practice fire drills. We've been doing fire drills for 80 years, and how often is there really a fire? I believe the SRO is there to educate people and build relationships. Every outcome isn't going to be peaches and cream, but you're there to help them, to give guidance.

I was assigned to TRAC at the end of 2012 and have been here since then. If there's a kid having issues at home or school, or on the edge of getting into the wrong things, we'll go to the kid's house. We'll sit down, have a meeting with mom, the kid, whoever else is involved in his well-being. We try to find out why this is happening, what resources they need. We get to the bottom of it, and come up with a plan. We work with all the inner city agencies and nonprofits that provide services. Maybe there's a truancy issue, and we find out the reason the kid isn't going to school is because he needs help with the work. So we reach out to the people we work with at SUNY, and they will hook him up with tutoring. Some of the kids have mental illness, or learning disabilities, so we connect them with services. We don't only help kids, but families as well. Maybe mom needs more parenting skills, and we have agencies that help with that. If the kid is going back to the same environment, they will forget what they've learned. So we have to change that environment.

It takes a lot of getting after, sometimes, for these kids to succeed. You can't give up. You can't lie to them. We always do our research about everything, so there won't be any disappointment. We say, "This is what we're going to do, and this is what you need to do." When I say I'm going to do something, I'll do it. It builds the trust. We'll go into the schools, go to their court hearings if they're on probation. We act as their advocate and mentor.

There's one kid I remember who was out in the streets, doing things he wasn't supposed to do. We worked with him and his mom. We kept pushing; he was not feeling it, didn't want to talk to us. At one point he had a probation warrant out. We caught him, arrested him, sat with him in family court. He got 35 days in the youth facility. In that short time, he had an epiphany, did a complete turnaround. After that he stayed out of trouble, started doing well in school, started asking us to help him get a job. Being away from his mother, being away from everything—sometimes kids need that time. We need these facilities for kids, because sometimes they don't have that support at home. Sometimes home is an environment where they're not being watched or disciplined, and they're just out there running around. I feel that without us standing on him, pushing him, it could have gone the other way.

For some of these kids, these behaviors are about survival. When I was young, I was hungry, so I would steal. Just because I would steal, was I a criminal? I was put on probation. But I didn't steal just for the act of stealing. It was what I needed at that time. I took things because I did not have them.

My son used to work in loss prevention at Lord and Taylor in the mall. He would catch a lot of people. One day he called me and told me, "I realized that a lot of these people who are coming here stealing, they don't have anything." I knew that, but to hear it from my child really touched me. He was thanking us for providing for him when he was a child. He felt he couldn't work there anymore. It felt like he was doing something bad, stopping them from stealing.

Sometimes kids start doing things like stealing for survival, and they can get addicted. They start to enjoy the sensation of going in and taking something and not getting caught. That's when it becomes criminal, because they're doing it to get some kind of excitement out of it. I would define a criminal as a person who takes advantage of situations and takes advantage of weak individuals, and tries to get away with unimaginable things because they think it will better themself. Like all the online schemes and scams, taking advantage of older people—that's disgusting. But someone who goes into a supermarket and takes an apple—is that wrong? Yes. Is it criminal? No.

You don't want society to shun someone because they've done that one action. Even though if you're a juvenile, your record gets expunged, it does still follow you a little bit. And adults, too—if someone makes one mistake, it shouldn't sit with them for life; you shouldn't judge them because of that. We've all done so many things, but we learn from them.

Right now I'm the only person in my unit. My partner got promoted to sergeant, and our office manager took a different job. The city does want to keep the program going, but there's a shortage of manpower right now. Retirement is up. People used to be lined up to take the civil service test, and now no one is taking it. We're all suffering because of the civil unrest in 2020, and the stuff we had to go through with COVID. The George Floyd incident woke people up, and it did damage. People turned their backs on us. The mayor's office, the city administration, the community. And we weren't the ones who did anything wrong. No good law officer thought that was a good thing. That was disgusting. We don't support that.

After the George Floyd incident, crime didn't go down. Crime went up. Homicides in Albany doubled. Shots-fired incidents doubled. The community wants us to go out and prevent crime, get these guns off the street. But you can't do that if your hands are tied. Now, every time you see action with an individual, people say you're harassing him. No, he just shot three people. He's not being harassed; he's being arrested! Good officers are getting backlash.

Civil unrest ruined our society a little bit. Officers are hesitant to pull an individual over, because they don't want to be berated on TV. As an officer, you shouldn't be out there second-guessing. It could be life and death. Police aren't pulling people over for certain things, are not dealing with certain issues because of the backlash. I understand it, but there has to be a support of the individuals that do their jobs every day. Crime is out of control. You can't tie people's hands when this is a hands-on job, and it will always have to be. Police officers are not all bad. We do respond to bad things. That's our job. Without us it would be anarchy out there, even worse than it is now.

I know my job. I know what I need to do. I do it every day. There's no different way of dealing with people who are out here killing each other, robbing and stealing. You can't just go hug them. We've got to stop it, and then find a better solution to reverse their actions. It's just like when you're growing up. If there's no consequence for your actions, you will continue to do wrong.

There's a reason officers carry weapons. We have to be that much more cautious. People are trying to do harm to others. There are kids being abused, kids being touched inappropriately. Women are being raped. Cars are being broken into. Banks are getting robbed. People are missing the point of policing. They need to support police departments, and try to understand what we do. We make it very transparent. We have so many programs, for kids, for community members, to learn what we do. Call us up, you can do a ride-along and spend half a shift in a patrol car with an officer. They will answer all your questions. Don't just talk to one individual, talk to a few. If we're holding an event, come to the event. You can't criticize unless you really understand.

2020 was a turning point. A lot of people were being threatened. People would go to your house. Guys are worried about their families. Who wants to do a job like that?

For me, it's different. It's a passion. I'm from this community. I love helping people. I want to see things go right. I want things to be good. That's why I love doing what I do every day. With my upbringing, struggling, going through things, I don't get flustered. It's tiring, but you can protest all year, and it's not going to stop my focus and drive. I'm going to work hard.

One thing I've learned is that you don't know at first what makes a person do certain things. You can't just go on your emotions. You have to sit there, speak to them, listen and learn. Take time to really grasp what you're dealing with. That's what makes you a good police officer—and a good individual. It's not an easy job. It's become easy to me over the years, because I love what I do. It's my passion. And every day I'm learning something.

Lawan Cancer has served as a police officer in Albany, New York for 14 years. Since 2014, he has been working with To Reach and Connect, a program that offers services to at-risk youth and families. Before becoming a police officer, Mr. Cancer held many other jobs, starting with selling newspapers at the age of 11. His experience includes working in fast food, being a resident aide for disabled adults, being a school security officer, and working at Berkshire Farms Center and Services for Youth. He graduated from Albany High School and holds an associate degree in office management and supervision from Hunter Valley Community College. Mr. Cancer is involved with many community ventures and is the proud father of three sons and one daughter.

6

FROM CORRECTIONS OFFICER TO MENTAL HEALTH COURT

New Approaches to People Who Commit Crimes

Blair Rowlett

As I looked into the cell where Mary was billeted, I felt a deep despair. She was genuinely terrified of me and my colleagues. We meant her no harm, but there was nothing we could say or do to convince her of that.

"Mary, no one is going to steal your baby," I said.

"Get away from me, Satan. You can't have him!" she replied.

She was not faking this portrayal of herself as the Virgin Mary giving birth to Baby Jesus. For her, this was entirely real. To her, we were dark, demonic creatures there to steal her child as soon as he entered the world. While Mary was not pregnant, she was incarcerated, and it was my job to fix the situation—to figure out how to safely and effectively get her into the hospital for mental health care that could not be provided to her at the jail. That incident, occurring shortly after I transitioned from being a corrections officer to working in community corrections, would make me reevaluate everything I knew about the system. It was clear to me, in that moment, that jail was no place for this woman; and perhaps no place for anyone like her.

In 15 years of work in the justice system, I've learned a lot about the complicated, and often tragic, relationship between mental illness and criminality. Now, I'm doing what I can to make the system work better for people with mental illness.

Becoming a CO

Like a lot of people, I didn't have any intention of becoming a corrections officer. I admit that I, like many people, looked down on the profession. I thought of them as "knuckle draggers" or "turn keys." (I later came to loathe the term "guard," too.) I'd applied for another job at the jail, and when I was turned down, the captain had told me I should consider being a corrections officer. I felt offended that he would

DOI: 10.4324/9781003169468-9

consider me for that type of role. Didn't he know I had a college degree? But after a while, without other career leads, I called him back.

In October of 2005, I became a correctional officer with the Strafford County Jail. The facility is located in rural New Hampshire, but it is unique because it holds state and federal contracts to board non-county inmates. This makes it far more diverse than the surrounding area, and the leadership is composed of forward thinkers. There is a focus on rehabilitation. It is known around the state for the great programming offered to the inmate population.

My first day on the job was really scary. I felt that everyone who was wearing a different uniform from me surely wanted to kill me. I stuck close to my training officer, watched him like a hawk, and listened to every instruction he gave me. "Never let an inmate hold the door for you, because it gives up your back." "Never give personal information about yourself, because it makes you vulnerable." "Be firm but fair, and always consistent. Respect and integrity are the most valuable tools on your duty belt," he told me.

Day two at the jail was equally exciting. I watched, listened, learned, then went home to call my parents and tell them all about it. Day three was a reality check. It happened to be a scheduled training for oleoresin capsicum spray, also known as pepper spray. In order for COs to be certified to use OC spray, they must first understand how it feels when it is applied. This is so that they won't use it carelessly, and also so that they can effectively respond to a situation if exposed to cross contamination. The average store-bought hot sauce has about 500 Scoville Heat Units. The training OC we used registered at 800,000 Scoville Heat Units. The best way to explain the feeling is this: imagine pouring hot sauce into your eyes, then multiplying that by about 1600. The day-three phone call was a bit less enthusiastic.

The OC spray training was not my favorite, but it did start to make me realize that COs deserve a lot more credit. Their level of dedication, in many ways, is unmatched. You agree to a training where you get sprayed with hot pepper oils because down the road, it's inevitable that you will be sprayed again while attempting to gain control over another human to break up a fight, or save a life. You have to decide early on that you are there for it; most decide that they aren't.

And that's only the physical part. The mental and emotional toll that certain experiences cause can be too much for people. Correctional officers are the outcasts of the criminal justice system: out of sight, out of mind. COs spend more time in jail or prison than most offenders do, and that can be mentally taxing. There is a very high turnover rate in corrections. People burn out quickly. I remember some police officers coming into the facility and saying, "I don't know how you guys do it." It really does take a certain type of person.

As the days and weeks and months progressed, I left the shadow of my training officer and began running units on my own. I was responsible for up to 72 male inmates in a direct supervision jail. That means there were no walls or bars or barriers between them and me in the unit. I was out in the dayroom, at a desk—just me. That is when I started to realize that the ones in the jail wearing a different uniform from me were also people. They all had stories. Some of those stories were clearly not true, some were overly polished and self-serving, but regardless, all of those people had backgrounds and feelings and personalities that made them individuals. I learned a lot about people and our society as I got to know them.

While people in jail talk about wanting to get out, life on the outside can be hard for them. I remember when I first started as a CO, there was a male inmate who was talked of as "running the unit." All of the other inmates respected him. Despite having no money on his account, he always had plenty of commissary in his cell. No one messed with him and if there was a fight, we always suspected he was the one to order it. He was charismatic, well put-together, and muscular. He never got into trouble and was always polite to officers. He would talk about how much of a big deal he was on the outside. He would talk about his money and cars and properties. But a few months after his release, he came back on new charges. He was skinny and dirty; he had no money and his clothes had holes in them. When I saw him, he looked embarrassed and ashamed. A senior officer explained to me that this is what he does—"He goes in and out of the system. He gets sober and on his medication here, then he gets out and goes back to drugs." In the jail, he thrived, in a way, but in the community he would flounder.

There are people in jail that, aside from being a human, you have nothing in common with. When you work in corrections, you don't get to choose if you interact with them or not. You are stuck inside of a secure facility and everyone, staff and inmates alike, has to do their part to make it function. There are some genuinely bad people, undoubtedly, but the more I worked, the more I understood that it was less "us versus them" than I thought. Most of the people there wanted to accept their wrongdoings, do their time, and get out; or fight their case and get out. I learned that while I viewed them as criminals, that didn't have to forever define them. Most of them still had a future afterwards, something to look forward to.

There were some people that I believed were truly evil, and I didn't believe there was help for them. While I could only see them as criminals, I tried to treat them fairly. After all, it was my job not to punish them, but to maintain the care, custody, and control of the facility and those inside.

A Turning Point

Less than a year after I started at the jail, I had one of the most defining moments of my career. On September 20, 2006, covering a shift for a coworker, I was assigned to the medical unit, where inmates who have severe medical and/or mental health issues are housed. There are only four cells, but there is also a nurses' station and four examination rooms, as well as a couple of other offices.

One of the cells had three males in it. Two of the males were labeled maximum security inmates because of their behavioral issues, but were housed in the medical unit rather than the maximum security unit because they had made suicidal statements. The third was in medical for reported mental health issues. The inmate who was not max status was allowed to come out of his cell to use the phone. He asked permission and I allowed it, per the policy at the time. This required me to key open the door to allow him out and secure the door behind him with the other two still inside of the cell. He remained on the phone for about 10 minutes while I watched him and the other inmates in all four cells. Nothing appeared to be out of order. When he was finished with his call, I went back to his cell and keyed the door open again. He stepped to the side and one of the other inmates lunged at me.

I could not tell what happened exactly, but I knew that my vision was altered. I wear glasses so I didn't feel anything directly in my eyes, but my view was obstructed. Before I could see what was happening, someone grabbed me and began to pull. I pushed my feet into the ground, trying to move in the opposite direction. That's when I felt someone else grab me from behind, trying to pull me into the cell. Between the two of them, they were able to lift me off of the ground.

My most valuable resource in that moment was located on my left shoulder: the two-way mic that was connected to my radio. I knew that I needed to reach that in order to get help.

It was dinner time and the entire nursing staff was in the cafeteria down the hall. I had just returned from my break; no one was scheduled to be back for at least another 20 minutes. I didn't know what would happen in those 20 minutes, but I knew what *could* happen. The two inmates who had dragged me into the cell were the type that I didn't see a future for. They were the type that I would see as criminals, by my definition. Their behavior in the facility prior to this incident was abhorrent. Their compliance would ebb and flow depending on whether or not they had their way. They were unproductive in the jail and didn't take advantage of any programming available to them. These two were not the type that spoke or acted in a way that suggested their future would be productive. They viewed the relationship between inmate and officer as "us versus them."

I had no traction in my lower body because my feet were off the floor, but I used all the strength of my upper body and pushed. I pushed hard enough to create a small amount of space between myself and the man who was bear-hugging me in the front. I grabbed my shoulder mic, keyed it, and yelled, "Backup to medical, backup to medical!" The inmate in front grabbed at my hand to pull it away from the mic. He said, "Don't even fucking think about it!" But he knew it was too late. Instead of continuing to jockey for my mic, he and the other inmate shoved me to the floor in the back of the cell. I still could not see well, but I heard the sound of the cell door slam shut. I wiped a white powdery substance from my glasses and could see the three inmates running around the unit with a fire extinguisher and an oxygen tank. I radioed again: "Backup to medical. I am secured in M-3 and there are inmates out in the medical unit. Bring the PepperBall system."

Shortly after that last radio call, other officers arrived to the unit and quickly subdued the three inmates. I was released from the cell and taken to the booking area, where there was an eye rinse station. The white powdery substance turned out to be Ajax that the inmates had saved up when cleaning their cell. I was fortunate that my glasses had protected me; I could potentially have been blinded.

It was nearing the end of my shift, but I needed to write a report about the incident as the three inmates would later be charged with assault and attempted escape. Aside from intakes, the booking area is where inmates are taken who cannot be managed in the other units within the facility. Each of the three inmates in this incident were taken to individual cells in booking called "dry cells." (They have no access to running water. These cells are necessary because inmates with behavioral issues will sometimes try to flood their cells when they are not getting what they want. This can be done by clogging the toilet, then flushing it repeatedly.)

When I sat down at an available computer to type my report, I found myself facing the dry cells. The inmate who was originally out on the phone sat quietly with his head down, but the other two kicked and screamed and made threats. One of them repeatedly called me a "nigger" and laughed about what they'd done. I don't remember exactly what they said, but I do remember thinking that they were exactly where they were supposed to be, and that I was going home soon.

I finished my report and was preparing to leave when my lieutenant stopped me. He suggested that I should show my face to the other inmates in the medical unit before I left. "Make sure they know that didn't get you down," he said. The cell where I'd been attacked was closed, as it was now a crime scene. I walked around to the other cells and to my surprise, the other inmates offered nothing but support. A male inmate said, "Rowlett, I was trying to get out. I would have kicked all their asses if I could have!" I told him I wasn't hurt, and that they would have to face the consequences of their actions. There were two other cells, with a female inmate in each. One of them jumped up when she saw me and started crying. She said, "Rowlett, are you ok? I was so worried. I was banging on the cell and screaming for help!" "Me too, Rowlett, we were both so scared," the other said. I told them I was fine and not to worry.

I tell this story to point out the obvious. Yes, these men were criminals. They planned an attack and they carried it out without remorse. But even more important to the shape of my career was the response I got from the other inmates. They were not cheering on those men; they were angry with them and they wanted to help me. They didn't believe that because they were incarcerated, they had to blindly side with other incarcerated persons. Being incarcerated, or being labeled a criminal, was not how they defined themselves. So why should I only see them that way? My training had taught me to interact with inmates with integrity and respect, and I'd done that. But I hadn't known that strategy would not only help me in the work; it also built a rapport that was not fear-based respect, but genuine and humane.

Community Corrections and Mental Health Court

I decided that if I was going to stay in this field, I was going to do more. Perhaps that incident made me feel like I was spinning my wheels a bit. As trite as it sounds, I truly did want to help people. After almost two years working in the jail, I accepted a position within the county as a community corrections pretrial officer.

In this role I helped people comply with release conditions and stay out of jail. While I was working in that position, my agency began to make a shift in thinking about how mental health figures in criminal activity, and created the Mental Health Supervision Program to work only with clients who had been diagnosed with a mental health disorder. The goal was to offer supportive case management to both pre- and post-trial clients who had different needs. Because of my background and experience at the jail, I was able to move into a position on that team, working with both pretrial clients and those transitioning out of incarceration. COs often learn de-escalation tactics and mental health first aid skills without even realizing they are doing it. Those skills sit right on a duty belt alongside handcuffs and OC spray, and in my experience, are used far more often. Working in the jail helped me polish these skills in preparation for transitioning to a role in the community where I felt I could do the most good.

Working with people in this capacity meant calling them by their first names, referring to them as clients and not offenders, and understanding that they had far more liberties than inmates—and I had far less control over them. The jail is its own fragment of society. It is often difficult for incarcerated persons to transition back to life on the outside. I found that there was a transition for me and my views as well. My perception of this population had changed when I began to work in the jail, and it changed again as I started working in the community.

Every client that I was assigned had been charged with a crime, but was innocent until proven guilty. I found that that was not the way that they were viewed by most of society, however. Most of the clients I worked with were low-income and poorly educated. It was a shock if I had a client who owned property or had a college degree. Most of my time with clients was spent helping them find housing, employment, and services.

The Mental Health Supervision Programs aimed not only to gain compliance from clients while on release, but to offer connections, services, and support that would last beyond their court orders. I began to work with people whom I had seen cycling in and out of the jail. I would see them come in showing severe signs and symptoms of mental illness. They would stabilize during their incarceration as a result of medication, a complete detox from narcotics, or enough time for symptoms to subside. With my role in the community, I could work with people while they were stable to try to help them meet their basic needs and avoid further incarceration.

If I had to define what a criminal is, I would say: a person who commits a crime willingly and knowingly. At that moment they are a criminal, but that doesn't last forever. A person isn't forever defined by one act, or for some, multiple and repeated acts. I know this because I have seen incredible success stories for people who have been given an opportunity with the right support and guidance.

When people have mental health disorders and trauma history, their symptoms are often exacerbated by their surroundings when they are in jail. I've seen people harm themselves and others. I've seen people refuse to eat for days. I've seen people smear themselves with their own feces. I've seen people get completely naked and masturbate in front of anyone who would walk by. When I began working in the community, I saw extreme remorse and embarrassment from the people who acted this way while in jail. They reported that they were not in control of themselves and would have never acted that way if they were well. I cannot simply say that the crimes they committed before arriving at the jail were done knowingly and willingly.

Schizophrenia is from the Greek words *skhizein*, to split, and *phren*, mind. A person suffering from symptoms of schizophrenia is experiencing their own reality that is separate, split off, from *the* reality. If that person at that moment commits the crime of assault, are they to be held responsible? Yes. Are they a criminal? By my definition, no, but we still live in a society where all members have to be held accountable. How do we do that when we are saying a person was not acting willingly and knowingly? This is something that the criminal justice system has struggled to answer as we come to better understand mental illness. A positive response to this growing knowledge is the development of specialty courts.

In 2007, Strafford County implemented a Mental Health Court, an alternative-to-sentencing program, because we understand that incarceration does not treat mental illness. It was not the first ever, but it is the one that I am most proud to be a part of; I now serve as Director. I've often said that not every criminal is mentally ill and not every mentally ill person is a criminal. I review all applications to determine if a person is eligible. There are certain criteria that can be bureaucratic and monotonous, but one thing I always consider is the person's state at the time the crime was committed. The men I mentioned in the escape attempt reported being mentally ill to avoid punishment; they are not the people Mental Health Court is meant to help. I do not want to include people with criminal thinking in a program designed to support and guide people with mental health disorders in the criminal justice system—they are two very different populations.

My application reviews are in-depth and I review records from treatment providers to help make each decision. If I read that a person was fully engaged in treatment, had positive feedback, and no concerns surrounding the time that they committed the crime, it doesn't necessarily exclude them, but it does raise a flag for me. I don't want to allow persons knowingly and willingly engaging in criminal behavior, which would mean they are not being driven by their illness, to participate in the program. It is designed to not only promote engagement in treatment for one's own well-being, but also to prevent further crimes from being committed.

Success Stories from Mental Health Court

Over the span of my 15-year career in law enforcement, working with the Mental Health Court has by far been the most rewarding part. I've been able to witness a person at their absolute worst, then watch them work hard and push through adversity to get to a place where they can be proud of themselves. Everyone in the system has different baselines, different capabilities, and different ceilings of success. I had a client once who had schizophrenia and a brain injury, and whose baseline was the ability to take his medication, attend his appointments, and show up to court. He was on disability and would be for the rest of his life. He would require wrap-around services through his treatment providers for the rest of his life. This client was able to complete the program. Usually, we ask participants to write a speech about their experience to give at their graduation, but this man pulled a harmonica out of his fanny pack and played a song for us. That was his success ceiling, and that was just fine.

I had a young female client who was diagnosed with borderline personality disorder. She would engage in harmful and self-harming behaviors when she was upset. She pleaded guilty to assaulting her ex-partner. While in the program, there were times when she would meet with me and I would see the marks on her arms where she had used a Paper Mate eraser to rub her skin until it came off. After completing the program, she enrolled in nursing school, and hasn't been involved in the criminal justice system since.

I had a client who was a Marine veteran. He came back from a tour with severe PTSD and began drinking to cope. He pleaded guilty to an assault which he committed while intoxicated and having a reaction to a trauma-triggering moment. He entered the program, found sobriety and therapy, and graduated with one of the most eloquent and inspiring speeches I've ever heard.

I had a client who was in college when he experienced his first psychosis during a manic episode from bipolar disorder, which was undiagnosed at the time. He pleaded guilty to stalking an ex-partner. He participated in the program and told us about his aspirations to go back to school for a law degree. He has stayed in touch over the years to keep us in the loop. He emailed me copies of his acceptance letters to Duke University Law School and Yale Law School. While he said it was a difficult choice, he chose Yale.

In New Hampshire, participants who complete a Mental Health Court program have the ability to ask the court to annul their record one year after the completion date. The people who have gone on to have great success stories didn't really begin to thrive until their records were annulled.

The success stories are what have sustained my career. Simply viewing everyone as a criminal, and not seeing the changes that can be made, would be too onerous to bear. The individuals I described wouldn't be looked as criminals today. They are now law-abiding citizens who are productive members of their communities, and yet they all have a criminal act in their past. They all committed crimes, but they were all also sick at the time. That doesn't make their crimes entirely excusable, but they qualified for the opportunity to be rehabilitated and not just punished.

I am not soft by any means. I am firm, but fair. I understand the need to consider people as individuals, as being worthy, and as having potential. Having a criminal record is a stamp. That stamp can affect your housing options, your right to vote, your ability to get a driver's license, to become employed, to retain custody of your children, and more. I'm not suggesting we do away with criminal records, but what I'm highlighting is that once we label someone a criminal, that person will struggle to succeed even if we know their success is in everyone's best interest.

Labeling someone a criminal, and doing so for life, is counterproductive in a society. The majority of incarcerated people will be released at some point. If they will always be considered criminals, they will always be at a disadvantage. They will resort to criminal behaviors and commit crimes that will ultimately have a negative impact on our communities.

What Is a criminal? That question is as complex as they come, but I believe that a criminal is a person who is actively committing a crime and is doing so willingly and knowingly. There has to be accountability, but in this day and age, with all that we know, we can hold people accountable in a way that helps the situation instead of making it worse. Incarcerating people who commit crimes unwillingly and unknowingly, labeling them criminals beyond the moment of the crime itself and well into the future, and punishing them for those actions without rehabilitation won't do anything to prevent similar actions in the future. When society labels someone a criminal, views them as a criminal, and treats them like a criminal, it becomes a self-fulfilling prophecy.

Blair Rowlett earned her Dual Bachelor's Degree in Psychology and Justice Studies from the University of New Hampshire in 2005. Shortly after graduation, she began her career at the Strafford County House of Corrections, where she became a decorated correctional officer. In 2007, she transitioned into a position with the Strafford County Community Corrections Program. In addition to overseeing the county's Bail Supervision Program and Post-Trial Supervision Programs, she currently serves as the Director of the Strafford County—Rochester Mental Health Court. Ms. Rowlett is a Trauma-Informed Response Instructor for Law Enforcement, a Mental Health First Aid Instructor, and a trainer for local police departments' Crisis Intervention Teams. She has created a training curriculum for new correctional officers at Strafford County. She is currently a member of the Mental Health Advisory Group for NH Mental Health Court State Standards.

7

LABELING, YOUTH CULTURE, AND TRUST

Lessons Learned by a School Resource Officer

Patrick Schmucker

What Is a criminal? One would think that after more than a dozen years of law enforcement service, earning a PhD in the field, and becoming a professor, I'd be able to answer this question easily. But that's not the case. If we look for common definitions of a "criminal," we will find statements like: "in a strictly positivist legal scene, one convicted of a criminal offense in a court of law" or "one who is guilty of committing a crime."[1] But that means that *every* person who has ever been guilty or convicted for anything, even receiving a traffic citation, is a "criminal" by definition. That includes me, and I don't think of myself as a criminal.

A lot of people have committed a traffic violation, or used alcohol while underage, or downloaded a movie illegally, and aren't considered criminals by themselves or others. Yet when people are labeled "criminals," very often that label doesn't take into account the totality of the circumstance surrounding their behavior, nor the lifelong impact the label of "criminal" can have. As a law enforcement veteran, I too have issued such labels without enough understanding of causes or effects. The following is the narrative of how over the course of my law enforcement career, and my journey within the scholarly world of criminal justice, I have learned to stop issuing labels without due cause.

I will be focusing on two specific encounters I had with different juveniles, and one criminal act, in which the labels of "criminals" or "delinquent adolescents" were, or could have been, assigned. These incidents range from disrespect, to theft, to conspiracy in an armed robbery with a deadly weapon and attempted murder. Through incidents like these, and educating myself, I learned that these specific actions, in context, do not necessarily warrant the title of "criminal" or "delinquency"—and that these labels can harm more than they help.

DOI: 10.4324/9781003169468-10

A Rocky Start

The first encounter was with a young man who showed me that our delinquent actions during our adolescent years should not create labels that form foundations for who we are to become in adulthood. This is a person I initially thought of as a "thug" or "punk"—labels that, as I have seen in my professional experiences, can be the starting point of suspecting a person of being a "criminal." While this was not a badge-of-honor kind of incident for me, it was one of the greatest moments in my police career, as it made me learn about people, and taught me not to just hand out labels.

In the summer of 2010, after being a police officer assigned to the patrol division for a little over two years, I became a school resource officer. The South Carolina school I was assigned to had seen an increase in crime over the past few years. Drug deals, vehicle break-ins, thefts, and fights were weekly events. I started the job with the mindset that any action that did not fit within the school norms—that is, being in class, learning—must be deviant actions. Disrespect to authorities and hanging out or roaming in the parking lot, hallways, or restrooms appeared to me to be outside the societal norms of a school setting—and therefore required intervention by me, before they led to criminal actions. I created these classifications of deviance before getting to know anything about the diversity and culture of the school, and the students who attended.

On my first day as an SRO, school was not in session, but the basketball team was holding summer practices in the gym, and the football team had also finished a workout not long before my first encounter with a student. Just after lunchtime, I was conducting a vehicle patrol of the school grounds. I drove in the front of the school near the gym area, as that was where most of the basketball team had parked their vehicles. As I passed, a student stuck up his middle finger and yelled at me: "Fuck the Police!" I was shocked, and amazed that a young student had shown such a high level of disrespect, out of nowhere. This clearly needed to be dealt with, and I stopped my vehicle. As I exited the car, the student started to run into the gym, so I yelled, "Come here, boy!"

He didn't listen, and I followed him into the gym. Inside, I addressed the level of disrespect with him. I told him that as a police officer, I would not tolerate being disrespected in such a manner—especially because the disrespect was unwarranted. I found out he was a member of the football team, and was still at the school four hours after the workout as he had no way of getting home before his parents got off work. Therefore, he was just hanging around. I turned him over to the head football coach and an administrator of the school. I then carried out the rest of my duties. That student, I thought, was definitely a punk. I had never been disrespected in such a manner in my short law enforcement career. I felt confident that I'd handled the incident correctly, and that my preconceptions about the level of delinquency at this school had been right. I was wrong in two ways.

I found this out the hard way when I was called into the Chief of Police's office, and questioned about why I thought it was alright to call a young African-American juvenile a "boy." In my view, I had done nothing wrong; the student was a boy. I didn't know the term was offensive, because I didn't understand the local Southern culture. After about an hour-long lecture about what it meant for a White officer to address any African-American male in such a manner, I could see it was time for me to learn about the community and students who attended the school. The following week, I asked one of the senior officers who was born and raised in the area to teach me about the different cultures of the community.

What I learned shocked me. I come from a small college city in Michigan, with the population comprised of mostly middle-class White families. As far as I could see, everyone in the city was equal in terms of economic standing. My time in the United States Marines had introduced me to a number of different cultures, but it had not prepared me for the magnitude of the cultural and economic differences within the small community I was living and working in. On one side of the street, you would have a million-dollar home on the waterfront; take a few steps across the street, and it was not uncommon to see extension cords running from residence to residence so people could share electricity. The current US Census lists the area as having a minority population of 21.8%; this was much higher than where I had grown up. I had a lot to learn about my neighbors and their diverse cultures.

I also learned that I'd been wrong about this young man. When I took the time to look past this student's disrespectful act and got to know him personally, he turned out to be as far away from a "punk" or a "criminal" as one could be. He is one of the few students I still stay in contact with today. This encounter helped show me that one act does not define who we are as people. It also started me thinking about how to get the most out of our community youth, even when they had committed a crime.

Gaining Trust

Learning about the youth culture of my community helped me gain an understanding of why some adolescents could be appropriately labeled as "criminals," while others just wanted to fit in. One of the key elements I learned about the youth culture in my community was that they held the personal trait of trust high on their value scale—and they did not trust the police. They had been raised hearing stories, or getting firsthand knowledge, of being lied to. They had observed failed promises by the police. I was fighting an uphill battle, trying to gain the trust of the youth. Understanding the importance of trust led me to design what I called my "choice program" to address an increase of thefts within the school.

I had three goals for the program. First, to increase the number of recovered stolen items; that was the main goal. Second, to gain the trust of the students within the school. Lastly, to decrease arrest rates for thefts within the school, in turn also decreasing the number of students who were labeled as "criminals." My plan was simple. After a theft investigation had been concluded and a suspect had positively been identified, I would wait before signing an arrest warrant. I would talk to the suspect and give them two choices. The first choice: return the undamaged property, or make arrangements with the victim to replace the stolen item, and no charges would be filed. The second choice was to not trust me, and not return the stolen item, and be charged with larceny. The program gave the power of choice back to the students, as they could now set their own destiny. It should be noted that the program operated with no need of internal or external funds.

As you might imagine, my "choice program" was not a big success at first. This was mainly due to the lack of trust within the community toward law enforcement officers. But trust levels can change with just one act of keeping to your word, which was the case in the second encounter I will describe.

This incident occurred during the spring months of the school year, when the school was observing an increase of theft reports. This was primarily due to the increased levels of unattended items; physical education classes were being held outdoors as well as spring sports, with a total of 10 teams. At the end of one school day, a student reported their new iPad had been stolen out of their bookbag, which had been left in the bleachers of the gym while the class was outside running the track. I obtained all the information about the stolen iPad, including the serial number. I started my investigation by speaking with the gym teacher, who stated they had left a hurt student in the gym area to watch over all the bags. That student stated they only left the area one time, to use the restroom. This was the timeframe I focused on when reviewing the four security cameras located in the gym area. After two days of reviewing security footage, I found the suspect. An African-American male had walked into the gym as the student went to the restroom, and started going into the different bookbags. He pulled the iPad out of the victim's bookbag and put it into his own bag. I traced the suspect through the building using other security cameras, and watched him place the iPad into a locker. It took about another day before I was able to identify the suspect. I interviewed the suspected student early on a Thursday morning. As I did with all my theft cases, I initiated the "choice program." At first the student, like so many others, chose to not speak to me about the incident. So, I tried something I had not done before. I tried to make a personal connection with him, rather than just letting him walk out. Before ending the interview, I reiterated that if the iPad was on my desk by the time I came to work the next day, I would not charge him. Then, I told him at some point in your life you are going to have to take a leap of faith and trust the police. The student just rolled his eyes, walked out of my office, and went to class.

Later that same day, I was outside conducting my lunchtime foot patrols of the school campus, when over the school radio I was requested to report to my office to meet with a student. It was my iPad theft suspect, who wanted to speak with me about the incident. The suspect looked right at me and said, "Ok, I am going to trust you." He said he could get me the iPad right away if I could take him to his residence. I agreed and drove him to his house, where he obtained the stolen iPad.

It took about 20 minutes to drive back to the school, so we just started to talk. The student asked me again, "Are you really not going to charge me?" I told him I was a man of my word, and I would not. But I also told him that I didn't work for the school district, and he might still get suspended from school for the theft. "I will take that over being arrested any day," he said. He then told me this was the first time he ever trusted a law enforcement officer and it took him three hours to bring himself to do so. I told him I was glad he trusted me, as I was here to help and nothing more. I then asked him why he chose to steal the iPad. He just looked at me, and said, "Did you see where I live?" He went on to say that it was hard going to school, watching all the different students use smart phones, iPads, and laptop computers, knowing that his parents could never afford to buy those things for him. He started to tear up, and said, "I just wanted to fit in, and be seen as an equal."

I lost track of this student over the years, but the statement he made on the drive back to the school has always stayed with me. This was also the turning point of me gaining the respect of the youth within my community, as an officer of his word. The more I learned about juveniles and youth culture and how the label of criminal can impact them, the more I thought about his statement: "I just wanted to fit in, and be seen as an equal." It had a major impact on me. It made me think about what were we doing wrong as a community that makes a young man steal, in order fit into the local youth culture. Secondly, I questioned whether this act was worthy of issuing the label of "criminal" to a young man who just wanted to be like the other local adolescents (unlike one who is a repeat juvenile offender). Lastly, was it worth putting a juvenile in the juvenile justice system, which was going to do nothing but give them a slap on the wrist?

Juvenile Justice and the Danger of Labeling

At the time, it seemed to me that the juvenile justice system did nothing to deal with young people whose actions cross the line and become criminal acts. During my time as a law enforcement officer, this was the most disheartening aspect of the job: watching the same juveniles commit the same crimes over and over again, with what appeared to be no repercussions for their actions. I know this idea was shared by many officers across the county, but we never took the time to understand how the juvenile system worked. In fact, I did not even fully understand the main mission of juvenile justice until I became a professor, after years of educating myself on why the juvenile justice system operates in the manner it does.

From the commencement of the inaugural juvenile court in Cook County, Illinois in 1899, the main focus of the juvenile justice system was to regulate and reform the behaviors of juveniles who chose to violate the law.[2] It wasn't created to lock people up, but to educate our troubled youth, with hopes of reducing the juvenile recidivism rates. This is why the juvenile justice system relies on diversion programs. These keep juveniles out of the formal channels of the justice system by suspending the formal proceeding before judgement has been rendered, and referring them to outside treatment programs. Diversion programs can take many different forms: anger management, mental health counseling, substance abuse treatment, and so on.

While these programs are a wonderful means of treating the possible root cause of the actions, they still might be creating labels, which can also be damaging. Larry J. Siegel points out that people establish a criminal career once they have been labeled for an action; they shape their personalities around labels such as "criminal."[3] In other words, once a person thinks of themself as a criminal, they are more likely to take criminal actions. In Siegel's words, critics of diversion programs "charge that they substitute one kind of stigma for another" (246)—that a diversion program might trade the label of "criminal" for another harmful label, like hothead, druggy, or mentally unstable. So, while these programs are very helpful, we need to be mindful of the other types of labels which can be created by these programs, which can be just as damaging.

To put this into context, say we have a juvenile who is addicted to opiates. If the addiction is left untreated, it could possibly lead to criminal actions such as theft, burglary, or selling drugs, and the youth would be labeled as a "criminal." The better outcome is to place the juvenile in a treatment program—but that in itself could create an informal label like "druggy" that would make the addiction harder to escape. Even after treatment, if the juvenile views themself as a druggy, it could lead them back to that lifestyle and possible criminal activities. Keeping these labels from being formulated can reduce the impact of these issues on our youth.

Avoiding the Label

The last incident I'll discuss has to do with the importance of stopping the label before it circulates. While I was not professionally linked to this incident, I was very personally linked. During my years as a law enforcement officer, I moonlighted as a high school assistant wrestling coach, and created bonds with many of my student athletes. There was one wrestler I looked at as one of my own. He was hardworking, trustworthy, and dedicated to both his sports, as well as his schoolwork, family, and friends. He was the type of student who would give you his lunch money, if you did not have any. He was always smiling and in good spirits. His hard work paid off: he was a star linebacker for the football team, and the state champ and wrestler of the year for our state in 2013. Upon graduating high school in the summer of 2013, he chose to play football at a prep school. He could have wrestled at a number of universities or colleges within the state, but he wanted to play football. So, though we'd advised against his choice, all of his coaches supported it. Then, during the early hours one December morning, I received countless text messages from former students, community members, and school staff asking if I had seen the news regarding this former student. It was then I learned he had been arrested for attempted murder, first-degree burglary, and attempted armed robbery.

I could not believe what I was hearing and reading. I thought, *No way, not him.* The following afternoon, I learned that he had given a ride to his roommate and another acquaintance to a local apartment complex. These two men attempted to rob the apartment, and a gunfight broke out. In the aftermath, one of the two men he had driven to the apartment died of injuries from the gunfight. The young man

I knew was arrested at the local hospital, as he had taken one of the other men there for treatment after being shot. Some of his other coaches and I were asked to be character witnesses during his trial, but were never called to testify. In the end, he pled guilty and served three years for his part of the criminal act. His relatively light sentence was based on the fact that he never left the vehicle.

After his release from prison, he returned home. I am proud of my community, which might have shamed this young man, and labeled him as a criminal. Instead, I never heard one bad thing spoken about this young man, either from a community member or any member of the local criminal justice system. I believe the label of "criminal" was never placed upon him because the community knew his true character. This young man proved all of us right. He is now a wonderful father of two, has recently gotten engaged, works hard every day to support his family, and understands the wrong choices he made that night. This may not have been the case had the formal and informal labels been issued to him upon his release from prison and his return home.

Experiences like the ones I have described have shown me that it's very hard to fully understand and answer the question "What Is a criminal?" My personal view of a criminal has changed over the course of my professional and academic journey. Especially with adolescents, it is key to know all the underlying facts before labeling someone a "criminal," as doing so may have irreversible effects on that person and the community where they live. In the three cases I have discussed, labels of some type could have been issued, but were not. In all three, there was a positive outcome. Perhaps more important than defining what it means to be a criminal, is recognizing how powerful it is to avoid labeling people as such.

Patrick Schmucker is Assistant Professor of Criminal Justice and coordinator of the criminal justice program at Huntingdon College in Montgomery, Alabama. He holds a BS in business and accounting, an MS in criminology, a master's degree in education, and a PhD in criminal justice. Professor Schmucker is a veteran of the United States Marine Corps, was a production manager within a prison industry, and worked for over 12 years in law enforcement in South Carolina. During that time, he served as a patrolman, school resource officer, public information officer, and SWAT operator.

Notes

1 David N. Falcone, *Prentice Hall's Dictionary of American Criminal Justice, Criminology, and Criminal Law*, 2nd ed. (Upper Saddle River, NJ: Pearson Education, 2010), 57.
2 Clemens Bartollas and Frank Schmalleger, *Juvenile Delinquency*, 2nd ed. (New York: Pearson Education, 2015).
3 Larry J. Siegel, *Criminology: Theories, Patterns, and Typologies*, 12th ed. (Boston: Cengage Learning, 2015).

8

A POLICE CHIEF'S JOURNEY TO HARM REDUCTION

Brendan Cox

I grew up in a working-class family, the youngest child living in a multigenerational house in Albany. My father worked two full-time jobs and grabbed as many hours of overtime as possible. We weren't rich but we certainly weren't poor. I never went cold, hungry, or wanting. I grew up in a mostly White, middle-class neighborhood, and went to school with mostly White, middle-class kids.

My father didn't work all the hours he did for no reason. He did it so that myself and my sisters could have opportunities he and my mother did not. We each had our choice of high school, which enabled me to go to a private all-boys school for high school. We each got to go to college, which neither of my parents had the opportunity to do.

I graduated from college in 1992 utterly unprepared for an actual career, as most 21-year-old people are, but eventually took the civil service test for the Albany police department. I had lived and worked my entire life in Albany, my family was from Albany, and it seemed logical that I would serve my community there. After pushing through all of the necessary steps, I was sworn in as an Albany police officer on February 10, 1994.

The Rookie

At that time the police department split the city into two large geographical areas. I was assigned to Division One, a mix of patrol zones that included densely populated areas of poor and marginalized communities with high crime rates, along with more suburban middle- and upper-class neighborhoods that had less crime.

This is the time in my life when I started to realize there were two separate cities in Albany, and that I had grown up not only in a different part of the city, but in an entirely different world than the one where I was working. While I had spent time in different parts of the city (and my parents were from West Hill, one of the

DOI: 10.4324/9781003169468-11

marginalized communities that I now patrolled), I had never been exposed to the level of poverty, trauma, and despair that I was now seeing. The police academy hadn't prepared me for this.

In 1994, Congress passed a federal crime bill that included funding for 100,000 new police officers to take care of supposed "super predators," and $9.7 billion for building new prisons to put them in. The war on drugs was in full swing, and for a young cop that meant an exciting, fast-paced job. It was exactly what I had wanted. I loved that you never knew what was going to happen on the next call. The rush of adrenaline was exactly what I was looking for. It was one thing to be reliable—answer your calls, back people up, patrol your zone—but it was completely another level to be one of the officers making proactive stops on the street and arresting people, usually for drugs.

The number-one drug in those days was crack cocaine. Sure, there was cannabis, but a cannabis arrest was usually reserved for someone who gave you a hard time. There was a little bit of heroin around, and you would certainly make an arrest for anyone with that or a needle, but in the 90s opiates were not what they are now. It was crack cocaine that was running rampant. That is what the proactive cops were looking for, and making names for themselves by doing street-level interdiction. In the 90s crack was blamed for everything from street violence, to teen pregnancy, to high school drop-out rates, to poverty rates. In my first two years I was into the game. I enjoyed it. I liked trying to catch the street-level action of the dealer. Like many young cops, I thought I wanted to become a detective in the narcotics unit. This would be how I would make my difference, how I would help people, how I would change things.

We tend to forget that drugs are everywhere, in every neighborhood, among all people, but in the war on drugs the frontline was always communities of color. In those times, we arrested many people for drug possession, possession with the intent to sell, and the actual sale of narcotics. As in many places in America, these were mainly young men of color. Once someone was arrested and put in jail, that individual lost opportunities for education, employment, housing, treatment, and multiple other services. In New York, the age of criminal liability was 16. When I think about the many high school juniors and seniors whose lives were destroyed by the war on drugs and the draconian policies of the 1990s and beyond, it brings shame and regret for having been a part of it all.

During those years, I did some damage. While never intentional, and certainly guided by the laws and policies of the day, it was still real, and I own it. I soon came to realize that the exciting cat-and-mouse "game" of narcotics policing was too easily corrupted. Money was always front and center, as any of the officers who worked evening or midnight shifts went to arraignments, and thus we were incentivized to arrest people in order to collect overtime hours.

It started to be clear to me that the war on drugs was one of constant conflict. I wanted to be a part of solving things, of seeing them get better. I didn't see that in making drug arrests or in going on raids with the narcotics unit. Sure, it was exciting, but it seemed pointless, a never-ending saga that put us at odds with the community. We were not solving any issues; we were exacerbating an already bad situation. We certainly never stopped the flow of narcotics into our community through street-level drug interdiction.

A Shift in Focus

My career ultimately took a turn through the supervision route. I took the sergeant's exam the first time I was eligible and scored high enough to be promoted with a little over four years of service. After a few years as a midnight patrol sergeant I moved to a detective sergeant position in the Children and Family Services Unit. The CFSU was responsible for investigating any crime committed against or by someone under 16 years of age, domestic violence, elder abuse, and our sex offender registry. The next few years would open me to developing an understanding of adverse childhood experiences and the many aspects of trauma that shape so many people's lives.

I eventually became the commander in charge of investigations, overseeing all of the investigatory units in the department. During that time, the department took a strategic shift towards hot spot policing and crime mapping analytics to determine patrol resource deployment. Between 2006 and 2009 the department became laser-focused on Part I crimes (homicide, rape, robbery, aggravated assault, burglary, larceny, motor vehicle theft, and arson) as New York State pushed to lower the crime rate outside of New York City. The department embraced the addition of a state-funded crime analysis center, embedded crime analysts into a crime information and intelligence unit, and focused patrol commanders to a more proactive geographic response to crime patterns. The older, more community-based walking beats were collapsed into an expanded unit that included 33 officers who could be tactically directed to any of the identified hot spots to immediately shut down any spike. I would eventually come to inherit and oversee the strategy when I was promoted to Assistant Chief in 2008 and oversaw both the detective and patrol functions of the department.

The tactics we were using—hot spot policing, broken windows policing, and many other patrol-heavy strategies—can reduce crime. CompStat, an accountability tool, can be used to ensure police supervisors are using resources in a strategic fashion and are making headway in a manner that can be measured. However, these strategies and tools can also shut out the community, make the police an occupying force, reduce opportunities to utilize non-criminal justice responses, and lead to poor police/community relations. That is exactly what was happening in Albany. The community and the police could not have been farther apart, and the chasm couldn't have been larger than with communities of color. The three traditionally marginalized neighborhoods in Albany could not have felt more divided. The police department could show large reductions of crime, but what we could not show was positive relationships. We were an occupying force, plain and simple. This created an erosion of trust in the police and reduced the likelihood of cooperation from the community. Community members were less likely to call the police to report a crime, or to help solve crimes.

In 2009, there was an incident in which the police chief told another assistant chief that the homicide of a White college student was more important than that of other homicides that we were investigating, and used a racial slur in this statement. Most of our homicides were Black males in their late teens and early twenties. The reaction to this incident eventually led to the resignation of the chief, and a chance at a reset for the department and community.

This reset came in the redesign of the department into a more community-based philosophy that looked at public safety as a partnership. I became the department's representative to make recommendations to implement a community policing philosophy. I found myself drawing on my time with the Children and Family Services Unit and what I had learned about trauma and adverse experiences. We began looking at alternative responses to crimes that were driven by issues that the criminal justice system hadn't been able to address. And truth be told, those crimes were being committed by people whom our educational, social services, and community-based providers had all failed as well.

Under the guidance of our new chief, we changed the way public safety was looked at and delivered. Instead of being an occupying force, we worked with our community partners to ensure that the police and community worked together. During this process there were many community meetings to talk about what this vision could be. These meetings also served as a healing process for the community, as many members took the opportunity to voice the harms that had come to them at the hands of the police. Much of this harm had happened under the guise of the war on drugs and our efforts to reduce crime. But these were harmful practices and policies that had caused long-term damage to individuals and the community itself. We couldn't just say "Sorry" and move on. There needed to be more. People were demanding more. And we were finally listening.

Let me stop at this point to say that I haven't said much about major investigations in my career. In my time in the Children and Family Services Unit, and then as the commander of investigations, I oversaw my fair share of horrific crimes. I helped implement anti-gun violence strategies and address street level violence. I also oversaw our registered sex offenders. While some people needed to be sent to prison, there were only a few that I would identify as being sociopaths, or people that I saw no redemption in. They did exist, but that was the exception, not the rule. While I am far from my 23-year-old self who thought that punitive actions were required to change behavior, I am also not in a place where I can say that no one I arrested, or oversaw the case against, should be in prison. There are a few people that I hope never get out, simply because I believe they will never stop hurting other people.

However, the overwhelming amount of people that get arrested absolutely have redeeming qualities and need interventions other than punishment and imprisonment. We need to find a way to address the root cause of what creates the situation that led to the crime in the first place. We need to stop criminalizing substance use, mental illness, and poverty. We need to start recognizing trauma for what it is and find a way to treat it as such, especially with young men and women of color. This is what brings me into this next part of my career and where I am at today.

Harm Reduction

While I was working in the Children and Family Services Unit, I was on the board of directors at a local community-based agency that was focused on domestic violence and youth issues. At one of our board meetings, another community-based provider made a presentation about a mobile syringe exchange program they were starting. The program would provide clean syringes to drug users in order to prevent the spread of diseases like HIV and hepatitis C. This was around 2006, and these services were fairly new to upstate New York, though they had been established downstate for a few years. The presenters told me they had been trying to set a meeting up with the chief and mayor with no luck. That was of little surprise to me; if you've spent years arresting people for using drugs, it's a strange idea that you would try to help them do it more safely.

I eventually got approval to work with the agency, but in an unofficial capacity. This meant that neither the police department nor the city would give the program a stamp of approval by officially acknowledging its existence, but that I could do what was needed to help get them off the ground. I was able to assist them in placement of their van, and opened up lines of communication so that we could alert them if there was a spike in overdoses. They could also call if participants were being stopped by officers or if they had any issues in the neighborhood. This became a great relationship, and benefited many in the drug user community as the program operated unimpeded. It also had the effect of reducing the number of officers who were stuck with needles—a common occurrence during a search for drugs. That experience laid the groundwork for how I would eventually approach changing the police/community relationship.

In the 2010s, as we were trying to reset our police department, we started to work with community agencies to find alternatives to arrest. We piloted a mobile juvenile assessment center with funding from New York State, with the goal of reducing juvenile arrests and the use of detention. That pilot was unsuccessful, as it was unwieldy and had mixed reviews from all parties involved. Our next attempt was a move to stop arresting men and women involved in sex work. There was one section of the city in which we traditionally received a large number of complaints from business owners. We had our crime analysts conduct a study of the factors that were driving sex work in the city, and across the board the issues came back to substance use disorders, domestic violence, and mental health needs. The overwhelming majority of sex workers had at least one of these factors occurring, with some having all three. Once we had gathered this intelligence, we invited service providers to a meeting to discuss how they could provide services in cases where we would otherwise make an arrest. Everyone agreed that we should conduct outreach efforts, but those efforts would need to take place late in the evening, and the providers told us they did not have the resources at that time of day. In fact, one of the providers asked if we could just continue to make arrests, and they could get access to the people prior to court.

So up to this point we had only had success in one area. We were running an outreach program to our homeless population in coordination with our service providers. It took place during regular business hours. We were able to get people connected to services by voluntarily bringing them to a one-stop help center. It was at least a step in the right direction, and helped demonstrate a collaborative approach, with businesses providing safe spaces and donated supplies, while service providers offered their skills and infrastructure.

For community-based policing to work, it is important to have good relationships with all people and agencies in your communities, even those that would seem to be on opposing sides. When we were doing our reset, we made a point of reaching out to the people that often opposed us. Those groups included the largest civil rights agency in the city, the Center for Law and Justice, which had been founded due to the killing of an African American man by the Albany police department in 1984. The fact of the matter is that there were times in our history that we were on the wrong side of things, and that included recent history. The Center for Law and Justice had standing and legitimacy in the community. It was important that we listened to what they had to tell us, and that they were part of our rebuilding process.

That relationship led to an opportunity to really change what we were doing about crime. The Center's executive director, Dr. Alice Green, invited us to a meeting at the offices of the Open Society Foundation in New York to hear a presentation on Seattle's innovative approach to address racial disparities within the war on drugs. Law Enforcement Assisted Diversion (LEAD) is a pre-booking initiative that allows police officers to use their discretion to divert a person to long term, intensive, harm reduction-based case management, rather than arresting them. LEAD provided an answer for us that we had not been able to put our fingers on: getting social workers to meet the police in the field and take over right on the spot. This is one of the key pieces we were missing during our previous attempts at diversions.

LEAD also further introduced us into a world we were familiar with but didn't exactly understand: harm reduction. Harm reduction is a public health philosophy that seeks to reduce the harms that are associated with certain behaviors, like the use of illicit drugs. Harm reduction seeks to meet a person where they are at, literally and figuratively. The key to harm reduction is that it doesn't leave the person where they are. Instead, it seeks to help them make positive, incremental change through a person-centered approach that works with an individual by building a relationship, and helps the person identify goals they would like to achieve and services they would like to access. A harm reduction philosophy comes without judgment and stigma; it is a humanistic approach. It takes the punitive and coercive approach of the criminal justice system out of the equation. It recognizes that behavior change takes time, and many people have deep-seated trauma that can only be addressed through long-term strategies that support the person, not force them into a corner.

Of course, I had already been doing work in harm reduction, without realizing it, through my unofficial collaboration with the syringe-exchange program. But harm reduction work is so counterintuitive to us in law enforcement that I did not make the connection right away; I didn't realize syringe exchanges were part of the same world as this new initiative. Pretty much on that day in Manhattan, we agreed that we would replicate what Seattle had done in Albany. It took a while to make it happen, but Albany's LEAD program would go live on April 1, 2016.

From Chief to LEAD

I became the acting chief of the department on April 1, 2015. On April 2, 2015 in the early morning hours three of my officers stopped a man, Donald "Dante" Ivy, whom they suspected of carrying a gun. As it turned out, the man was not carrying a gun, nor was he committing any crime. The interaction became physical, and the man went into cardiac arrest and died. It turned out the man suffered from mental illness, and many of the signs the officers took for criminal activity were actually due to his mental illness. While the officers had reasonable suspicion to stop him, he was never involved in any criminal activity. He had just gone to the corner store late at night, something he did to avoid dealing with large numbers of people.

There were three separate investigations into the case: an internal one, a grand jury that was convened by the district attorney, and a civil rights investigation by the Justice Department. All three investigations cleared the officers and department of wrongdoing. As a department we responded by changing a number of policies and increasing training and community engagement. I will always question what I could have done differently to prevent that death. Dante was a Black male walking in a marginalized neighborhood. We had increased/focused patrols out in that neighborhood to reduce gun violence. The officers were doing what we were asking them to do.

I am a strong believer in police reforms and in criminal legal system reforms. I am a strong believer in ending the war on drugs. And I believe if I had done more to reform the system from within, that maybe Dante wouldn't have died. We were highly transparent during the investigation and when we reported the findings. We tried to have an open-door policy with the family so they always knew what we knew. Many people in the community struggled with the fact that a man was dead, and yet no one was being held accountable, no one held the blame. I blame myself. I should have changed more and quicker.

I held that post of Chief until January of 2017. I am proud of the work that was done with the men and women of the department and the community I served. The people I worked with sacrificed much to make the city a better place. The community was filled with people that wanted a safe place to live, but not at the cost of living in a police state. People gave their time to groups like the Albany Community Policing Advisory Committee, which helped redesign how we engaged the community and taught me about the trauma that our traditional policing tactics created.

This is what made the decision to leave the Albany police force an easy one. I was offered the position of director of policing strategies with the LEAD National Support Bureau. What I wanted at that point was to help move the national discussion on policing. The Albany police department had been recognized as one of the top 15 departments in the country in implementing the recommendations of the Task Force on 21st Century Policing commissioned by President Obama. I felt maybe I could help move the needle on a different level. So, I retired from the police department, and now I work full-time for LEAD.

LEAD offers a systemic new option to respond to people repeatedly arrested for a variety of low-level offenses due to unmet behavioral health needs or associated poverty. Rather than the binary choice of arrest/don't arrest, LEAD diverts the person out of the criminal legal system and into long-term, harm-reduction, street-based case management. LEAD allows police officers to use their discretion to recognize that crimes driven by addiction, mental illness, poverty, or homelessness are better served by addressing the root cause of the issues, not through punishment or coercive action that is just going to create more trauma and harm.

In addition to traditional arrest diversion, officers can also make a social contact referral into the same case management services. That means if an officer knows someone who's been caught up in the system before, they don't have to wait until the next time they may commit a crime, but can make a straight-up offer for services. This has proven popular, as many officers use this for the people they have frequent contact with but no real solution for. This is not only good for the person being offered the services but can reduce calls for service for the officer and the department.

LEAD recognizes that police should not be the only route through which people get the resources they need, and in 2021 we introduced a community-based referral system known as Let Everyone Advance with Dignity. This allows for neighbors, business owners, or other community members to contact the LEAD project manager directly to refer potential participants into services. This now can act as an alternative response to 911 and reduces the need for police responses.

Law Enforcement Assisted Diversion/Let Everyone Advance with Dignity take us from a criminal justice approach to a public health approach when dealing with substance use, mental illness, and homelessness. A public health approach recognizes that we need to retool our systems to address the populations needs upstream in a more holistic manner that addresses the actual needs, not just the symptoms.

Reflections on Crime, Punishment, and Doing Better

If we think about what we traditionally have done through punishment and coercion, we have utterly failed. The United States is roughly 5% of the world's population but we own 25% of the world's incarcerated population. We increased the prison population by 700% for non-violent drug offenses from 1980 to 1997, and yet the rates of drug use continued to rise. We continue to believe that we can coerce someone to drug treatment without ever trying to determine why it is they are taking drugs. And most of the reasons we outlaw particular drugs (marijuana but not alcohol, for example) are based in racial or ethnic bias and discrimination. While we threw hundreds of thousands of people away to prison, we have also allowed hundreds of thousands to die from the opiate crisis.

The war on drugs was set in motion by people who are cruel and inhumane. It is time to end it. That means ending police action when it comes to personal possession and consumption of illicit drugs. Whether through legalization or decriminalization, it needs to be done. Legalization gets us to a place where we can regulate the market and ensure there is access to a clean drug supply, but more people can agree on decriminalization. Either way, we need to take broader harm reduction approaches and give people access to safe consumption sites and on-the-spot access to medication assisted treatment.

People need to stop judging those that use drugs, and let the experts lead the way. When I argue for safe consumption sites, or legalization, people often say I must be condoning the use of dangerous drugs. I am not, but I am saying the criminal legal system has no place in the enforcement of personal use and a regulated market would be far safer than the illicit market we have today. When people have to turn to the street corner where they can only buy fentanyl, we are not keeping them safe. We are just keeping the cartels in business, and people dying in all parts of the world.

My beliefs after over 27 years working in the criminal legal system is that we need a complete and total overhaul. If the murder of George Floyd didn't confirm that for people I do not know what will. Substance use, mental illness, and homelessness issues need to be handled by professionals in those fields first. While there may still be a need for police officers to respond to certain situations, police should not be the primary agency dealing with these complex issues.

We must continue to find ways to break down barriers between the police and the public that they serve. Public safety is a cooperative effort, and it can only happen if there is a trusting relationship. Right now, that trust is hard to find. We have been trying to build trust through community policing, and while I have been a huge proponent of this philosophy, it has started and stopped so many times that many people have lost faith in what the term *community policing* actually means. To me it is about building relationships—which brings us right back to harm reduction.

In harm reduction we always talk about relationships. We also talk about meeting people where they are, respecting that, and being there with them. If what they are doing is harmful, we do not leave them there, but we also do not cause more harm and trauma trying to force them down a pathway just because we think it is the correct way.

Perhaps following the principles of harm reduction could be a new way forward in policing efforts. We can be community centered, trauma informed, relationship driven, and look for individualized approaches to problems. Far too often we have tried to make change using singular strategies. That is one of the ways we wound up with the problem of mass incarceration—we thought arresting everyone and putting them behind bars would stop them from committing crimes in the future and deter others from doing so in the first place. That has failed. It's time to work with people and the community in a different way.

This is a complex issue; life is a complex issue. Just like I tell my two sons, draw a couple of different cards and your life may be totally different. You may be the person living on the street, or serving 15 to life for a horrible decision you made when you were 16 years old. We are all human beings. It's time our lawmakers recognize that and stop creating lifetime criminal-involved people. With the appropriate services, time, and resources we may actually make a difference.

Punishment and coercion are not justice.

Chief (Ret.) Brendan Cox is the Director of Policing Strategies at the LEAD Support Bureau, where he provides strategic guidance on the implementation of Law Enforcement Assisted Diversion/Let Everyone Advance with Dignity to jurisdictions around the world. Chief Cox was previously employed with the Albany, New York police department, from which he retired as Chief of Police in 2017. He served in numerous capacities in the Albany police department, including overseeing its Special Operations Unit and Children and Family Services Unit. He rose through the ranks to become the Commander of Investigations, Assistant Chief of Operations, and Deputy Chief. In July of 2015 he was appointed Chief of Police. Chief Cox has a Bachelor of Science degree in criminal justice from the University of Dayton and a Master of Public Administration degree from Marist College. He is a graduate of the Police Executive Research Forum's Senior Management Institute for Police. He is a member of the New York State Juvenile Justice Advisory Group and was appointed to the New York Governor's Workgroup to Draft Legislation for Regulated Adult-Use Marijuana Program in 2018. He is an Executive Fellow with the Police Foundation, a speaker for the Law Enforcement Action Partnership, and a member of the Global Law Enforcement and Public Health Association. He sits on several local boards of directors, including the Albany Police Athletic League and the LaSalle School of Albany.

III
Ripple Effects

9

CHILDREN OF CRIMINALS

The Hidden Victims of the Justice System

Anna Roberge

I first entered prison when I was 13. I walked with my head down, scared of making eye contact with those around me. Keeping up a staring contest with the floor, I reached for my younger sister's hand and brought it close to me as we sat down to wait on cold, hard wooden benches. I could tell she was nervous too, as her foot tapped against the ground. When I finally decided to look up, losing my staring contest, I saw everyone around me sitting in the same position: uncomfortably upright with their hands in their laps. None of us were here because of crimes we had committed, but we were being punished all the same.

My mom was standing in the corner, holding my younger brother. I watched as she wiped away a tear that dripped down her face. Finally, the stone-cold silence was broken: I heard the name "Roberge" called from behind the desk. I was the last of my family to walk over to the gate, with my hands tucked deeply away in my pockets, holding back tears. I wasn't sure I really wanted to go through.

As we prepared to visit my father, another family was being turned away. A little boy and his mother were being told that they could not visit his dad because the mother was wearing an "inappropriate shirt." The shirt was a blue button-up, completely modest. But according to the guards, the buttons made it unacceptable. Everyone in the room seemed to sigh; everyone knew the pain of being turned away. I think my mother saw the look on my face. Although it meant losing our spot in line, she turned around and ran out to the mother.

Moments later they were back inside, with smiles on their faces. The mother was in one of my mom's shirts, with no buttons. Waiting longer didn't matter to me as I watched the family being let through the metal detectors to go see the father. My mother always taught us to look out for others, and she never failed to show us how it was done. Throughout the entirety of my dad's imprisonment, this was just one of the ways she became my true hero.

DOI: 10.4324/9781003169468-13

After what felt like hours, our name was finally called again. This time, I stood up with a little less lead in my legs. Knowing that the little boy had been able to walk through those doors was like a wave of warmth. We handed the guards our birth certificates, they checked our clothing, and we walked through the metal detectors. Fear was wrapping around my body. We were about to walk into a room full of prisoners. We were about to see my dad: a prisoner, a criminal. Was he going to be different? Was the room going to be safe? I stuck close to my siblings, wanting to protect them, even though I knew there wasn't much of anything that I could actually do.

Bang! The huge metal door behind us slammed closed and I could hear the maze of locks clicking. Suddenly my siblings started running. Startled, I ran as well, imagining I was running away from this prison, away from the pain. But reality hit, and reality was my father. His gentle hands, bright smile, and warm hugs were gone. Prison had taken away my father, I thought.

Throughout the entire visit I was preoccupied with watching the little boy play with his father. He was sitting on a worn-out carpet that looked like it hadn't been replaced in 20 years. They were both playing with toy cars that were definitely from the last century. But the boy looked at his father, in his jumpsuit branded with a six-digit number, and smiled. He was happy.

The guard yelled a warning: five minutes left. Everyone started saying their goodbyes. I gave my dad one last, forced hug and walked towards the metal door, holding my breath to avoid letting a single teardrop fall. Then I heard a noise that will ring in my ears forever. The little boy was sobbing. He wouldn't let go of his dad. He knew it would be days, or more, before he could see him again. It bothers me that I never got a chance to see that boy smile again. He could have been crying the entire drive home (I found out it was four hours). I will never have the chance to know if he was okay.

I know that there's a good chance he wasn't.

Children of incarcerated people are not rare. According to a study done in 2014, about 1 in every 25 children has a parent who is currently incarcerated.[1] While there is a lot of focus on the enormous number of people incarcerated in the US, their children are usually overlooked. However, the imprisonment of a parent is severely detrimental to children's emotional and mental wellbeing. Many call children the "hidden victims" of mass incarceration.[2]

As I sit here writing this, the sound of his sobbing still rings in my ears as if I was standing right back there at the prison. That young boy did nothing to deserve the pain he will live with forever. None of us did. I was fairly lucky, and lost my father for a year and a half; many parents' sentences are much longer. Some children will never be able to forgive their parents, some will never be able to see them, and some will live the rest of their lives visiting their parents only in prison. Some will forever live with their parents' legacy.

Before my father went to prison my life was almost "normal," if I can even use that word. My parents were together, we had a nice house, they had good jobs, and we were a happy family. After he left, we were a family of criminals. The crime not only defined my dad, but it defined his four kids and wife as well. I couldn't walk into a room without seeing heads leaning together to whisper, and people staring. Was I a criminal too? Because my dad made a mistake, did that mean I also made a mistake? It became an overwhelming feeling, too much for a 13-year-old to handle, so I began to believe it.

I never visited my father after that first time. Society, and the actions of those guards, pushed me into a dark place where I felt stuck. I didn't want to be seen by anyone. I was embarrassed. My life would never be normal again. Newspapers, social media, and word of mouth spread stories, true and false, about my father. His crime was inescapable. Turning to friends sometimes resulted in the loss of a friendship. Turning to teachers resulted in judgmental looks. Turning to family meant demonstrating weakness. I began to fall into a cycle of sadness and despair that I felt I would never escape. I started to view our justice system in a negative light, and felt resentment towards all police officers and prison guards.

However, despite all this negativity, I had a great amount of support. In this situation, I was lucky; I had more help than most people will get. My family worked together to push through the difficult days and nights. My school counselor made sure I got the support and time to process that I needed. My cross-country coach built my confidence back up. Therapists, family members, friends, mentors, coaches—most were there to hold me up, to provide me with a shoulder to cry on. But the people who weren't there for me and my family made an even larger impact. The guards who didn't let in the little boy, who declined my family several times, who made my mom cry—I don't think I will ever move past them. They not only punished criminals; they created them.

Researchers have found that there are five major consequences for children who have incarcerated parents: becoming more likely to commit a crime, psychological problems/antisocial behavior, low educational attainment, low economic well-being, and disruption of parent-child attachment (Martin 2017). All of these effects can be connected to the way children of criminals are made to feel like criminals themselves.

The correlation between having a parent incarcerated and criminal activity can be difficult to understand. If you've seen a parent punished for a crime, wouldn't you know better than to commit one yourself? But children of incarcerated people experience the constant feeling that they are already criminals. As I experienced, society and the judicial system make it difficult for the child to live down the crime of their parent, forcing them into feeling like a criminal too. Some children are able to become more resilient under this burden, while others succumb to the pressure and pain, committing a crime. Children with incarcerated parents are six times more likely than other children to engage in criminal activity (Martin 2017). If those kids were properly supported, that statistic could be changed.

But sometimes these children are hard to support, as they are at increased likelihood of developing antisocial behavior. When a child is made to feel different, or that they play a negative role in society, they are likely to pull away from others. It is common for children to ignore those trying to help, because they believe they are not worth the help. They believe that no one truly wants to help them, so they begin to push away. When I watched a guard yell at my mom and watched my friends slowly disappear, I felt like a criminal; I didn't trust anyone to help me; I retreated into myself.

Those feelings can also account for the low educational attainment present in the majority of children who have incarcerated parents. Most of us have experienced the death of a close loved one, and know that during the grieving process it becomes difficult to be productive. Now imagine taking that difficulty and living with it every day, for years. It's easy to see why you'd struggle to achieve high standards. In addition, most of these children also experience adverse circumstances, shame, and stigma—all of which act as roadblocks to productivity.[3] It would require an immense amount of resilience and support for the children to have the drive to keep up with their education. To keep from giving up, children struggling with this experience will need support from teachers, parents, and adults that they look up to. I valued grades my entire life, but when my dad was incarcerated I wanted to give up on everything. The only reason I did not lose my high academic achievement was the support I had from my mother, siblings, and grandparents. They pushed me to continue being the best version of myself.

We know that education is important for future success and good careers. Thus, a lot of children of incarcerated parents fall into economic instability and decreased happiness throughout their lives. This in turn puts them at a higher risk for engaging in criminal activity, especially with the foundation of risk that was built by having a parent incarcerated. With guidance and support they may persevere through school, leading them to a better future. Effective forms of support include one-on-one tutors, teachers taking time to check on the student, and most importantly, ensuring the student has positive reinforcement instead of the negativity attached with lower grades.

While community support can mitigate the harm of having an incarcerated parent, support within the family is essential to the healthy development of children. When family members of incarcerated people feel criminalized themselves, parent-child and sibling bonds can be threatened. If family members begin to go their separate ways after a traumatic event like a criminal conviction, a child may begin to be unattached from their family, thus increasing the likelihood of engaging in criminal and antisocial behavior. Families that maintain bonds through the difficult time of incarceration support children by reinforcing the positives in life and the love that they still have. In order for families to maintain this bond, it is important that they receive social support within the community where they reside. It will be difficult for this bond to evolve if they are alienated by the community, creating feelings of unworthiness and loneliness.

Understanding the consequences suffered by children of incarcerated people should make it easier for a community to provide the children with support that they need. Instead of gossip and judgmental stares, we need to start lending a helping hand or shoulder to cry on. The more we make children feel like criminals, the more likely it is to come true. Regardless of what their parents have done, children never deserve the feelings it creates for them.

Nor do incarcerated parents deserve to watch their children suffer. Throughout my experience within the prison system, I have met rapists, murderers, robbers, and more. Never once have I believed that any of them deserve to watch their children suffer. Everyone makes mistakes. I admit that even I make mistakes. These prisoners make larger mistakes, and need some help getting back on track. This does not warrant abuse or shame. Whatever society inflicts upon the prisoners is inflicted on their children as well.

I still think about that little boy, how he smiled at seeing his father, how he cried at leaving him. Could he have become a criminal himself? He has lived his entire life feeling like a criminal who did nothing to deserve that shame. Did he have support networks, or did he spend his days being judged and humiliated by his peers? The answer to that question will affect whether that little boy might have committed crimes of his own, whether he might someday be locked away from his own children. I want to spend my life making a difference in the lives of innocent children like that boy. By offering them support, by understanding their difficulties, we can all make a difference.

With this in mind, I have devoted my life to supporting children in the same situation as myself, while also learning to work within the justice system. My mother pushed me to use my life experiences as a way to help others, to push myself to become a better person. Without the support of this incredible person, I would never have been able to look at my situation as anything but negative. Now, with a completely different view on this life-changing event, my future direction has been altered for the better. I plan to earn a therapist's license and open a practice to help children with parents in the justice system, along with other juveniles. I would also like to work with the police, in order to make change to the justice system from the inside. The imprisonment of my father caused me a lot of pain, but with the help of my family, friends, and community, I have learned to use this pain to make things better.

Anna Roberge is an honor student at the University of New Hampshire, where she is dual-majoring in Justice Studies and Human Development and Family Studies. As a member of the Hamel Scholars leadership and service program, she works to help those dealing with the justice system. Having experienced the incarceration of a loved one, she is a strong advocate for restorative justice. She hopes to pursue a future in counseling justice-involved juveniles. It is Ms. Roberge's goal to show children whose parents are incarcerated that they are not alone, while also helping incarcerated parents to persevere. Prison can be a long and painful road. Ms. Roberge wants to educate inmates on how to navigate this challenging experience, while also understanding the gravity of their crimes.

Notes

1 Paola Scommegna, "Parents' Imprisonment Linked to Children's Health, Behavioral Problems," *Population Reference Bureau* (December 2014). https://www.prb.org/resources/parents-imprisonment-linked-to-childrens-health-behavioral-problems/
2 Eric Martin, "Hidden Consequences: The Impact of Incarceration on Dependent Children," *National Institute of Justice Journal* 278 (May 2017).
3 Rebecca J. Shlafer, Tyler Reedy, and Laurel Davis, "School-Based Outcomes Among Youth with Incarcerated Parents: Differences by School Setting," *Journal of School Health* 87, no. 9 (September 2017).

10

LIVING UNDOCUMENTED

Alex Masias
Translated from Spanish by Justin Mixon

I would say a criminal is someone who has committed a crime—like a *matanza* [murder], like a more significant crime. The *Migra* [Immigration and Customs Enforcement police force] discriminates against you just for coming here. They act like you don't have any value. But why would they think of me as a criminal? I just came here for a better life. Criminal is a very strong word used against someone. In reality, I haven't committed any crime.

My Life in Honduras

When I was younger, I never thought I would come to the United States. My parents had already lived for several years in the US, in Pennsylvania. They left me and my older sister with my grandmother in our hometown in Honduras.

I was happy there with my grandmother. She was really my mother to me. I had friends, and I enjoyed going to school. But then when I was about 15 years old, gangs of young criminals were organizing in my hometown. One of the older gang members started a relationship with my sister. He was always telling me I had to join his gang and that I needed to sell drugs at my school. Eventually, I had to stop going to school because I kept running into these gang members who were threatening me when I would walk to and from school.

My sister died because of this gang member. Then, I knew I had to leave Honduras right away. It was not safe for me there. I knew I would miss my grandmother, but she said that I could leave to get away from the gangs. I was 16 years old when I left Honduras.

I saved money for a couple of months and then took buses up through Guatemala and Mexico until I got to the US/Mexico border. At one point, I had to pay a bribe to a Guatemalan police officer who drove me in his police car to the next border checkpoint with Mexico. That cost me a lot of the money I had with me.

DOI: 10.4324/9781003169468-14

At the US border, I went with a group of young immigrants across the Rio Grande into Texas. We crossed the river in the daytime, and we knew that we would just turn ourselves over to the US border patrol, who would pick us up on the other side.

Eventually, the US government sent me to a children's shelter for a few weeks, and then released me to live with my mother in Pennsylvania.

Arrested by ICE

It has been very hard for me to stay in the US. When I first got here, I hired a lawyer to represent me in court. Then I lived with my dad in Harrisburg, Pennsylvania, working and paying my bills. I never missed a court date.

One day I saw an ICE officer on my block. I knew they were looking for my dad in Harrisburg. He had some sort of a fight with his girlfriend. I saw that there were four ICE patrol cars. I had walked to my uncle's house nearby to get a ride to work. I saw another patrol car behind my dad's house. A fifth one. Two pickups and three cars.

They had blocked my uncle's car. They had blocked the street. I was walking to the traffic light. One of the ICE guys came up to me and said "Hey," but he didn't say he was with immigration. So I walked away. Then he was following me for like ten minutes, walking. Then I started to run. The ICE officer was very tall, but he couldn't catch me running. He still never said he was anything—ICE, or police, or anything. I eventually jumped into a dumpster, but they found me there, maybe because someone else had seen me jump in. They put handcuffs on me.

There in the street the officer asked me if I had a passport. He took my keys and said, "Let's go to your house. You can use these keys to get your passport. We need your passport. We need to look at things in your house, to see if you are the person here in this court document appointment paper."

I refused to go back to my house. He said he knew which house I left from. He asked which one of my keys went to my house. They showed me a photo of another guy they said lived in my building. They said he had a deportation order. They were looking for him. I did not know that guy in the picture. Still, I refused to go back to my house with ICE.

I showed him that I had an asylum case in the court. They called their office. They took me to some office. One of the ICE officers was going to let me go. But the other one, the one that caught me, he was very angry, and said they had to arrest me because I was running.

Unfortunately, I didn't have my lawyer's number with me. But I did ask another guy who was arrested there to tell his girlfriend to look up my mom on Facebook and call my mom. I knew she would call my lawyer. When I got to the ICE office, they made fun of me for jumping in a dumpster. They called me stupid.

They made me sign a paper. They didn't tell me what was written on the paper. Then they forced me to give a fingerprint. I kept that paper. The paper said that

I did not want to see a lawyer. The paper said that I wanted deportation right away, without going to court. But that was not true—I did not want to be deported.

Then they took me to a large prison in York, Pennsylvania. The first day was the worst for me. I had never been in jail before. I thought the worst would happen. I thought someone would harm or kill me there. I met this one guy with lots of tattoos, including one with a Death Saint image. He said he stabbed someone and was in federal prison before they brought him to this immigration prison for his deportation.

I was scared and sad. I thought they were going to deport me quickly. I knew that if they sent me back to Honduras, the gangs would see me as someone with money after living in the US, and that they would target me even more than before.

In ICE Detention

About three days after I arrived at the jail, the same guy, the tall White guy from ICE who found me in the dumpster, he came to try one more time to make me sign the deportation order. I refused to sign.

They took my things and gave me an orange jumpsuit/prisoner uniform. The food was terrible—no salt, bad taste. There were people in my cell block who had been there six months because they refused to sign their deportation orders. The guys who had been there six months said I should take the deportation because there was no hope.

My mom had to borrow money from my brother—a thousand dollars. My uncle Will loaned $2,000, and my mom put together $1,000. That was to pay for the bond. My mom also had to borrow money to pay the lawyer. Lots of people had lawyers who would not go to the prison, lawyers who just did the hearing by computer screen. I wanted my lawyer to be there in person. I was worried that they would leave me there locked up or get me to take "deportation express," but I knew ICE was trying to trick me.

I still had an asylum case with a different judge in Philadelphia in immigration court and I already had a lawyer. Fortunately, my lawyer came to the jail to see me and convinced the judge to release me so I could live with my family again. I remember seeing my lawyer through the tiny window in the jail. I felt relieved. I had been so worried. I thought I might never get out without being deported.

Hostility at Work

I now work for a company driving a very large box truck and delivering construction materials to job sites. I now have a work permit because of my asylum case. I have been at this job about two years. As a delivery driver, the company always gives me an *ayudante* [helper] for unloading materials at a job site. The helpers are usually temporary workers, someone who is not an employee. It is my job to report the hours for these temporary workers, the helpers.

One time about 5 months ago, I had a problem with a helper who was assigned to me. He had worked with me one time before. We got along fine the first time he worked with me. The first time we worked together he was friendly. We talked in English. I have a motorcycle and we talked about that. His brother has a motorcycle. He said that he had worked in roofing. He said roofing is much harder than driving a truck.

This time, when we got to the work site to deliver construction materials, he became very angry. He went to the back of the truck and slammed down the lift gate that we use to unload materials from the truck. He was yelling and said he did not want to work. I said I would have to cut his hours on the timesheet if he didn't work.

He surprised me. He said "You, who are you in your country?"

"You should go back to your country!"

"Why don't you go back to Mexico?" (I'm from Honduras and not Mexico.)

"You don't speak English."

"I don't know where you are fucking from."

He said, "You come here to steal our jobs." He said a lot of things to me. He was very angry. He got very red in the face. He was breathing very hard and loud. He asked, "Do you want to fight me?"

I said no. I thought about calling the police. Instead, I texted my boss.

On the way back to the office for my delivery company, he was still angry. It was hard to be in the cab of the truck together. I thought he was going to grab the steering wheel or hit me while I was driving. He finally calmed down, pulled out a marijuana joint and started smoking. I had my COVID mask on. I was worried that I would lose my job or get in trouble because he was smoking marijuana in my work truck.

I know that immigrants get deported for using drugs. I don't use drugs. I wanted him to stop smoking, but at least he calmed down. That's why I didn't say anything to stop him.

There was a supervisor at the office who helped me when I got back. The supervisor scolded the helper man who was angry with me. They fired him.

I know a Latino man like myself, but who works at another company at these construction sites. He is maybe 58 or 60 years old. He said he was here in the 1990s and the discrimination was even worse. But everywhere I go, all the construction sites, it's mostly Latinos. The roofers, cement work, framing, drywall—almost all Latinos.

What I want for the future is to buy a house in the US and have a family here. Right now, I live in a trailer home. It's not easy, but I have friends and family. I am grateful to have so many people who have helped me.

Translator's note: I came to know Alex Masias in 2017, when he was applying for asylum. He was afraid of being deported to Honduras because gangs were threatening to kill him. Since then, I have been submitting evidence to the court and preparing for his final asylum hearing. Alex has worked hard to adapt to a new country. As an immigration lawyer, I see a lot of cases like Alex's—young men and women fleeing gang violence in Central America. Alex wants the immigration judge and ICE to see him as a good person, someone who does not want to harm the United States. He wants the judge to use his discretion to help Alex stay here in the US. Unfortunately, judges in immigration court have very little power to let someone stay just because they are a good person or hardworking. I would like to see the immigration courts and agencies treat people with dignity. These are caring, worthy people just like you and me. Putting immigrants in jail and deporting them will never work to decrease the flow of people coming to the United States. As long as there are jobs for them here, they will come. Law enforcement agencies should focus less on treating poor immigrants like criminals, and instead look at the companies that hire them.

—Justin Mixon

Justin Mixon is an immigration and family lawyer in Jenkintown, Pennsylvania, primarily serving Spanish-speaking clients from Central and South America. Mr. Mixon litigates Special Immigrant Juvenile Status, asylum, and other immigration cases in court and with United States Citizenship and Immigration Services. From 2014 to 2017, he worked at the nonprofit HIAS Pennsylvania representing immigrant youth. He graduated from the University of Minnesota Law School in 2002 and was an elementary school teacher in the Philadelphia School District for four years. He became fluent in Spanish as a Peace Corps volunteer in Guatemala from 1995 to 1998.

Alex Masias elected not to provide a biography.

11

THEY SEE ME AS A CRIMINAL

The Unrelenting Policing of Black Bodies

Seren Sensei

As a child, I was riding in the car with my father. He liked big trucks: Cadillac Escalades and Ford Expeditions with loud music, blacked-out windows, and the interior dash lights turned down so no one could see inside. We were riding out one night—I remember it was night—and a police officer pulled up behind us with lights flashing. My father pulled over, preemptively took out his license and registration and held it in his left hand, turned up the dashboard lights, and rolled down his driver's side window *before* turning the car off and placing his hands on the steering wheel.

He said, "See how I'm keeping both hands on the wheel?" as the cop, a White man, walked up. It turned out we had been pulled over for the blacked-out tints, which were darker than regulation in the state of Maryland, and we were let off with a warning. But my father kept both hands firmly on the wheel and never moved them the entire time we were stopped, except when he handed the license and registration cards to the police officer (which he verbally communicated that he was handing over). Later on, he explained to me that he never moved his hands off the wheel so the officer didn't have a reason to shoot, and that he kept the interior of the cab bright so the two of us were entirely visible in the dark and not asked to get out. I was 10 or 11 years old. It was my first one-on-one encounter with police, and my first understanding of the concept that **police will hurt you if you are Black**. They will harass you. Your very Blackness is criminalized; your existence is seen as a threat.

My mother and stepfather keep pictures of citizens resisting police and other armed forces on their refrigerator to this day. One stands out in particular: Indian citizens dressed all in white, pelting patrol officers with sticks. The police cower on the ground. Another was emblazoned with recognizable Black figures: Malcolm X, Muhammad Ali. My grandmother opposed practically all forms of White

DOI: 10.4324/9781003169468-15

authority, from the mail lady to the chief of police to my second-grade teacher, who was fired after she grabbed a classmate by the ear for cracking jokes in class. She dragged him down the stairs to the principal's office with so much force that his seven-year-old body flew through the air. Seven years old, he was already being labeled a "troublemaker," already being policed.

My grandmother wrote a *strongly* worded letter to the superintendent, and the woman was fired. I attended District of Columbia Public Schools, known as DCPS, and in high school I was subjected to a police presence that included School Safety Officers (SSOs), metal detectors (conveyor belt detectors for backpacks; wands and body scanners), and a security ID card to swipe before you were let in; it had to be worn around your neck at all times on school grounds. If you swiped in late, a call was triggered to your parents and a paper slip printed; acquire too many slips and it was a citation. It wasn't until I was an adult that I marveled at the way policing and prison culture had been normalized to us. Even the long lines of waiting and the honey-bun vending machines under flickering white lights were replicated in our high school. It was implied that of course some of us would end up in prison; we belonged there.

SSOs also freely roamed the campus outside, regularly stopping students to ask why they weren't in class, although we were allowed a free lunch period and could travel to nearby shops if we chose. Stopped enough times outside, and you would earn a dreaded TRUANCY slip. "Truancy" is defined as unauthorized absence from compulsory education, and in DC it is monitored by the Metropolitan Police Department. According to DC law, if a child reaches five unexcused absences, a plan must be developed between students, family, and administrators to improve attendance; after 10, the child is referred to family services, and at 15, students aged 14–17 can be sent to juvenile court. (These rules vary from state to state: in California, for example, four truancy slips can equal schoolchildren being sent to juvenile court, as well as possible charges for their parents.)

So I didn't have any great awakening about the state of police and policing of Black bodies in this country. I have experienced it firsthand for what seems like every day of my life. I got into protest work with Occupy Wall Street in 2012, and witnessed the police destroying a peaceful encampment in the middle of the night. I marched through tear gas and rubber bullets in Ferguson and wrote a free lawyer's phone number in Sharpie on my arm in case I was locked up and my possessions seized, including my cell phone. But there's an aura of pride around arrests due to nonviolent protest. It's not the same as being arrested for physical violence, and the first time I was arrested, it was for fighting.

I'd been fighting a girlfriend—with whom I'd had a physically and emotionally abusive toxic relationship for years. She was smaller and meaner than me, nicknamed Mighty Mouse—proven all too accurate when she put her foot through the windshield of my car or broke down a door I'd locked against her. A neighbor had called the police as we argued, and when the police came to arrest us for a DV—domestic violence—they expressed surprise before they locked us up: "It's two girls?"

The police refused to physically separate us, because we were the same gender. We were put in squad cars together, fingerprinted together, and placed in holding one after the other. It seemed a cruel irony that I was thrown into a pit with the one person I'd been fighting to get away from. The day had been cold, and I wore a coat into jail over my pajamas. They hadn't let me retrieve a hair tie so my hair—natural curls slightly past my ears at the time—whipped around my head in a frenzy.

When I arrived, I immediately staked out a corner spot on a bench for myself, curling up with my back against the wall. My ex took up a claim on the opposite end, and we ignored each other for the next 48 hours. I felt numb. I shivered through those hours, but not out of cold, as I'd kept my jacket buttoned up tight. I shivered in order to feel something, rocking back and forth, the vibration of my limbs tapping against the wall and bench underneath me. It felt surreal, like a hallucination or a fever dream. Those vibrations reminded me that it was all really happening.

I was put in group holding for two days instead of one because it was a holiday weekend. I was arrested on a Sunday, and the judge wouldn't be in until Tuesday—too bad for *us*. Group holding was one big cell in the uptown Manhattan precinct, a dimly lit concrete box with rows of wooden benches snaking across it and a couple open toilets in the back. The women were thrown in one at a time, save for a rowdy group of Dominicans in smeared make-up, short shorts, and ripped fishnet stockings whom their arresting officer seemed to know personally.

They bantered back and forth about how much money they'd be losing out on that night, being locked up instead of on their "dates." I remember a homeless woman being thrown in in the early hours of light, and she threw up. Women that smelled of booze and piff and occasionally the cloyingly sticky scent of dope. Women draping themselves across the barred doors of our cell, stretching their hands and arms out as far as they could go as they pleaded for cigarettes, or a phone call, or a sandwich.

"Arms in!" the police officer on duty would snap, banging back against the bars. I called my mother when I got out and told her where I'd been. She laughed. "Got locked up? Yeah, you're one of us."

"One of us." A member of a family with so many police run-ins they had become legend. Police presence seemed an inheritance in my life, an unavoidable consequence of my genes, my family. On my mother's side, there were infamous stories of my grandfather shooting a man.

My father was incarcerated when I was around five, and those years are a blur of time that I don't remember very well. I'm very close with my family members on his side, and have a vague understanding that they stepped up to assist my mother in his stead. Aunts, uncles, cousins, and my beloved paternal grandmother watched me, took care of me, and became my friends, siblings, and confidants. My paternal cousin became a sister to me, and the second time I was arrested, it was with her, in the most benign of circumstances: after leaving a housewarming party for a friend. The party was only a few minutes away from her house. She noticed before me the cop car in the rearview mirror.

"What Is he doing?"

We weren't speeding, smoking, or drinking. The music was loud, but that's not a crime (unless you're Black, of course). The car followed us into her residential complex, and stopped across from her townhome. We remained in the car. Five minutes later, several police cars pulled up, with at least four White male officers (YET AGAIN) jumping out with guns drawn, because two unarmed Black women had parked in a residential neighborhood. They forced us to get out, claiming her car was stolen—it wasn't—and tackled me when I maintained that it wasn't stolen. They put my handcuffs on so tight that they pinched my skin and left bluish-purple bruises all over my arms. I sat in the backseat and listened to the woman dispatcher's voice crackle out of the radio. It sounded like a betrayal. I wondered if she was White or Black. One of my arresting officers appeared to be "spicy" White, with the kind of olive-toned complexion that immediately brings to mind the Mediterranean Sea, or maybe Kim Kardashian.

He seemed to be aware of the racial dynamics of the situation. Out of nowhere, he said, "Don't make this a race thing."

I was shocked. I was sure I must have heard him wrong. There was no way he just said what I thought he'd said.

"Excuse me?"

"Don't make this a race thing." He turned around slightly, facing me from his position in the front passenger seat, with a thick plane of impenetrable hard plastic serving as a partition between us.

"I was born in Africa. So don't even think about making this a race thing." I guess the complexion wasn't Kim K. It was French Montana.

I leaned forward. I wasn't sure how to respond, wasn't even sure what I was going to say, until I opened my mouth: "And do you consider *yourself* Black?"

He seemed taken aback. "What?"

"Do you consider yourself Black?"

He didn't respond. The minutes ticked by as we sat in the car in the dark. The silence stretched out as neither one of us moved, staring at each other. I wondered what he would say. I think I might have appreciated honesty. Maybe he could have said that he wasn't Black, and I was, and that's why I was where I was, and he was where he was. The power dynamics played out across both of our faces. Then he turned around and faced the front without another word.

"That's what I thought," I said, leaning back in my seat.

Later on, while lying in my cell, I thought back to those words. I wonder if I shouldn't have said them. But then I felt a wave of indignation: I'm a fucking American citizen, too. I have rights, goddamn it. And these fuckers aren't going to just roll over me quietly just because they're fucking cops.

Maybe unsurprisingly, I was not allowed a phone call. I was printed and had my mug shot taken by a tall Black man with a gold tooth, who asked me why I looked so calm in my picture.

"Because I know I didn't do anything wrong."

I did feel calm. I also felt angry; a rage so hot it boiled up like lava inside me. I felt it scream when I was forced to change into a scratchy cotton jumpsuit, my blue jeans and t-shirt disappearing into a plastic bag along with my cell phone and wallet. It roiled as I was placed into my solitary cell, lying down on my cot, the bright fluorescent lights searing my eyelids even as I closed them. It burst when the Black woman across from me couldn't stop crying.

"Shh, shh. It's all right," I said. "They'll let you go in the morning. It's not a big deal."

"It is," she replied, in between sobs. "They said I was drunk. I'm not drunk. Now I have a record. It's always going to show that I was arrested. And for a DUI!"

The fear of arrest is two-pronged: on the one hand, they can lock you up, throw you in a holding cell, and look around in shock when you turn up dead in the morning, like Sandra Bland. On the other, if you survive the night, arrest records loom over Black bodies like invisible bogeymen. Lawyers focus mainly on criminal records, which occur after you've been charged. But with mere arrest records, police can wrongfully or falsely arrest you, hold you, and later on let you go without formally charging you with anything or dropping charges later on—and the arrest can loom over your history, popping up when you go up for a job or apply for an apartment. The fear is always there. *Will it show that I was arrested?*

I think women, especially Black women, might fear a pull-over or arrest for an alleged DUI most of all. In the dark, in the cold, an officer—usually a man—can take you out of your car and do whatever he wants to you. The Oklahoma City police officer Daniel Holtzclaw infamously wielded his authority in this manner, raping and sexually assaulting as many as 13 Black American women. "Holtzclaw targeted them during traffic stops and interrogations, forcing them into sexual acts in his police car or in their homes. Prosecutors say he deliberately preyed on vulnerable black women from low-income neighborhoods," says a Democracy Now report.[1]

On Thanksgiving several years ago, I was pulled over on my way home from my parents' house, where I hadn't been drinking. It was a freezing November night, and I was wearing a green party dress, sweater, and very lightweight stockings. When the two White male officers made me get out of my car and take a field sobriety test, I obliged, blowing into breathalyzers, walking a straight line—in high heeled boots, no less—and even reciting the alphabet backwards.

"Even though you have completed the field sobriety tests," they said, "We still believe that you have been drinking to the point where it would be unsafe for you to drive home."

My jaw dropped. Despite my family's objection to authority, my mother would've done something like cry on cue to get out of this one. She could conjure waterworks with a snap of a finger. Unfortunately, that talent didn't pass to me, and the only emotion I'm able to conjure at will is rage.

"I'm not drunk!" I raged, feeling my voice rise. I couldn't control myself. It wasn't just; it wasn't right! I've never been one to temper my feelings, and don't feel I should be asked to strictly because I am Black, or a woman. I remain convinced that had I been White, the next words out of my mouth would've gotten me off the hook: "And I live five minutes away. Can't you just give me an escort or something?"

"I'm sorry, but we must insist you sit down now." I sat on the curb. The cold seeped from the ground up through the concrete, so that I wrapped my arms around my legs and rocked back and forth to keep my teeth from chattering.

"My headlights are on," I said. "May I turn them off?"

"Do not move off that curb."

I stayed on the curb. I watched as the lights grew dimmer and dimmer, eventually flickering out. We were on a well-lit main road, but a sliver of fear began to wind its way up my spine. It was dark *enough*, and the wind blew my skirt around my legs. I wrapped my arms around myself even tighter to keep more than the chills at bay. The officers sat in their police cruiser, windows rolled up tight while their headlights shone directly on me like a spotlight, ensuring I didn't move. After two hours, they let me go.

"You're lucky that we didn't arrest you."

Lucky that they didn't arrest me? Lucky that they forced me to sit on a curb for two hours and abandoned me on a winter night? Or lucky that they didn't rape me? Lucky that they didn't saddle me with an arrest record in that moment? (I ended up with one twice over anyway.) A Black body, a Black woman's body, being policed seems as natural as breathing, and as unavoidable as death.

Arrays of names have piled up over the years; some of them were blasted across headlines and some weren't. Sandra Bland. Mike Brown. Akai Gurley. Kalief Browder. Vonderrit Myers hit me especially hard. The St. Louis police shooting of the teenager occurred moments after he left a corner store with friends; the shop owner, who had known Myers and his friends since they were children, released the footage from the store. I watched it. Unlike the bizarre torture porn of Walter Scott getting shot in the back while fleeing police, or the snuff film of George Floyd being slowly, agonizingly murdered over a span of nearly nine minutes, the Myers video showed three Black children—CHILDREN—goofing off, sharing a sandwich and drink while they were rung up by the clerk. I cried watching it. At that moment, I thought about my connections with these other stories, other people with Black bodies that police eyes saw as criminals.

I felt I knew him, knew a million boys just like him. Myers wore his jeans and t-shirt in the ultra slim-fitting style that is currently popular, making it damn near impossible for him to be carrying the weapon St. Louis PD claimed they saw, that led to his death. No weapon was ever recovered at the scene. Mainstream media launched a smear campaign against the teenager, pulling pictures from his social media and leveraging accusations that, like Mike Brown, he was "no angel." Whether or not he had a weapon, do Black people have to be angels to be worthy of life? No charges were brought against the officer.

I'm no angel. I threw away the clothes I wore when I was arrested, both times. I washed my hair; I scrubbed my skin, yet I couldn't get the stench off me. It's an acrid stench of authority, authority seized by abusing people, especially Black people. Maybe it's the smell of so many lives lost? Sucked away, disappeared. It reminds me of the fragrance of weeping willows, mint julep, and cool lemonade on a hot day after a lynching, where there are no arrests made and, in fact, the police most likely helped string **The Black** up.

I've been asking this question to Black people: how often have you actually called the police for help? How fearful have you been of calling? And when you have called, have they actually been helpful? Overwhelmingly, I've found that we rarely call; we often fear violence, escalation, or retribution; and police are rarely helpful. They serve their purpose as enforcers of the State against Black bodies, and do little else.

During my most recent brush with police, this was made evident. I was participating in the protests that swept the nation in 2020. Contrary to Ferguson, and similar to Occupy, that protest was predominantly White. Police stood on the curb and in the road, keeping a wide berth from the large crowd that spilled across the sidewalk and out into the street. They directed traffic around the group while protesters yelled and held signs that said "Black Lives Matter."

A couple of officers stood clustered together at the beginning and end of the block, chattering with stragglers as they walked up. It was an incredible contrast to what I had seen at the predominantly Black protests of Ferguson, and I wondered how amicable this all would be if it were less White? Based on a lifetime of experience, I thought I knew the answer. I'd seen something similar at the 2017 Women's March. Two White women next to me remarked on how "safe" their march was. "No looting, no burning! This is how it's done."

I said, "Well, there are no tear gas or rubber bullets for the Pink Pussy Hats, either."

Police violence sounds like these words: "No angel." "No charges." It sounds like the flash of the camera when they take your mug shot, the siren, the knock on the door, the voice: "It's the police." There is a smell in the precinct, sickly sweet, cold air conditioning run-off mixed with Glade plug-ins and sweat. Stale pizza. Donuts. Chinese food. Brimstone, lit matches—Hell. It smells like blood and teargas, the unwashed bodies rounded up and thrown in a cage, vomit, the salty brine of the sea . . . an ocean of tears?

I can still hear that woman sobbing sometimes. She wasn't drunk.

Seren Sensei is a filmmaker, writer, and artist. Her writing has been printed in such publications as NAACP's *The Crisis* magazine, *NYLON*, *Kweli Journal*, and *Riot Material*, and referenced in *Jacobin*, *Vulture*, *Complex*, *Newsweek*, *AJ+*, *People*, *Vice*, *Walker Art*, and more. Specializing in race, culture, and sociopolitical theory, she has released three seasons of the docuseries *The [Black] Americans* to explore and archive Black American culture. She was a 2016–2017 cohort with At Land's Edge pedagogical program to combine art and activism, and in 2020, was named an Indie Memphis Black Filmmaker Resident for her screenplay, *KITT*. She was also named a 2020–2021 "Time, Space, Money" HRLA Resident, exhibiting a video installation on police brutality protests at Actual Size Gallery in Los Angeles.

The first chapter of her speculative fiction novel, *Blue Zone*, was published digitally through Arch St. Press.

Note

1 "When Cops Rape: Daniel Holtzclaw & the Vulnerability of Black Women to Police Abuse," *Democracy Now!* December 15, 2015, www.democracynow.org/2015/12/15/daniel_holtzclaw_convicted_of_serial_rape

12

FROM THE HOLE TO THE WHOLE

A Filmmaker Learns to Look for Joy

Jennifer Fischer

Albuquerque, 2021

The images of broken bodies have become too much. The voices crying in the street, so loud, are still not heard. The list of names that have become trending hashtags is too long. It tumbles and jumbles my mind, sends me spiraling back in time to another place. I need to ground myself. I pick up the phone and call Will, whom I haven't spoken to in years. There's no need to text ahead and arrange a phone call like I do with so many friends these days. Will always picks up the phone. It is as if no time has passed since our last conversation, at a film festival in Los Angeles in 2015, as if just yesterday we were chatting at that LA theater after the screening of our short film, *The wHOLE*. Me, lead producer; Will, lead actor. Usually, this easy ability to pick up as if no time has passed is associated with those friends we've had since childhood, the ones we share deep-seated connections with. They know our family, our past, our history, and those shared signposts are the reason that we can pick up right where we left off.

Will and I don't have that. He was born and raised in South Central. He's short and compact, with dark skin, a baseball cap often on his head and trendy glasses on his face. I was born in Indiana, grew up in Oklahoma and Texas, am frighteningly fair, with a messy bun and contact lenses. Despite outward differences and chasms in childhood experiences, conversation flows easily between us. Shared concerns and brief, but powerful, shared experiences cement our connection.

Will updates me on his life now in Rosamond, CA. "I love the quiet life. It's like peace. I don't hear helicopters, no sirens." He is making masks now, doing his part to fight the pandemic. His home community in South Central and the Black community, in general, have been hit hard by COVID. He returns to South Central often, crossing an invisible border into a landscape so different from the rest of LA.

DOI: 10.4324/9781003169468-16

He's there to sell the masks, t-shirts, sweats, cups. He seeks to bring some positivity to the troubled community that was his home for so long.

Our conversation circles back to Ezell Ford, a friend of Will's who was shot by police officers in 2014. Recent events keep pushing me back in time to the moments Will and I shared. Time, a once rigid border, has become porous as the pandemic wears on. Before, time was a rigid thing measured by school drop-off, yoga class, soccer practice, my teaching commitments, work meetings, doctor's appointments. Now, time has no form, no clear function. It is expansive one day, precise and yet fleeting the next. "How is it *still* March?" we ask, as 2020 turns into 2021 without bringing the change we'd hoped for.

In the static reality of pandemic life, my mind takes me to a variety of places through the fictional stories I read and watch, the essays and tales I write, and the vivid dreams that visit me each night.

The unexpected result of all of this are these increasingly frequent forays back and forth through time and space. The time machine I imagine is not a phone booth or DeLorean, but a red 1966 Ford Mustang, the one my dad and I fixed up together when I was kid; the one he sold to help me pay for college. I find myself sliding into its bucket seats and traveling back to the experiences that keep tugging at my sleeve, like a child demanding attention. Filming *The wHOLE* with Will, and the death of Ezell Ford that occurred at the same time, is one of those moments that just keeps tugging at me. So, I buckle my seatbelt and travel back seven years.

Portland, Oregon, 2014

The engine revs, the brakes squeal, and I'm in Portland, Oregon on a sticky summer night. There with me in a small basement apartment are Ramon (writer/director of *The wHOLE*; he is also my life partner and the father of my children), Daniel (the cinematographer for the film; he handles lighting and camera), and Will (the lead actor).

The three of them drove to Portland from Los Angeles on Saturday; 16 hours straight in a giant black Escalade, carrying all of our film and lighting equipment. I flew up late Sunday evening, leaving our two young children with my mother back in the tiny town outside of Los Angeles where we live.

We're in Portland because we can film for four days and will have access to an entire prison for the same amount of money that would get us one day in one cell in Los Angeles. The county facility in Portland where we are filming has never been occupied by guards and inmates. The cost to operate it is too high, so now the county struggles with what to do with the space. There are only so many things one can do with an empty prison. It is used for filming; it has become a fictionalized representation of itself.

As the cast and crew for the project came together, so did the film's title. The hole, with an H, is what most in the prison industry call solitary confinement. *The wHOLE*, with a W, reflects the pervasiveness of incarceration in the US: its reach, its impact, its completeness. Intentionally, we cast a lead actor who has been incarcerated and other formerly incarcerated individuals were involved in the project as producers and writing consultants. Guards and others working within the system were consulted as well.

When the crew is all together in Portland that Monday morning in August, I see the *whole* reflected back to me. Adam, our key grip, has been incarcerated. Another actor and our sound guy have family members who are guards at prisons. Still others working on the film have friends or family members who have been or are currently incarcerated.

The "mass" aspect of mass incarceration is clear as I get to know the small team involved in telling the story of a fictional character's struggle to adapt to 23 hours a day in a 6' x 9' cell.

When you enter a solitary cell, you cross a border like no other. Compassion, understanding, books, stimuli of any kind, social engagement with others, are all gone. The range of reasons one is placed in solitary is astounding: from physical violence toward another inmate or guard to someone saying you are associated with a gang to having too many sharpened pencils in one's cell. The experience of solitary confinement is pervasive. All of the formerly incarcerated individuals we worked with for the project spent time in solitary confinement at some point during their months or years in prison. Their crimes varied, as did their gender, age (some were minors) and innocence (some were exonerated after years behind bars), but the one commonality between them all was spending time "in the hole." All told, our cast and crew spent a collective 40 years behind bars and a collective seven in solitary confinement.

On Monday night of August 11th, Will, Daniel, Ramon and I are in the basement apartment of an empty-nester couple who live in an affluent neighborhood in Portland. They are supporting the film by offering us free housing, which we are happy to take. The basement is usually only occupied during holidays by a college-aged son. The refrigerator is skillfully stocked with a wide array of microbrew beers. Very Portland, I think, as I prep meals and snacks for the next day of the film shoot.

We've made it through our first day of filming. It's been a good but long 14 hours. Daniel and Ramon are going over the shot list for the next day. Will is relaxing, and we want him to do so, to recharge. What we are asking of him, emotionally, is immense.

I hear his phone ring as I mix pasta and pesto sauce together in the kitchen. Then, I hear nothing, but I feel the energy shift. I step out of the kitchen to catch a glimpse of his face. This call is not good. I step back into the kitchen, wanting to give him privacy.

Soon, all four of us are in the living area of the basement and Will opens up about the call. As he tells us the tragic news that reached him on his cell, we see it come through on our own phones, our social media exploding with it.

Will's neighborhood buddy is dead. Ezell Ford, the person, has quickly become #EzellFord, the hashtag. The official story is that Ezell was acting erratically. The police arrived and shot him.

"There's no way Ezell was a threat," Will explains. "He'd never hurt anyone, but they killed him." Will makes Ezell real to us, more than the social media story that's growing as we watch.

Ezell was an integral part of Will's community, a community in which people looked out for each other, and everyone looked out for Ezell because of his development delays. Everyone in the neighborhood knew Ezell had a slew of mental health issues—everyone except the officers that came on the scene. They were not connected to the community, not aware of Ezell's history, that Ezell wasn't a danger to anyone. They didn't understand that Ezell needed help.

The atmosphere is slightly different the next day when we step inside the prison and set to our specific tasks. Will changes out of his normal clothes and into an orange jumpsuit, the make-up artist sets up her things, the camera and sound crew start laying cables, Ramon consults his script. Ezell's death hovers above us all, reinforcing the importance of our work, of why we want to convey that everyone deserves their humanity. As I set out bagels and granola bars, I feel a little nauseous.

Los Angeles, 2013

I rush back to my time machine; I need a break. The dizziness of that day in 2014 stays with me as I stumble out, expecting to be back in the present, in Albuquerque with my 9 and 11-year-old children playing outside. Instead, I'm disoriented as I find myself imagining a different time and space. I am in Val Verde, a tiny town outside of Los Angeles, and it's the summer of 2013. Ramon and I are enjoying a rare moment to ourselves; the two-year-old and not-quite-four-year-old are both asleep. For once, Ramon and I are not too exhausted to talk. It's been a while since we've had a moment like this. We speak openly about what has been weighing on each of our hearts and discover that both of us have been following the media surrounding the Pelican Bay Prison Hunger Strikes.

Individuals in solitary confinement in Pelican Bay State Prison, a maximum security facility in Northern California, are on a hunger strike to highlight the inhumane reality of solitary confinement: 23 hours, seven days a week, in a small cell, alone. Food slid into the cell through a small slot in the steel door. The lights, always on. The corridor, never quiet, but accented with shouts, incoherent rantings, and the brutal sound of various endeavors at self-harm or prison guard punishments.

Our previous film recently completed its film festival circuit and academic tour. We need a new project. It instantly becomes obvious to us that *this* is what comes next. The stories of Pelican Bay call to us. We will create our own story, inspired by it. The seeds of *The wHOLE* are planted that night in the living room of our small house. At that moment we are sitting on an Ikea couch staring at the blank screen of our large TV, the kind where the back sticks out. The piano given to me by dear friends sits in the corner next to a black bookcase stuffed full of DVDs. I can't fathom how this seed will change our artistic trajectories and personal lives.

Albuquerque and Los Angeles, 2021

I hear the time machine's engine rev up and I peel out of there. This time, the machine dumps me back in New Mexico, where I live now. The couch, TV, and bookcase of DVDs didn't make it. From that living room and moment, only the piano and *The wHOLE* remain. In New Mexico, I steady myself so that I can focus again on my conversation with Will, as he reminisces about Ezell.

"I used to go right there," Will explains. "Consistently, to his house. I know his dad, his brothers. We ran around in the same circles. One of my best friends, if not my very best friend, grew up in that area, all his life. His grandmother owned two houses over there. He and Ezell were tight from kids. They had a great relationship. That is how I met Ezell, through my best friend. There is a mural there now, honoring Ezell, near where he was shot and killed." The landmark of Ezell's mural grounds him in time and space.

Will's mind drifts to a moment in his own past, not too far back, to an afternoon a few weeks earlier:

> It is so crazy there. Actually, you see it a lot more now. You get the constant pressure from the police, pulling you over and challenging you. They call in other officers, call for more backup, and ask more questions, even though there was no law broken. They don't want to let people go. This is still happening on Broadway, steps from where Ezell was killed. That division of police is still acting in that way. Everyone who stays in that area has come to expect that treatment, that harassment. The D.A. can change, but what does that change for us? You aren't changing the police who are directly connected to the community. They "protect and serve" the community as *they* see fit.
>
> It happened to me. I was driving in my wife's truck, and the cops pulled me over. I have a license. I have registration. I have proof of insurance. I am on 68th and Broadway, a block or two from where Ezell was killed. They search my car. They ask my name. They do all of that. I should be free to go, but instead they call in another set of officers, keeping my ID in their hand. The sergeant comes and runs my ID and calls up past offenses, notes that I served time. That has nothing to do with what I am doing today. I am selling t-shirts. I am selling face masks. I am doing something positive. I have no guns, no drugs. What is this about? What happened in the neighborhood? Did something happen? Do I fit the description? Everyone fits the description because we're all Black, but I never get an answer, just the feeling that it was because they wanted to hold me.
>
> It's just another attempt for them to humiliate me, and for nothing. They were doing that because they can. They are the law. We must abide by the law.
>
> Because I drive a nice truck, they look and assume that it's stolen, but it's not. It's paid for. We see it every day. It's common. If you don't get jacked by the police in a week in South Central Los Angeles, you are blessed.

In speaking with Will, I am reminded of how this label of "criminal" boxes him in, creates an invisible border he can't quite cross. It won't let him go, despite how many years it has been since he last served time. Despite the fact that he's not on probation and has no recent violations of any kind. Despite the changes he's made in his life. His focus now is on the peace and quiet of Rosamond. On t-shirts and masks, on encouraging friends and family to get vaccinated, on his children and grandchildren, on always picking up the phone for a friend, a friend like me who asks him to go back to a hot, sticky, and painful August night.

This is the night that keeps drawing me to the time machine as I watch my children grapple with the reality of George Floyd's death, of Breonna Taylor's, of so many others', now that these stories are part of their worldview. I go back there when my children hear their father share his degrading experience of being stopped-and-frisked in New York City while visiting as part of a prestigious Black Public Media fellowship for *The wHOLE*. Tears in my sons' eyes as they consider that others saw their father—a teacher, a filmmaker, a game designer, a generous and kind man—as a threat, as dangerous. It's the night I return to as I consider how close I came to losing my life partner in New York City that afternoon. I can't let go of that night because I believe that maybe if I can relay this story—Will's story of loss and pain—then others will start to empathize with his experience, and change will come.

Here, Now

And yet, as I reflect on our conversation, I realize that Will is showing me the way out of this time loop. Very little of our conversation was actually about Ezell or even about Will's recent encounter with law enforcement. Mainly, we talked about the shared experience of parenting during a pandemic, of our common desire to keep our communities and family members safe. Will spoke of imagination and opportunity, of joy and hope.

That is what Will focused on, but I almost missed it because I was listening for something else. I was stuck in a certain time and space. I was limiting his story because of my obsession with his pain and trauma. I didn't hear him as he pushed open the door and walked out of the cell, crossed the border, and invited me to step out of my stupid time machine. Will wanted me to join him in the here and now, where he shares his joy and his hopes and dreams. He is striving for something new and different. It is joy and hope that we need more of. My own son recently said the same thing. "I just need more joy, Mom. Can we just focus on the joy?" he asked in his newly changing voice.

"Can we?" I ask myself. If an understanding and awareness of Black pain were all that was required for change to come, wouldn't we already be there? It is not that we are unaware. It is not that these stories are not swirling around us all the time. Maybe we're not really listening, we're not opening our minds, expanding our imaginations so that they hold something new, something different. There is magic in listening. I need to actually hear Will's words, his dreams, his hopes, and share those.

Will (like others who have been incarcerated) *served* his time. The debt to society has been paid. A clean slate is like a bucket full of LEGO with no instruction manual. You can build whatever you want, and Will wants to build something new. He is dreaming, raising children and grandchildren, and making masks. He is encouraging neighbors and friends to get the COVID vaccine. He is striving for positive change and growth in his community, despite what history offers, what a recent drive into South Central offered.

I re-tune the radio in the imaginary Mustang, and I hear Will now.

> We can't keep putting a band-aid on the problem. We have to fix it. We have to get in the community and talk and listen and build trust. We can't assume that we know what is best. Whatever the situation is, we can fix it. Let's stop everybody giving up. I'm tired of that because we aren't getting anywhere. If we give up, then no kids get to grow up there. That's not fair. I have kids. There are kids being born in this world every single day and it isn't fair to them.
>
> I know this community. I wish someone would come to that area and teach kids how to code. If those kids were making video games, even the parents would play them. They could be doing something else, something constructive. But they are lost. People with power and money need to come back and create these opportunities, put the money together, and build a building that brings opportunity. We probably won't be able to save everybody, but we will help people. Let's start somewhere. If we continue to ignore the problem, we'll be stuck and talking about this same thing 20 years from now.
>
> I wish that more people were more interested and involved in our community instead of being so scared of it. There are jewels over there if you know how to shine them.

Fear and jewels. That is what I think of now as I step out of the time machine and push myself to be fully present to *this* day, to *this* moment in *this* space. I think of the way that our fears inhibit us and keep us from seeing the jewels in front of us, the possibilities, the opportunities that we should create, the breadth that our imagination needs to reach. I see, too, that sometimes it isn't fear, but "good intentions" that cause problems. **We focus on bleeding-heart stories, on pain, when we could be mining for joy.** Will invited me to shift my focus from the potential for pain to the potential for joy. Yes, he's seen more than his fair share of pain, caused some as well (as we all have), but he doesn't stay there. He doesn't get stuck in the pain. He doesn't live that narrative anymore, and it's not fair of me to ask him to.

During our film shoot that August, Will spent every lunch break making all of us laugh, even as our film asked him to crawl back inside pain and make it visible for others. He crawled out of that pain every day at lunch, and again every night, and reminded us of the joy he has in his life, the joy he brings to ours.

I'm back in the time machine again. Just this one last time, I tell myself. I return to sticky Portland in August where everyone else gets VooDoo doughnuts but me. I can't remember why I never got a doughnut. It's the day after Will's fateful phone call. I am making a phone call of my own. My shy three-year-old's voice comes through on the other end as he reluctantly talks about his first day of preschool. Will sees the tears welling up in my eyes as I think of this milestone that I missed. He nudges me with his hip. "It's okay. He knows you love him. It's okay," he tells me.

"Thanks," I reply, grateful for his words and for that experience, for what we all created together.

That film premiered at Amnesty International's 50th Anniversary Human Rights Conference. It has been used by those advocating for change. It has moved audiences, touched hearts. It will continue to do so. It will continue to bear witness. That film also imprinted a connection between Will and me that has lasted seven years and that I believe will last much longer.

I look back and see all the pain shared during that time, but I also see the joy. The joy of creation, the joy of story, the joy of collaboration, the joy of new friendships growing out of a shared experience, the laughter that filled the halls of that empty prison facility for four days. The joy I find now in a phone call to Will, who reminds me that life is not "this or that." Instead, it is "both, and." Life is expansive. We can honor Ezell's memory, honor that loss, *and* look toward a brighter future. We can tell stories that encourage empathy *and* imagine futures full of joy. We can focus on positive growth inside of ourselves *and* let it flow into our family, our friendships and our community. We can go from the hole to the whole, and we can invite others to dream with us.

Jennifer Fischer is a writer, film producer, and activist. Her writing focuses on filmmaking, parenting, and social issues. *Smuggled* (2012), her film about immigration, screened at over 100 universities, colleges, and community organizations throughout the United States and abroad. Her short film *The wHOLE* (2015), about solitary confinement, premiered at Amnesty International's 50th Anniversary Human Rights Conference. Her work has been featured by multiple media outlets, such as NBCLatino, NBCBLK, ABC, Fusion, Univision, Vice News, and others. She holds a BA from Sarah Lawrence College in International Cultural and Media Studies and an MA from Harvard University in Middle Eastern Studies, where she received a prestigious FLAS Scholarship.

IV
Scholarly Perspectives

13

WHAT CAUSES CRIMINALITY? SOCIOLOGICAL, BIOLOGICAL, AND PSYCHOLOGICAL THEORIES

McKenzie Wood

Under a simplistic view, criminals are simply bad people who choose to behave in harmful and illegal ways. Decades of research in the social sciences, however, have shown that many factors influence an individual's likelihood of committing a crime, from their genes to their environment. This chapter offers a brief overview of some prominent theories and debates that can inform approaches to the question "What Is a criminal?"

Sociological Explanations

While individual differences are important, sociological research has found that socioeconomic status, neighborhoods, and associations have links to criminal response. Thus, more than just who we are, but also the life we are born into, where we live, and with whom we associate determine our behavior.

Social Class

Some convincing studies have determined that individuals, particularly youth, in lower social classes are more likely to commit serious offenses than those in higher social classes, though the same pattern does not seem to hold true for minor offenses.[1] Other research has argued that chronic offenders are almost universally poor, with earnings at or below the poverty line.[2] People born into lower social classes are at both legal and social disadvantages, with those who are poverty stricken more likely to get in trouble with the law. In one famous study, William Chambliss spent years following two groups of young boys: the Saints, who came from upper-middle-class families, and were generally expected to succeed in school and life; and the Roughnecks, hailing from lower-class families, who experienced frequent encounters with the police. Despite engaging in the same amount and

DOI: 10.4324/9781003169468-18

types of criminal activity (actually, the Roughnecks probably committed less criminal activity than the Saints), their social class and associated stigma resulted in the Roughnecks being held accountable for their crimes, while the Saints' behavior was either ignored or minimized by authorities. Just like their adolescent experiences, their adult experiences also differed. The Saints largely ended up in professional careers (such as doctor, lawyer, or manager), while many of the Roughnecks ended up in illegitimate work (bookie) or imprisoned.[3]

Prominent sociological theorist Robert Merton states that "children commit delinquency only when their backs are against the wall."[4] Poor adults as well may commit crimes because they have no other options. For example, Shaina Bell, a homeless mother, was arrested for leaving her children (ages nine and three) in the hotel room they were living in while she reported for her shift at Little Caesars. After receiving misdemeanor charges for child endangerment and spending a night in jail, she told reporters, "I had to go to work. . . . I would never do anything to harm my kids."[5]

Whether crime is a direct effect of social status, or an indirect result of other social problems that come in conjunction with being poor or experiencing relative deprivation, is unknown. The relationship between poverty and crime might best be explained by scholar Kenneth D. Tunnell, who states, "Although most underclass individuals do not commit crime, it nonetheless is often seen as a distinct characteristic of underclass occupants."[6]

Environment

Crime can be associated with geography. In some studies, weather or temperature patterns have been linked to violent crime. For example, a study out of Finland found that an increase in ambient temperature led to an increase in violent crime, proposing that violent crime rates can increase 3% with every two-degree-Celsius rise above average temperatures in some locations.[7]

Many people associate crime with cities, but some urban areas become breeding grounds for crime, while others do not. Research suggests that criminal communities experience social disorganization and have higher levels of cultural conflict than areas with lower crime rates.[8] Social disorganization is defined by breakdowns in social institutions, including education, health care, and community. According to Ernest Burgess, a sociologist who studied cities such as Chicago, these breakdowns are most likely to occur in Zones of Transition, or areas immediately between places of industry and modest working-class homes. These areas will have the most traffic, as people move in and out, traveling to and from work, and will also contain individuals and families who are left behind by urban sprawl. Those who do not have the funds or resources to relocate will be forced to reside in areas of the city that are more subject to crime.[9]

In areas with higher social disorganization, crime may appear a normal part of neighborhood activity. As theorist James F. Anderson stated, "Most criminologists believe that 'bad places' rather than 'bad people' are responsible for crime and the continuation of such behavior."[10] This suggests that the environment in which one is raised can lead to criminality, rather than a particular child's individual attributes. After looking at areas with the highest rates of crime, Clifford Shaw and Henry McKay found that neighborhoods that were originally high in delinquency remained high in delinquency 30 years later, even though the original residents had died or moved away.[11]

While there is convincing evidence that where you are raised contributes to your likelihood of becoming a criminal, it is important to note that even in neighborhoods with the highest crime rates, the majority of residents are still law-abiding. Conversely, some individuals from low-crime communities are criminal, despite never experiencing social disorganization or cultural conflict. Furthermore, even though certain neighborhoods within cities experience more criminality, those same areas are also subject to additional social ills, such as physical dilapidation, poverty, transient populations, high rates of diseases, infant mortality, and unemployment among residents.[12] This leads some to believe that it is not the neighborhood itself, but the deprived conditions and extreme disadvantage residents of socially disorganized neighborhoods experience that lead to crime.

Socialization

Theories of social learning suggest that the mechanisms that teach us how to put on deodorant, ride a bike, or do math are the same learning pathways that teach us the attitudes, values, and techniques of criminality. Therefore, theories of socialization suggest that if we surround ourselves with criminals, we will become criminal ourselves.

Organized crime and gang activity can be seen as criminal peer groups, so it makes sense that growing up or living among mob bosses or gang leaders will result in criminal socialization. For emerging gang members who have been exposed to gang violence from a young age, becoming a participating part of the gang seems like a natural transition. As one gang member noted, "What I might do for my gang you might not do. You've got people out there taking bullets for their friends and killing people. But I'm sure not one of you would be willing to go to that extreme. These are just the thinking patterns we had growing up where I did."[13]

One critique of social learning theories of crime is that they do not establish which part of the learning process comes first: do we meet criminal people and then become criminal ourselves, or do we have preexisting criminal tendencies that attract us to those who are criminal? Another criticism is that most people who grow up around criminals do not succumb to crime. However, a general consensus among many researchers is that criminality is learned. As social learning theorist Robert DuRant noted, "Children learn violent behaviors in primary social groups, such as the family and peer groups, as well as observe it in their neighborhoods and in the community at large."[14]

Psychological Explanations

Psychological theories focus on the brain and on individual traits. They explain why a certain person does a certain behavior, as opposed to explaining crime at the community or social level.

Psychopathic Personality Traits

In February of 2012, 17-year-old Thomas M. Lane III entered Chardon High School wearing a t-shirt with the word "Killer" inscribed across the front. He shot ten rounds in the cafeteria, hitting six students, and killing three. When interviewed by a sheriff deputy, Lane, known as T.J. to his family and friends, confessed to the killings, and admitted he did not have a motive. After confirming he was not suicidal or depressed, he simply acknowledged, "I don't understand myself."[15] Over a year and a half later, after a motion to try Lane as an adult was accepted and his attempted insanity defense denied, Lane pled guilty to multiple counts of homicide. During the sentencing hearing, as victims and their families sobbed, Lane again shocked the court by unbuttoning his blue shirt to reveal a white shirt underneath, with the word "Killer" handwritten in large black letters. He smirked and smiled as the judge handed him a sentence of life without the possibility of parole, and, never showing remorse, left the courtroom after yelling obscenities to those in the gallery and pointing his middle finger at the families of those he had killed.

T.J. Lane's abnormal yet frighteningly cogent courtroom behavior serves as an example of psychopathy. Psychopaths possess a collection of traits, or symptoms, related to callousness, lack of empathy, poor behavioral controls, pathological lying, superficial charm, impulsivity, lack of remorse or guilt, manipulation, and criminal versatility. Although the exact number of psychopaths is unknown, it is estimated that about 1% of the male population meet the criteria for psychopathy. Psychopaths are found at high levels in the prison system, with about 15–25% of male prison inmates, and one out of every four inmates in maximum security prisons, qualifying as a psychopath.[16]

It is believed that many notorious psychopaths have experiences with abuse, neglect, and betrayal. T. J. Lane was taken out of his parents' custody at the age of three, reportedly due to parental drug use.[17] However, research is unclear about whether these childhood factors contribute to the formation of psychopathy. While there is evidence that childhood abuse and neglect are related to criminal behavior,[18] the question of why most people who grow up in terrible, cruel, or abusive homes remain law-abiding remains unanswered. The current opinion on psychopathy is simple: some people live with a psychopathic abnormality, making them more likely to become criminal.

Intelligence and Education

Intelligence is a vital component in making rational decisions, solving problems, and learning from experience.[19] It has long been assumed that individuals who demonstrate poor reasoning skills are likely to have lower levels of intelligence than people who consistently make good, pro-social choices. Early intelligence studies find that those in correctional facilities have lower intelligent quotients (IQ) than those not incarcerated, and current studies indicate that those imprisoned have, on average, a tenth-grade education or less.

There have been suggestions that those with lower-than-average IQ may struggle with day-to-day tasks and may inadvertently engage in criminality. For example, someone who has difficulty managing their finances or balancing their bank account may write a bad check and end up in trouble with the law, regardless of their criminal intent.[20] Larger studies linking criminality to IQ determine that criminals in general have a lower IQ than their non-criminal counterparts. This intelligence predictor was significant, with IQ relationships to criminality remaining stronger than both race or socioeconomic status indicators.[21] Additional research reports that on average, offenders have intelligence quotients eight points below the average non-offending population.[22] Macro studies mirror the micro level findings, with counties with populations that have lower average IQ scores experiencing more burglaries, larcenies, motor-vehicle thefts, robberies, and aggravated assaults than counties with populations that have higher average IQ scores.

Although it appears there is a causal link between IQ and crime, mitigating circumstances have been used to explain this effect. For example, some believe that lower IQ makes a student less likely to excel at school, thus having fewer scholastic opportunities, and possibly turning to crime in an effort to be accepted.[23] Other theorists view IQ as "augmenting the effects of other behavioral traits, rather than as a core cause of crime itself."[24] Whether the influence of intelligence on behavior is direct or indirect, intelligence quotient score appears to remain a contributing attribute to criminality.

Brain Injuries

Acquired brain injuries contribute to a slew of adverse behavior, including disinhibited reasoning, apathy, lack of planning, difficulty developing strategies, becoming easily distracted, and antisocial behavior.[25] Additional studies have confirmed the link between brain injuries and aggressive behavior, but some results leave questions as to whether the aggressive behavior existed prior to the brain injury, or whether it might be mitigated by a supplementary factor. For example, a large-scale study of traumatic brain injury patients confirmed that 25% exhibited signs of aggression, but researchers also found that aggression was heavily correlated with depression, another symptom of individuals with brain injuries.[26] While criminologists and medical doctors are still learning about the effect of brain injuries on conduct, the general impression remains that brain injuries, particularly in the frontal lobe, can impact ability to make pro-social choices and may influence behavior.

One kind of brain injury that has recently received a good deal of attention is Chronic Traumatic Encephalopathy (CTE), a brain disease caused by recurrent blows to the head—such as those experienced by football players. CTE is not detectable while an individual is alive, so the existence can only be determined upon death. After football star Aaron Hernandez died in prison, having been accused of killing three people, his brain was evaluated and it was determined he suffered from CTE. Scans of his brain revealed that some parts were enlarged, others shrunken, and overall had an abnormally excessive amount of the tau protein. Jovan Belcher, who played four seasons for the Kansas City chiefs, was also confirmed to have a CTE diagnosis, with the disease only discovered after he murdered his girlfriend and took his own life. Several more former football players have been accused of murder, such as Rae Carruth, Ray Lewis, and Lawrence Phillips, and several more have taken their own lives. Of the 20 former football players who have died by suicide since 2005, 16 have confirmed CTE diagnoses.[27]

Biological Explanations

Biological theories purport that criminality is a result of our genetic makeup, thus making criminal behaviors innate, or a natural characteristic of certain individuals. Biology is subject to evolution, indicating that some of our behaviors are the result of evolutionary responses to threats or circumstances that may no longer exist in modern times. Therefore, criminal urges that might have once guaranteed our survival are now unnecessary and a violation of our social code. The following section will address common themes associated with biological theory, including low resting heart rate, chemical makeup, and criminal heritability.

Low Resting Heart Rate

Several studies have linked low resting heart rate (less than 60 beats per minute) to criminality.[28] An average resting heart rate for an adult is between 60–100 beats per minute, and while a low resting heart rate can signify cardiovascular health, it can also indicate a propensity for criminal activity. The exact connection between heart rate and criminality is unknown, but it has been suggested that low resting heartrate is related to lower arousal in the brain, signifying that an individual who is less likely to be aroused is more likely to be bored, and will seek out stimulating circumstances, such as sensation-seeking, risk-taking, and crime.[29] While risk-taking behaviors have been linked to violence, the major criticism of this concept is that is does not explain why some with low arousal turn to crime, and others turn to adventurous, lawful activity, such as skydiving, mountain climbing, or other extreme sports.[30] Additionally, it is difficult to account for changes in resting heart rate due to increased exercise or frequent physical activity. Despite the unknowns related to the heart rate crime connection, low resting heart rate continues to be one of the most consistent biological indicators of crime.[31]

Chemical Makeup

The chemical makeup of our bodies may create conditions that favor criminal inclination. Abnormal levels of serotonin, a neurotransmitter related to information processing, have been linked to violence in males and suicide.[32] Extremely high or low levels of dopamine, a neurotransmitter providing pleasurable sensations, is linked to deviance.[33]

Sex-related hormones, such as testosterone, estrogen, and progesterone, have also been connected to crime. It has long been believed that testosterone, the hormone stimulating male secondary sexual characteristics, has been linked to aggression, even though some research shows this relationship, although present, is weak.[34] The increased level of testosterone in males, compared to females, has commonly been used as an explanation for why males tend to be more deviant, violent, and criminal than females.

Although notoriously used as a sexist punchline, the notion that women are more aggressive or criminal during PMS (the pre-menstruation phase of their menstrual cycle) has found limited scientific support.[35] It has been suggested that a high number of women in prison for violent crimes committed their offense during their premenstrual period. Interestingly, women in their premenstrual phases experience an increase in "male-like" hormones, and a decrease in "female-like" hormones, such as estrogen and progesterone, thus supporting the idea that males might be chemically inclined to be more violent and criminal than females.[36]

Heritability

Heritability is the extent that traits or characteristics are due to genetic influences.[37] Biological crime theorists have proposed that some people are born with a higher likelihood to commit crime than others.[38] This biological propensity is due to genetics, and thus is able to be passed by genetic heritability from generation to generation; criminal activity can be a family affair.

Criminologist Kevin Beaver examined family concentration and crime transmission and determined that 50% of all arrests are experienced by 5% of families, indicating that just a few families are committing half of the crime in society.[39] Additional research, collected by former prisoner Darryl Goodman, estimates that in the Pennsylvania prison system there are at least 243 incarcerated father-son pairs.[40]

The biological component remains strong enough that the criminal-familial relationship remains true, even when children of biological parents are adopted by law-abiding parents at a young age. A large-scale study of adopted boys from Copenhagen revealed that adoptive sons who had criminal biological parents were more likely to be criminal than adoptive sons who had law-abiding biological parents but criminal adoptive parents.[41]

If criminality can be inherited, and shared within families, then it logically follows that those with higher levels of concordance (shared traits), such as twins, would likely have similar criminal likelihoods. Identical twins, who share 100% of their genetic makeup, are subject to the most concordance.[42] Research reveals that anywhere from 22–30% of fraternal twins, and 52–60% of identical twins, share criminal behavior patterns, finding that if one twin is criminal the other twin is criminal as well.[43]

Conclusion

Missing from many of the above explanations is the compounding of nature and nurture, or the collision of genetic and environmental components. While some individuals have criminal instincts, it is likely a combination of social, biological, and psychological factors that determine our likelihood of criminality. As multiple scholars have suggested, "Genes are linked to antisocial behavior and empathy, but these traits interact with the environment. Some people's DNA may lead them to seek dangerous, exciting environments, thus reinforcing the genetic effect. Genes don't determine behavior themselves; rather, it is the combination of genetics and life events and situations that may contribute to violent behavior."[44] Ultimately, research supports that it is the interaction between biology and environment that generates criminal development; both need to be studied together to explain what causes criminality.

While science has connected each of the above-mentioned attributes with criminality, the existence of these attributes in an individual does not necessarily equate criminal causation. Even compounded they are not deterministic; many people who have multiple risk factors do not commit crimes. Criminologists remain just as interested in why someone may not be criminal as they are about why others become criminal. Many people can exercise rational choice, which may affect why crime looks more appealing to some people than others.

The science of criminology has undergone a maturation as researchers seek to explain biological, psychological, and sociological criminal phenomena. Theories and methodology continue to evolve, leading to ripe conditions for policy creation. While we may not know the "why" behind all criminality, policy allows us to tackle what we do know, often with successful results. For example, recent policies have been implemented to reduce levels of environmental toxins (specifically lead) in inner-city apartment buildings, initiate prenatal intervention programs for at-risk expectant mothers, and include genetic risk assessments in conjunction with criminological risk assessments in offender treatment programs.[45] Such policies aim to lower the risk factors that might cause criminality in the future. While the exact recipe for criminal construction remains unknown, and the signature question "What Is a criminal?" persists, research has much to offer in addressing and responding to the causes of crime.

McKenzie Wood is an assistant professor of criminal justice at Weber State University, in Ogden, Utah. A sociologist at heart, she has taught an array of classes, including Criminology; Victimology; Punishment and Society; and Crime and the Media. Her pedagogy involves teaching theoretical tenets and then assisting students as they make theory connections to their own life experiences. Professor Wood's areas of research interest revolve around criminal theory, crimes against women, crime prevention strategies, and the help-seeking behaviors of survivors. Most recently she has studied active shooter and armed intruder policies in healthcare and hospital settings. She has been published in various outlets, including the *Journal of Interpersonal Violence, Race and Justice*, and the *International Journal of Offender Therapy and Comparative Criminology*.

Notes

1 Delbert S. Elliott and Suzanne S. Agetan, "Reconciling Race and Class Differences in Self-Reported and Official Estimates of Delinquency," *American Sociological Review* 45, no. 1 (February 1980): 95–110, https://psycnet.apa.org/doi/10.2307/2095245.
2 Kenneth D. Tunnell, *Living Off Crime*, 2nd ed. (Lanham, MD: Rowman & Littlefield Publishers, 2006).
3 William J. Chambliss, "The Saints and the Roughnecks," *Society* 11, no. 1 (November 1973): 24–31, https://doi.org/10.1007/BF03181016.
4 Robert M. Regoli, John D. Hewitt, and Matt DeLisi, *Delinquency in Society: The Essentials*, 5th ed. (Boston: McGraw-Hill, 2003), 167.
5 Nadine Grimley, "Liberty Mom Deflects Haters, Gets $100K in Support Following Child Endangering Charge," *WKBN First News*, February 18, 2021, www.wkbn.com/news/local-news/liberty-mom-deflects-haters-gets-100k-in-support-following-child-endangering-charge/.
6 Tunnell, *Living Off Crime*, 17.
7 Jari Tiihonen et al., "The Association of Ambient Temperature and Violent Crime," *Scientific Reports* 7, no. 1 (December 2017): 1–7, http://dx.doi.org/10.1038/s41598-017-06720-z.
8 Clifford R. Shaw and Henry D. McKay, "Juvenile Delinquency and Urban Areas," in *Understanding Deviance: Connecting Classical and Contemporary Perspectives*, ed. Tammy L. Anderson et al. (New York: Routledge, 2014), 106–27.
9 Robert E. Park and Ernest W. Burgess, *The City: Heritage of Sociology Series* (Chicago: University of Chicago Press, 2019 [1925]).
10 James F. Anderson, *Criminological Theories: Understanding Crime in America*, 2nd ed. (Burlington, MA: Jones & Bartlett Learning, 2015), 108.
11 Shaw and McKay, "Juvenile Delinquency and Urban Areas."
12 Ibid.
13 Michael L. Birzer and Paul F. Cromwell, *In Their Own Words: Criminals on Crime*, 7th ed. (New York: Oxford University Press, 2017), 311.
14 Wake Forest University Baptist Medical Center, "Violence Is a Learned Behavior, Say Researchers at Wake Forest University," *Science Daily*, November 9, 2000, www.sciencedaily.com/releases/2000/11/001106061128.htm. See also Robert H. DuRant et al., "Exposure to Violence and Victimization, Depression, Substance Use, and the Use of Violence by Young Adolescents," *Journal of Pediatrics* 137, no. 5 (November 2000): 707–13, https://doi.org/10.1067/mpd.2000.109146.
15 Shelley Ng, "'F—all of You!': Ohio Teen Psycho T.J. Lane Gives the Finger and Smirks as He Is Sentenced to Life for Shooting Rampage that Left Three Chardon High School Students Dead," *New York Daily News*, September 11, 2014, www.nydailynews.com/news/national/ohio-teen-faces-life-prison-shooting-rampage-left-high-school-students-dead-article-1.1292702.
16 Robert D. Hare, *The Hare Psychopathy Checklist—Revised*, 2nd ed. (Toronto, ON: Multi-Health Systems, 2003), 412; Kent A. Kiehl, *The Psychopath Whisperer: The Science of Those Without Conscience* (New York: Crown Publishing, 2014). Identifying psychopaths is difficult, as psychopathy is not a clinical diagnosis. Psychopathy remains a legal label given by various institutions to determine risk of recidivism, categorization, and placement. In the criminal justice system, a psychopath is generally designated after one completes the Hare Psychopathy Checklist—Revised, and receives a score consistent with the psychopathy threshold.

17 Tracey Read, "Chardon High School Shooter T.J. Lane Sentenced to Life Without Parole in Ohio Courtroom," *The Times Herald*, March 19, 2013, www.timesherald.com/2013/03/19/chardon-high-school-shooter-tj-lane-sentenced-to-life-without-parole-in-ohio-courtroom/.

18 Cathy Spatz Widom, "Long-Term Impact of Childhood Abuse and Neglect on Crime and Violence," *Clinical Psychology: Science and Practice* 24, no. 2 (April 2017): 186–202, https://psycnet.apa.org/doi/10.1037/h0101743.

19 Larry J. Siegel, *Criminology: Theories, Patterns, and Typologies*, 11th ed. (Belmont, CA: Wadsworth, Cengage Learning, 2012); Anderson, *Criminological Theories: Understanding Crime in America.*

20 David C. Rowe, *Biology and Crime*, 2nd ed. (Los Angeles: Roxbury Publishing Company, 2002).

21 Travis Hirschi and Michael J. Hindelang, "Intelligence and Delinquency: A Revisionist Review," *American Sociological Review* 42, no. 4 (August 1977): 571–87, https://doi.org/10.2307/2094556.

22 James Q. Wilson and Richard J. Herrnstein, *Crime and Human Nature* (New York: Simon and Schuster, 1985).

23 Megan Moore, "Psychological Theories of Crime and Delinquency," *Journal of Human Behavior in the Social Environment* 21, no. 3 (April 2011): 226–39, https://doi.org/10.1080/10911359.2011.564552.

24 Rowe, *Biology and Crime*, 6.

25 David Frank Benson and Dietrich Blumer, "Personality Changes with Frontal and Temporal Lobe Lesions," in *Psychiatric Aspects of Neurologic Disease*, ed. David Frank Benson and Dietrich Blumer (New York, Grune and Stratton, 1975); Robert J. Sbardone, "The Executive Functions of the Brain," in *Neuropsychological Assessment in Clinical Practice: A Guide to Test Interpretation and Integration*, ed. Gary Groth-Marnat (New York: John Wiley & Sons, 2000), 437–56; Paul J. Eslinger and Antonio R. Damasio, "Severe Disturbance of Higher Cognition After Bilateral Frontal Lobe Ablation: Patient EVR," *Neurology* 35, no. 12 (December 1985): 1731–41, https://doi.org/10.1212/wnl.35.12.1731.

26 Ian J. Baguley, Joanne Cooper, and Kim Felmingham, "Aggressive Behavior Following Traumatic Brain Injury: How Common Is Common?" *Journal of Head Trauma Rehabilitation* 21, no. 1 (January 2006): 45–56, https://doi.org/10.1097/00001199-200601000-00005.

27 Sacha Pfeiffer, "A Terrible Thing to Waste," *The Boston Globe*, October 18, 2018, https://apps.bostonglobe.com/spotlight/gladiator/cte/.

28 David P. Farrington, "The Relationship Between Low Resting Heart Rate and Violence," in *Biosocial Bases of Violence*, ed. Adrian Raine et al. (New York: Springer Science+Business Media, 1997), 89–105; Rowe, *Biology and Crime*; Adrian Raine, Peter H. Venables, and Sarnoff A. Mednick, "Low Resting Heart Rate at Age 3 Years Predisposes to Aggression at Age 11 Years: Evidence from the Mauritius Child Health Project," *Journal of the American Academy of Child & Adolescent Psychiatry* 36, no. 10 (October 1997): 1457–64, https://psycnet.apa.org/doi/10.1097/00004583-199710000-00029.

29 Farrington, "The Relationship Between Low Resting Heart Rate and Violence."

30 Ibid.; Rowe, *Biology and Crime*.

31 Olivia Choy et al., "Explaining the Gender Gap in Crime: The Role of Heart Rate," *Criminology* 55, no. 2 (April 2017): 465–87, http://dx.doi.org/10.1111/1745-9125.12138.

32 Terrie E. Moffitt et al., "Whole Blood Serotonin Relates to Violence in an Epidemiological Study," *Biological Psychiatry* 43, no. 6 (March 1998): 446–57, https://doi.org/10.1016/S0006-3223(97)00340-5; Tyra Lagerberg et al., "Association Between Selective Serotonin Reuptake Inhibitors and Violent Crime in Adolescents, Young, and Older Adults—A Swedish Register-Based Study," *European Neuropsychopharmacology* 36 (July 2020): 1–9, https://doi.org/10.1016/j.euroneuro.2020.03.024.

33 Kevin M. Beaver, *Biosocial Criminology: A Primer*, 1st ed. (Dubuque, IA: Kendall Hunt Publishing Company, 2009).

34 John Archer, "Testosterone and Human Aggression: An Evaluation of the Challenge Hypothesis," *British Journal of Psychology* 82, pt. 1 (February 1991): 1–28, https://doi.org/10.1111/j.2044-8295.1991.tb02379.x.; Angela S. Book, Katherine B. Starzyk, and Vernon L. Quinsey, "The Relationship Between Testosterone and Aggression: A Meta-Analysis," *Aggression and Violent Behavior* 6, no. 6 (November 2001): 579–99, http://dx.doi.org/10.1016/S1359-1789(00)00032-X.

35 Willard R. Cooke, "The Different Psychology of the American Woman," *American Journal of Obstetrics and Gynecology* 49, no. 4 (April 1945): 457–72, https://doi.org/10.1016/S0002-9378(45)90002-0; P. T. d'Orban and J. Dalton, "Violent Crime and the Menstrual Cycle," *Psychological Medicine* 10, no. 2 (May 1980): 353–59, https://doi.org/10.1017/S0033291700044123.

36 Pamela J. Schram and Stephen G. Tibbetts, *Introduction to Criminology: Why Do They Do It?* 3rd ed. (Thousand Oaks, CA: SAGE Publications, 2021).

37 Anthony Walsh, *Biosocial Criminology: Introduction and Integration* (Cincinnati, OH: Anderson Publishing Company, 2002).

38 Rowe, *Biology and Crime.*

39 Kevin M. Beaver, "The Familial Concentration and Transmission of Crime," *Criminal Justice and Behavior* 40, no. 2 (February 2013): 139–55, https://doi.org/10.1177/0093854812449405.

40 Samantha Melamed, "Generations of Philly Families Are Incarcerated Together," *The Philadelphia Inquirer*, January 25, 2018, www.inquirer.com/crime/inq/generations-philadelphia-families-are-incarcerated-together-20180125.html.

41 Sarnoff A. Mednick, William F. Gabrielli Jr., and Barry Hutchings, "Genetic Influences in Criminal Convictions: Evidence from an Adoption Cohort," *Science* 224, no. 4651 (May 1984): 891–94, https://doi.org/10.1126/science.6719119.

42 Rowe, *Biology and Crime*; Walsh, *Biosocial Criminology.*

43 Sarnoff A. Mednick and Karl O. Christiansen, *Biosocial Bases of Criminal Behavior* (New York: Gardner Press, 1977).

44 James Alan Fox, Jack Levin, and Kenna Quinet, *The Will to Kill: Making Sense of Senseless Murder*, 5th ed. (Thousand Oaks, CA: SAGE Publications, 2018), 65.

45 John Paul Wright and Danielle Boisvert, "What Biosocial Criminology Offers Criminology," *Criminal Justice and Behavior* 36, no. 11 (2009): 1228–40.

14

NO "CRIMINAL" HERE

A Conviction Where There Was No Crime

Jessica S. Henry

Before Ernest ("Ernie") Ray Willis was charged with killing two women in an arson-murder, he was not what you would ever have called a "real criminal." Willis drank too much, and had a petty record made up of drinking-related offenses to prove it. His employment was spotty, and his romantic relationships were not much better, with a trail of broken marriages in his wake.[1] But drinking and driving convictions, or driving naked through a drive-through, or even a series of divorces, were a far cry from the deliberate murders of which he was accused and ultimately convicted.

The basic facts were not in dispute. In June 1986, Ernie Willis and his cousin, Bill Willis, were living in a shared place. On June 11, the Willis cousins were up late partying with two women, Elizabeth "Betsy" Belue and Gail Allison, who stayed over in a separate room.

A fire broke out in the middle of the night. Only Ernie and Bill made it out alive.

From the outset, the sheriff suspected the fire was deliberately set. Arson experts claimed to find "pour patterns"—markings on the floor that suggested a flammable liquid had been poured inside the house to light the fire. Ernie, who made it out of the house first, became the primary suspect. Ernie explained to the authorities that he woke from the fire around 4:00 a.m. and tried to wake everyone, but could not get near their rooms because of the flames. He fled the house on foot; cousin Bill made it out through a window. When Ernie described what happened, law enforcement dismissed his explanations out of hand. They didn't think he seemed upset enough and, despite a severe burn on his arm, they didn't think that Ernie was injured enough to have survived the fire in the way he described.

Even though he had no motive and despite the lack of evidence against him, the police arrested Ernest Ray Willis on October 22, 1986. The prosecution moved

DOI: 10.4324/9781003169468-19

aggressively and charged him with a capital crime for the arson-double murder. If Ernie Willis was convicted, he would face the death penalty.

The Trial

While Willis sat in jail, waiting for his capital trial to begin, an extremely unusual thing happened. The State began giving Willis daily doses of powerful prescription anti-psychotic medications—Haldol and perphenazine. Willis had not been taking these medications before his arrest. Nor was Willis ever diagnosed as having a mental illness that required medication.

A federal judge who later reviewed Willis's case described the inexplicable decision to medicate Ernie Willis—and the heavy dosages of medication forced upon him—this way: "The dosages for Haldol (40 mg. per day) and perphenazine (8 mg.–32 mg. per day) that the State gave to Willis during the course of the trial were high doses, even for acutely psychotic patients. The maximum dose of Haldol for a severely psychotic person is 15 mg. per day. Willis received more than twice that amount at 40 mg. per day." The federal judge also found that this aggressive medication regime was "without medical need," meaning no doctor had ever made a finding that Willis was psychotic or in need of medication.[2]

The forced and unjustified medication regime had devastating consequences for Willis's case. Common side effects of these antipsychotic medications include "flat or little facial expression, inexpressiveness, rigidity of the facial muscles, fixed gaze, drowsiness, confusion and diminished ability to communicate with others," according to the federal opinion. Willis exhibited all of these symptoms, and then some. Willis was unable to communicate with his lawyer, or to follow along with the proceedings. During the four-and-a-half week trial, Willis sat silent and dazed, in a drug-induced stupor. The prosecution eagerly seized on Willis's flat affect by referring to his "dead pan, insensitive, expressionless face" and his "cold fisheyes," and describing him variously an animal and a "satanic" demon.[3]

Willis's young and inexperienced defense lawyer did not demand an explanation for the administration of the antipsychotic drugs, or object to the impact the drugs were having on his client and their case. Nor did Willis's lawyer object to the prosecution's highly objectional comments. Even worse, his lawyer did not put up much of a defense, failing to call any character witnesses, at least one of whom would have testified that Willis was a hero who had saved a boy from drowning. This would have been important in a case where the jury was tasked not only with finding a defendant's guilt or innocence, but also in deciding whether the defendant should live or die.

The prosecution's theory of the case was that Willis set the fire by pouring an unidentified accelerant on the floor. No evidence was presented about the so-called accelerant, but the prosecution called an expert to testify about the distinctive pour patterns that indicated the fire was an arson.

Despite the lack of actual evidence against him (and perhaps in part because of the lack of evidence *for* him), the jury deliberated for less than an hour before voting to convict Ernie Willis of arson-murder. It also deliberated less than an hour before deciding to sentence him to death. Willis was promptly carted off to his new home on Texas's notorious death row.

And the State promptly stopped medicating him.

After the verdict, even the trial prosecutor, J.W. Johnson, admitted the case against Willis was shockingly weak: "[T]here were no eyewitnesses, we didn't know what the flammable liquid was, and we never proved a motive—that [conviction] was astounding." Johnson added: "[W]e went into the trial with a 10% chance of winning. I didn't think there was adequate proof to convince 12 people."[4]

On appeal, Willis argued among other things that he was innocent, that he was improperly medicated, and that the prosecution had engaged in misconduct. The Texas Court of Criminal Appeals in 1989 dismissed his arguments out of hand (italics added):

"The facts of this crime demonstrate an utter disregard for human life. . . . Indeed, *they depict a man so determined to murder the very people with whom he earlier socialized* that he effectively sealed off their escape routes by pouring an accelerant (flammable liquid) on the door jambs to their bedroom and on the front and back doors to the house immediately before sending the house up in flames."[5]

The U.S Supreme Court denied his petition for review in 1990 without comment.

Ernie Willis, it appeared, was destined to die at the hands of the State of Texas.

Why the Word "Criminal" Is Arbitrary

This essay collection asks, "What Is a criminal?" It's a provocative and problematic question.

I want to be clear about one thing: I don't believe in using the word "criminal" to talk about people who have committed crimes. I believe that words matter. I don't believe that people are the sum of the worst thing that they've ever done. If you steal, you are not just a thief. If you use drugs, you are not just a drug user. Even if you take someone's life, you are more than just a murderer.

I learned this lesson up close when I was a public defender in the South Bronx. I lived and breathed the lives of my clients. They had families they loved, and families that loved them. They had hopes and dreams, disappointments and shame, moments of joy and of deep despair. They were funny and intelligent. They loved their children. The made good—and sometimes very bad—choices. My clients were poor people charged with crimes. They were often guilty of those crimes, and even sometimes guilty of causing tremendous harm to others.

But they were always much more than just "criminals."

My clients taught me about the inherent human dignity that exists within all of us. That you can break the law and still, first and foremost, be a human being worthy of attention and respect. The men and women who wind up in the criminal legal system may have done something illegal, but they did not lose their humanity when they entered the courthouse.

The word "criminal," when used to describe individuals, ignores all of that. A criminal is an "other." A "criminal" doesn't have rights or even feelings. A "criminal" can be locked in tiny steel cages and forgotten. A "criminal" can be abused and neglected behind bars. A "criminal" can be excluded from mainstream society when they are released. To be a "criminal" is to be someone less deserving and less worthy than you and me.

And that's just not accurate.

The people who get caught up in the criminal legal system are people. But here are a few things that tend to distinguish them. The people in the criminal legal system are almost always poor,[6] and poor people of color are disproportionately represented at all stages of the criminal justice system.[7] Police do their jobs differently and more aggressively in poor communities than in wealthy communities. Racism and poverty determine whom the police choose to stop, frisk, and ultimately arrest.[8] They arrest poor people and people of color for crimes such as drug offenses at far higher rates than people who are wealthy and White, despite similar rates of drug usage.[9]

Once a person is arrested, system biases against the poor and people of color are further magnified. Poor people can't pay even small amounts of bail, so they sit behind bars in pretrial detention waiting for their day in court. Wealthy people go home. This means that poor people—even innocent people—will sometimes take a plea to a crime they didn't commit if it means getting out of jail sooner, a choice wealthy people never face. People who can't make bail face different outcomes in their cases: research shows that people who are detained in jail pretrial receive prison time—and longer sentences—more often than those who were released pending trial. People who are detained pending trial are less able to assist their lawyers and prepare their own defense. They are unable to earn money that might help pay for investigators or experts, and they are unable to do the legwork themselves. They can't engage in activities that would demonstrate "good behavior" to a jury or a sentencing judge, such as community service, consistent employment, or positive academic performance. People held in pretrial detention often take pleas and, for the all the reasons mentioned, receive worse outcomes than those who can afford to make bail and resolve the case from the outside.

The upshot is that being a lawbreaker is not the only thing that earns you the label of a "criminal." A lot of it has to do with race and economic status, factors that shouldn't matter, but very much do. Some of it has to do with happenstance and luck. Yet, despite its arbitrariness, the word "criminal" lingers in the popular vernacular. As I mentioned earlier, I avoid the word. I know that refusing to use "criminal" won't fix a broken legal system that is so stacked against the poor and the most marginalized members of society. But I nonetheless believe words have power, and that we need to be deliberate about what words we use and what meaning they convey.

And there's another important reason why "criminal" is a word to be avoided. Sometimes it's just plain wrong.

Remember Ernie Willis, the convicted killer and remorseless "monster" waiting to be executed on Texas's death row.

A federal judge determined that Ernie Willis was entirely innocent.

Exoneration

Willis lost appeal after appeal. He came within hours—on multiple occasions—of being executed. But then an unlikely series of events occurred. A New York law firm took on his case. They sent five lawyers and an investigator to Texas. And what they found caused his conviction to finally crumble.

With the aid of his legal team, a new petition was put together. A federal judge examined his record carefully and overturned his conviction. The court found that Willis had been inappropriately forced to take medication that he did not need, and that the medication had entirely derailed his ability to aid his defense. In addition, the court found that the prosecution had hidden from the defense a document in which another man confessed to setting the fire that had killed the two women (there were questions about the credibility of the new confession, but it certainly would have cast doubt on Willis's guilt).[10] In addition, the prosecution had hidden a report issued by a mental health expert who said Willis was not a future danger and was not an appropriate candidate for the death penalty. The court also said that Willis had been denied an effective lawyer at trial.

But, most importantly, the court concluded that the fire was not—and had never been—arson. A new Texas prosecutor who reviewed the case in 2004 agreed. New arson experts determined there was no evidence that the house had been intentionally burned to the ground. Instead, the experts concluded, the house had electrical issues, which could well have explained the blaze.

No one had set the fire. No one had been murdered. There had been no crime at all.

The prosecutor moved to dismiss the charges against Willis.

After more than 17 years behind bars, on October 5, 2004, Willis was released and exonerated of all wrongdoing. Willis—the "remorseless," "stone-cold" killer—was entirely and completely innocent, wrongly convicted of a crime that never even happened in the first place.

If you don't believe it, consider this: over one-third of known exonerations involve a no-crime wrongful conviction, involving innocent people convicted of crime that literally never occurred.[11] A suicide is mislabeled a homicide. An illness or a natural death is misdiagnosed as shaken baby syndrome or murder. A false accusation results in an assault conviction. The police plant evidence resulting in a drug conviction. An accidental fire is wrongly determined to be arson.

But it's not just no-crime wrongful convictions that should make you pause. Actual crime wrongful convictions, where an innocent person is wrongly convicted of a crime committed by someone else, also occur with frequency. While the total number of wrongful convictions (both no-crime wrongful convictions and actual crime cases) is unknown and perhaps even unknowable, the best estimate suggests that about 4.1% of *all* convictions involve an innocent person wrongly convicted of a crime they did not commit.[12] That would mean roughly one out of every 25 cases involves a wrongful conviction. But even a far more conservative estimate—let's say only 1% –means that *thousands and thousands* of innocent people have been wrongly convicted of crimes they did not commit.

We can't know the number for sure, because most of the information about wrongful convictions comes from exonerations—when people are officially cleared of all wrongdoing by a court or a prosecutor. But exonerations are rare for a whole host of reasons. Over 95% of people plead guilty, and many guilty pleas include a waiver of the right to appeal. Even pleas that don't include such a waiver are hard to challenge; our legal system prioritizes the finality of a conviction over justice every time. Finding legal representation can also be a herculean task. Innocence Projects are overwhelmed with requests for assistance, and many innocence organizations have strict limitations on the cases they will accept. This can leave the wrongly convicted languishing behind bars without any legal assistance at all. And even for the fortunate few who are able to secure representation, the path to exoneration is littered with obstacles, making success a hard-fought and far too infrequent occurrence. Most wrongful convictions remain unknown and uncounted.

Once a Convicted Criminal, Not Always a Convicted Criminal

Willis was now a free man. He was released into the arms of Verilyn, a woman he'd met and married in prison. He eventually received compensation from the State of Texas for the decades spent behind bars. He bought a truck with some of that money. After Verilyn died, he continued to spend time with his sons.

But the wounds from decades on death row ran deep.

Prison medical treatment is notoriously lousy. The medical care on Texas's death row was no exception. Willis's diabetes had been largely untreated while he was incarcerated. After his release, he continued to have major health issues and eventually lost one leg, and then the other, to his battle with diabetes. Willis died at the age of 75, 17 years after his release from prison.

Willis (arguably) was one of the lucky ones. He was released and exonerated. He had family to turn to when he got out. That is not true for all people. Even among the exonerated, many leave prison after decades behind bars with no outside support. Family and friends have died or moved on, leaving them with no place to go and no one to lean on.

People who are newly released after exoneration struggle with financial security. It can take months—or years—to obtain a settlement once an exoneree is released from prison. In the meantime, they have no clear way, save the kindness of others, to meet their own immediate needs. And compensation by the State is not guaranteed. Only 45% of exonerees receive any compensation for the damage caused by their wrongful conviction.[13] Some states have no compensation statute for the wrongly convicted.[14] Some states with compensation statutes have significant limitations on the amount and type of financial award.

Exonerees also face non-monetary challenges once they are released. Prisons are violent, chaotic places, where people have no privacy and no autonomy. While some people, like Willis, move forward with their lives, some people who are wrongly convicted suffer severe trauma from their incarceration, and become consumed by bitterness, anger, and depression for the years lost behind bars. They may have become institutionalized, causing independent decision-making to be overwhelming. Therapy—which is expensive—is often critical, but unavailable, for reentry to society.

Exonerees also lag in job-readiness skills. Depending on when they were incarcerated, they may have never used a cell phone, and may have limited or no computer experience. They have to relearn how to think independently. They may have aged out of their former employment or be unable to keep up with the physical demands of potential jobs. Aside from a lack of job skills, exonerees also have a gaping hole in their resume that makes it hard to find work. How do you explain years with no work experience at all?

And that's the other piece of it. Exonerees are often viewed as "criminals" just because they spent years locked among those who in fact broke the law. Walter McMillian, featured in Bryan Stevenson's best-selling book *Just Mercy*, was an innocent man wrongly convicted of murder and sentenced to die in Alabama. Upon his release, McMillian developed dementia. Yet, advocates had trouble finding him a place in a nursing home because administrators at various facilities continued to view him as a "criminal," even though he was very publicly exonerated.

An official exoneration is only the start of shedding the "criminal" label that should never have been imposed in the first place. For some innocent people, that goal remains forever elusive.

Conclusion

Ernie Willis was an innocent man. At least, he was until he was legally declared "guilty" after a sham of a trial in which officials forcibly medicated him without a medical justification for doing so, hid evidence, and relied on unreliable fire science. He was a death row inmate and a convicted murderer, whom the State of Texas and the Texas prosecutors' office wanted desperately to execute (and almost did).

Willis was painted as the worst kind of "criminal," until a federal judge decided Willis's conviction should be tossed out.

Throughout all those years, before trial and after trial, before and after each state and federal appeal, during his years on death row, Ernest Willis was never anything more or less than what he always was: an entirely innocent man.

Calling Ernie Willis a "criminal" didn't change his essence, or alter what he had not done. But it did allow the state to abuse him at trial, lock him up on death row, and nearly kill him by lethal injection. More importantly, it allowed him to be treated, through every stage of the criminal legal process, as less than the important human being that he was.

We would all would do well to keep Ernie Willis in mind the next time we come across another so-called "criminal."

Jessica S. Henry is Professor of Justice Studies at Montclair State University. She is the author of the award-winning book *Smoke But No Fire: Convicting the Innocent of Crimes that Never Happened* (2020). After obtaining her JD from NYU School of Law, Professor Henry served as a public defender in New York City for nearly a decade before joining the faculty at Montclair State in 2005. Her research interests include wrongful convictions and severe sentences, such as the death penalty and life without parole. She is a commentator on national and local television and radio, and has been widely cited in the mainstream media. In 2022, Professor Henry was named University Distinguished Scholar. She also received the Montclair State University Distinguished Teacher Award in 2015. To learn more, visit her website at http://jessicahenryjustice.com/.

Notes

1 On the case of Ernest Willis, see the excellent reporting of Michael Hall, including "The State of Texas Tried to Kill Ernest Willis. But He Still Had a Lot of Living to Do," *Texas Monthly*, October 2021, and "Death Isn't Fair," *Texas Monthly*, December 2002.

2 Willis v. Cockrell, No. P-01-CA-20, (W.D. Tex. Jul. 21, 2004), https://casetext.com/case/willis-v-cockrell-4.

3 Hall, "Death Isn't Fair."

4 Jan Tomas, "Pecos County Jury Gives Death Sentence in Arson-Murder Case," *San Angelo Standard Times*, August 6, 1987.

5 Willis v. State, 785 S.W.2d 378, 378 (Tex.Cr. App. 1989), https://scholar.google.com/scholar_case?case=678898252682830197

6 Bernadette Rabuy and Daniel Kopf, "Prisons of Poverty: Uncovering the Pre-Incarceration Incomes of the Imprisoned," *Prison Policy Initiative*, July 9, 2015.

7 See, for example, Elizabeth Hinton, LeShae Henderson, and Cindy Reed, *An Unjust Burden: The Disparate Treatment of Black Americans in the Criminal Justice System* (New York: The Vera Institute of Justice, May 2018); "Racial and Ethnic Disparities in Correctional Facilities," infographic, *Prison Policy Initiative*, accessed April 18, 2022, www.prisonpolicy.org/profiles/US.html#disparities.

8 The overrepresentation of people of color in the criminal justice system is long-standing and well documented. For a primer on how the legal system is structured to disfavor Black and brown people at every step of policing, prosecuting, sentencing, and incarceration, see Michelle Alexander, *The New Jim Crow: Mass Incarceration in the Age of Colorblindness* (New York: The New Press, 2010). For a selection of scholarly writings on this subject, see: Elizabeth Hinton and DeAnza Cook, "The Mass Criminalization of Black Americans: A Historical Overview," *Annual Review of Criminology* 4, no. 1 (June 2020): 261–86; Hinton, Henderson, and Reed, *An Unjust Burden*. For specific examples of racial influence on policing and criminal process, see, for example: Cornell William Brooks, Roslyn M. Brock, and Barbara Bolling-Williams, *Born Suspect: Stop-and-Frisk Abuse & the Continued Fight to End Racial Profiling in America* (Baltimore: The National Association for the Advancement of Colored People, September 2014); David Arnold, Will Dobbie, and Crystal S. Yang, "Racial Bias in Bail Decisions," *Quarterly Journal of Economics* 133, no. 4 (May 2018): 1885–932; Carlos Berdejó, "Criminalizing

Race: Racial Disparities in Plea-Bargaining," *Boston College Law Review* 59, no. 4 (2018): 1187–249; Tushar Kansal, *Racial Disparities in Sentencing: A Review of the Literature* (Washington, DC: The Sentencing Project, 2005).

9 For example, a recent research report by the ACLU finds that Black people are 3.64 times more likely than White people to be arrested for marijuana possession, notwithstanding comparable usage rates. ACLU, *A Tale of Two Countries: Racially Targeted Arrests in the Era of Marijuana Reform* (New York: American Civil Liberties Union, April 2020).

10 Alexandra Gross, "Ernest Ray Willis," *National Registry of Exonerations*, last modified October 21, 2021, www.law.umich.edu/special/exoneration/Pages/casedetail.aspx?caseid=3755.

11 Jessica Henry, *Smoke but No Fire: Convicting the Innocent of Crimes that Never Happened* (Berkeley, CA: UC Press, 2020).

12 This estimate comes from Samuel Gross, a leading innocence scholar, who conducted a study in death penalty cases. He found that if all death sentenced defendants remained under a sentence of death indefinitely, at least 4.1% would be exonerated. Samuel R. Gross et al., "Rate of False Conviction of Criminal Defendants Who Are Sentenced to Death," *Proceedings of the National Academy of Sciences* 111, no. 20 (April 2014): 7230–35.

13 "25,000 Years Lost to Wrongful Convictions," *National Registry of Exonerations* (June 2021), www.law.umich.edu/special/exoneration/Documents/25000%20Years.pdf.

14 Eric Ferkenhoff, "After 43 Years in Prison on a Wrongful Conviction, Kevin Strickland Is Getting No Restitution. He's Not Alone," *USA Today*, December 9, 2021, www.usatoday.com/story/news/nation/2021/12/09/kevin-strickland-case-exposes-gaps-state-restitution-laws-wrongly-convicted-exonerated/8834538002/.

15

VERA'S FAMILY

The Community Context of Criminalization

Michelle C. Sermon

It's February, and my children are participating in the annual Black History Month celebration at their school in Washington, DC. The mood is festive and congenial, as excited parents flood the auditorium to cheer on their children's performances. I notice a familiar, yet unexpected, face in the crowd. Vera* is about 84 years old, stoutly built, with kind eyes, a friendly smile, and bobbed hair that belies her advanced age. She is seated with her three great-grandchildren. The younger siblings, fraternal twins aged about 7, are growing increasingly restless. They shift anxiously in their seats, talking loudly and standing up to gain Vera's attention, as the older sibling, perhaps 12 years old, attempts to help her great-grandmother settle them into their places. An assistant principal and kindergarten teacher, who appear to be familiar with this grandmother's particular situation, kindly greet the family and offer to take the younger children for a walk around the auditorium to release their restless energies. As we all settle in to experience the showcase of student speeches, dance performances, poetry readings, and musical renditions, I lose track of the family in the growing crowd and the excitement of the performance, but my thoughts remain with them.

The moment I noticed this grandmother, my heart sank. I wanted desperately to intervene, to let her know that I was there to help. I knew her from my role as a social worker who has worked professionally with her granddaughter and her family. According to the ethics of my field I could not acknowledge her first; she was too distracted in the moment to notice me. I am familiar with Vera and her unconventional parenting role through my professional work with her granddaughter, Alexis,* a young woman with whom I have worked for many years. At the time of this event, Alexis was experiencing one of her periodic incarcerations in the local jail.

I knew a lot about the history of Alexis and Vera, and of course as a professional I know about the impact of incarceration on families and communities. Still,

DOI: 10.4324/9781003169468-20

bearing witness as Vera struggled to manage her great-grandchildren in the school auditorium was an eye-opening and disheartening peek into how criminalization changes the reality of a family. As a mother of four young children myself, I deeply empathized with the complex, exhausting, unrelenting, and self-sacrificing situation of this grandmother. Instead of enjoying the latter years of her life at leisure, she is enmeshed in the triumphs and challenges of parenting in the twenty-first century. I imagined how she managed the various schedules, afterschool activities, technology needs, and homework support to help each of "her" children be successful, while maintaining her aging body and mind. I imagined the opportunities that the children would have to forgo because grandma just can't do it all on her own. And there's always the burden of fear: what happens to the children if something unspeakable happens to grandma?

When people talk about the criminal justice system, Vera's situation doesn't often come up. She is not a criminal; neither are her great-grandchildren. But their lives have been shaped by the way the term "criminal" is defined in our society.

I became a social worker because I wanted to serve and empower underserved and underrepresented individuals and communities. My first job was working with a nonprofit that provides services to incarcerated and returning citizens in Washington, DC. I engaged with clients in the local jail, federal correctional institutions, and the community. This was in no way my dream job. Nonprofit work is not financially lucrative; it's thankless and invisible, and even more so when you are working with populations that most in society have discarded. While I was new to social work and this justice-involved population, I was not new to the area, and I possessed an appreciation for the rich history of the local people and the places, now threatened by gentrification that was displacing many who had called this community home for generations. I could also relate to the people and community, as we shared commonalities as African Americans and products of the Great Migration of African Americans out of the Jim Crow South.[1] I found working with this population of mostly African American, justice-involved men and women with co-occurring mental health conditions more rewarding than I anticipated, and I learned to see their humanity despite their criminality.

I first met Alexis during my first year with the nonprofit, while she was incarcerated on a probation violation. On the occasion of our first meeting, Alexis appeared to be anxious, restless, irritable, and easily distracted, all signs of cocaine withdrawal. She asked me to contact her "mother," Vera, for commissary money and to retrieve her confiscated property from the local precinct where she was arrested. Over the next few weeks, I provided more services for Alexis, such as brief counseling sessions, phone calls to her "mother," and greeting cards for her children's birthdays. Over time, she began to share more details about her circumstances. I learned that Alexis had a significant history of mental health diagnoses, learning disabilities, and substance misuse beginning in childhood. She was raised by her grandmother, Vera, because her biological mother, Patricia,* Vera's daughter, was unable to care for Alexis because of her own substance use issues. Alexis was still a teenager when her first child was born, and Vera became the primary caregiver for both Alexis and her infant daughter. As a result of these early challenges, Alexis's substance use progressed to narcotics addiction, and she became regularly involved in criminal activities.

Fueled by untreated emotional and physical traumas, Alexis's addiction led to criminal behaviors such as petty theft, shoplifting, and solicitation to support her illness. Substance abuse and misuse are illnesses that, for some people, lead to a cascading set of circumstances that leave individuals unable to maintain employment and housing. As a result, many of those individuals engage in illegal activities to earn money to purchase drugs and alcohol. Alexis is one of those individuals, and she was eventually arrested and convicted of her crimes, beginning when she was a teen. While most of her convictions were for misdemeanor crimes, each leading to less than one year in the local jail and probation, Alexis has served more than 10 years of incarceration for violating the terms of her probation.

Probation is a form of community corrections, allowing convicted misdemeanants to serve out all or part of their jail sentence in the community under the supervision of a probation officer. The probation terms, determined by the court, at minimum require convicted misdemeanants to report regularly to their probation officer; secure employment and steady housing; abstain from drug and alcohol use; and avoid criminal behavior and rearrest. Any violation of the terms of probation can result in rearrest and an extension of the probation sentence. This was the case for Alexis, who was sentenced with probation as a young adult for a period of one year that has been extended after multiple probation violations and rearrests. As a result, Alexis has been incarcerated or justice-involved 10 times as long as her original sentence. With the revolving cycle of arrest and release, Alexis has not been able to successfully complete substance use treatment, secure stable employment, or find housing. In addition, she has not been capable of caring for her three children. That responsibility has been left to Vera, who assumes the burden to keep her great-grandchildren out of the child welfare system.

When not incarcerated, Alexis contributes to Vera's burden when she shows up unexpectedly to Vera's home—often intoxicated, agitated, and volatile, demanding money, making unrealistic promises to the children, and exhibiting physically violent behavior that forces Vera to report her to the police. Her trauma is conveyed to the next generation: her children. The impact of criminality on children and other family members is often disregarded; without proper emotional and psychological interventions, cycles of trauma and criminality persist, especially in communities of color. Despite Vera's best efforts, Alexis's children are at elevated risk of being "criminals" later in their lives. The children of incarcerated parents are hidden victims; support services that are made available to other victims of crime are not available to them. Depending on the strength of the relationship between a child and their incarcerated parent and the social supports available to the child, children may experience psychological distress, grief, and depression that often go unresolved. As a result, the children of incarcerated parents are more likely to experience poverty, have disciplinary issues, exhibit antisocial behaviors, perform below the average in school, and eventually become justice-involved.

Alexis's story is not new or unique. Many women, especially women of color, labeled as criminals, receive misdemeanor charges that lead to community corrections or probation for a period of 12 months to upwards of three years. Because their illnesses are criminalized, violations of their probation add more probation time as well as jail time, with little to no supervised mental health, trauma, or substance use treatment. They become caught in a cycle of criminal dysfunction that becomes easier to navigate than life free from criminal justice involvement. Their children, families, and communities are the silent victims of their criminalization.

If a criminal were defined as someone who does harm, Alexis would fit the bill. Her behavior is dangerous to her family and her community, as well as those affected by crimes like shoplifting. However, from my perspective, it's clear that her cycle of behavior is characteristic of someone who is suffering from behavioral and mental distress. It's when law enforcement gets involved that it escalates to criminality. Alexis didn't have to be a criminal.

How did we arrive at this place, where psychological and behavioral health conditions become criminalized? In what follows, I'll describe what I think are the three main forces that led to Alexis's situation: racial and economic dynamics in the community; changing approaches to mental health; and the "racial empathy gap" that makes Black women more vulnerable to those forces.

Racial and Economic Dynamics

The history of African Americans in Washington, DC is complicated. In the eighteenth century, enslaved African-descended people existed on forced labor camps (i.e. plantations). They literally built the city, including the US Capitol building and the White House. Emancipation for the enslaved in Washington, DC preceded the constitutional abolishment of slavery, but racial apartheid and legal segregation—as well as Black resistance—persisted in the city. By 1957 Washington, DC had become the first major US city with a majority Black resident population, although the White minority maintained political and economic power. Those dynamics—a large Black population, a White power structure—have continued to shape the city in the present. Recently, they have taken the form of gentrification.

According to the *Washington Post*, Washington, DC has the highest intensity of gentrification of any US city, with more than 20,000 residents displaced from low-income neighborhoods since 2000.[2] In DC, that economic displacement is also racial displacement. In 1980, African Americans made up 70% of DC residents (leading to its affectionate nickname, "Chocolate City"); today, they make up 40% of residents.[3] The drastic shift is not only in population. The city's changing priorities have impacted the availability of affordable housing, employment, and educational opportunities for justice-involved adults like Alexis. These factors lead to instability for vulnerable people, forcing many to either leave their homes or continue the unforgiving cycle of substance misuse, criminal behavior, and incarceration.

From Health Care to Prison

In addition to the changing demographics of the city, the privatization of health care and the prison industrial complex have exacerbated the conditions of vulnerable and marginalized, primarily Black, people in the city. Prior to the privatization of health care in DC in 2001, residents could access physical and mental health services from the publicly funded hospital and community-based public health clinics across the city, regardless of their insurance status or ability to pay. The hospital was located on a large 60-acre campus that included a trauma center, inpatient and emergency mental health services, inpatient substance misuse treatment services, pharmacy, social services, services for children with special health care needs, and later, the DC Correctional Treatment and Detention Centers (i.e., the jail).

Since 2001, DC has moved to a system of healthcare that prioritizes community-based care, provided through private managed care organizations that are contracted through the local government. Theoretically, this model is intended to manage costs while providing quality care. However, it has been criticized for the inability to provide low-income, high-need individuals the care they require to maintain mental health stability and recovery.[4] Many of my incarcerated or returning clients experienced frustration in trying to find health care. Some struggled to find a provider who would accept their insurance. Some insurance does not cover mental health services for more than three visits. Contracted community-based mental health services are overcrowded, and provide only medication management with a psychiatrist and sparse therapeutic interventions with mental health therapists (i.e., talk therapy).

In the past, people with mental illness were better able to rely on community support from families and neighbors who understood their difficulties and were less likely to call the police on them during a mental health crisis. With the loss of community and dwindling affordable housing resulting from gentrification, individuals unable to sustain their mental stability often interface with law enforcement and the criminal justice system before they receive appropriate mental health treatment. Lacking housing or behaving erratically can lead to a criminal record, and once a record exists, incarceration becomes a more likely outcome. This outcome might be in keeping with cost-saving goals and even profit. Privately owned jails and prisons promise to be built faster and more cost-effectively than publicly owned facilities.[5] For the people who are placed in them, the profit comes at the price of humanity. One of my colleagues who counsels incarcerated adults tells them: "You are a commodity, exchanged on the NYSE. There is a price on your head."

The Racial Empathy Gap

While gentrification, the collapse of mental health services, and mass incarceration are theoretically race-neutral, their effects fall disproportionally on Black people, and Black women in particular. Depending on whom you ask, DC ranks either first or in the top five of "states" with the highest rates of incarceration, at 1,153 per

100,000 residents (or 930 per 100,000 residents).[6] While the population of African Americans in Washington, DC is decreasing, the percentage of incarcerated African Americans has failed to show a proportionate decrease, but has remained stable and high. Of incarcerated men in DC, 87.4% are African American, and of incarcerated women, 79.6% are African American.[7]

These effects appear at a national level as well, as race contributes to observed disparities in the criminal justice system, affecting policing, jury selection, and sentencing. Nationally, African Americans make up 13% of the population, compared to 73% of White Americans.[8] In 2015, White Americans made up 77% of drug users and 71% of drug possession and distribution arrests. However, Black Americans and White Americans were sentenced to state prison for drug offenses at equal rates—31% each, despite the lower Black population. Of those sentenced to federal prison for drug offenses, the disparity is even worse: 38% are Black, and 22% are White. These statistics suggest glaring disparities in how Black and White Americans are treated in the American justice system.

Further, the gendered racism experienced by Black women exacerbates these disparities. Historically, Black women in the US, enslaved and free, have not fully enjoyed the privilege of protection under the law. While White women are socially valued for their feminine qualities, Black women are viewed as comparable to their Black male counterparts and are valued for their work, and the ease at which they can be exploited without recompense. History documents many cases of Black women resisting such exploitation and suffering harsh consequences of incarceration, sexual violence, torture, and death, from a justice system designed to protect all other sectors of our society except them.[9]

Compounding these facts is a lack of empathy for Black victims of racism and racial violence, perpetuating the impact of historical, intentional, and systemic exclusion of African Americans in American society. Expressions of empathy are critical to the function of human social interactions, as empathy enables people to understand the pain, actions, behaviors, and intentions of others. Racial empathy acknowledges that racial bias impacts the ways in which empathy is granted based on an individual's or community's racial lens.

In the case of African-descended people, research has shown that White observers react significantly less to the pain and suffering of people of African ancestry than of White people, correlating with the observer's individual implicit racial biases.[10] Another theory that explains the racial empathy gap is based on perceptions of privilege and hardship. People who are more privileged are perceived as experiencing more pain, and are thus extended more empathy. Those who have historically experienced more hardship or are "hardened" are perceived as experiencing less pain, and therefore receive less empathy. The limited empathy applied to Black Americans who experience the pain and discomfort of interpersonal, institutional, and systemic racism contributes significantly to the racial disparities observed in mental health services and criminal justice. It also contributes to our society's limitations in acknowledging that Black women with co-occurring mental health diagnosis and criminal justice involvement are as much victims as they are criminals—and maybe more so.

How would Vera's situation be different if our society bestowed similar empathy on her Black "daughter," Alexis, with her history of mental instability and substance use, as is granted to White women with similar circumstances, instead of criminalizing her illness?[11] I imagine that Vera would be able to assume her role as the doting great-grandma to her great-grandchildren, and enjoy her life of leisure in retirement. If it were not for the pressures of gentrification and institutional racism, both her daughter, Patricia, and granddaughter, Alexis, would receive the behavioral and mental health treatments they need. As a result, they would have employable skills, gainful employment, affordable housing in a safe neighborhood, and great schools that would prepare their children to reverse the conditions of intergenerational poverty and criminalization. Our society can accomplish this reality if we commit the same energy to eradicating general and gendered racism and assuring recovery and healing for behavioral health conditions as is committed to criminalizing those conditions. Our society would achieve the civilization imagined by the ideals of American exceptionalism.

*Names in this story have been changed.

Michelle C. Sermon is a licensed social worker who has worked with racially marginalized, justice-involved individuals, their children, and extended families. Professor Sermon's clinical expertise is counseling adults with trauma, severe mental illness, and co-occurring conditions. With almost 20 years of experience working with diverse communities, she is also an expert in diversity, equity, and inclusion, and serves as a consultant and facilitator for a diverse collection of organizations and industries. In her research, Professor Sermon uses history to elucidate the experiences of intergenerational racialization experienced as trauma by African Americans in rural, Southern US communities to develop and implement effective, community-specific healing strategies. Professor Sermon is an assistant professor in the Department of Social Work at Bowie State University, and holds a PhD in Social Work from the University of Maryland Baltimore, a Master of Social Work degree from George Mason University, and a Master of Science degree in Human Genetics from Howard University.

Notes

1 In this essay, "Black" refers to all people of African descent across the global diaspora, including African-descended immigrants in the United States. "African American" is a specific reference to people of African descent that are citizens of the United States.

2 Katherine Shaver, "D.C. Has the Highest 'Intensity' of Gentrification of Any U.S. City, Study Says," *The Washington Post*, March 19, 2019, www.washingtonpost.com/transportation/2019/03/19/study-dc-has-had-highest-intensity-gentrification-any-us-city/.

3 Alex Baca and Nick Finio, "Gentrification in DC Isn't Just a Black and White Issue," *Greater Washington,* May 25, 2020, https://ggwash.org/view/77621/gentrification-in-dc-is-not-just-a-black-and-white-issue_1. Malcom B. Morse, "True Justice: The Disturbing Truth About Incarceration in D.C.," *Georgetown Journal of Law & Modern Critical Race Perspectives,* February 17, 2020, www.law.georgetown.edu/mcrp-journal/blog/true-justice-the-disturbing-truth-about-incarceration-in-d-c/. Steven Overly et al., "Washington Was an Icon of Black Political Power. Then Came Gentrification," *Politico Magazine,* April 15, 2022, www.politico.com/news/magazine/2022/04/15/washington-dc-gentrification-black-political-power-00024515.

4 Jared S. Warren et. al., "Youth Psychotherapy Change Trajectories and Outcomes in Usual Care: Community Mental Health Versus Managed Care Settings," *Journal of Consulting and Clinical Psychology* 78, no. 2 (April 2010): 144; Michael H. Tang et. al., "Medicaid Managed Care and the Unmet Need for Mental Health Care among Children with Special Health Care Needs," *Health Services Research* 43, no. 3 (July 2008): 882–900.

5 James Austin and Garry Coventry, *Emerging Issues on Privatized Prisons,* US Department of Justice, Office of Justice Programs (February 2001).

6 Martin Austermuhle, "District of Corrections: Does D.C. Really Have the Highest Incarceration Rate in the Country?" *WAMU 88.5: American University Radio Local News,* September 10, 2019, https://wamu.org/story/19/09/10/district-of-corrections-does-d-c-really-have-the-highest-incarceration-rate-in-the-country/.

7 Morse, "True Justice."

8 Elizabeth Hinton, LeShae Henderson, and Cindy Reed, *An Unjust Burden: The Disparate Treatment of Black Americans in the Criminal Justice System* (New York: The Vera Institute of Justice, May 2018).

9 Dorothy Roberts, "Race," in *The 1619 Project: A New Origin Story,* ed. Nikole Hannah-Jones et al. (New York: One World, 2021): 45–61; Gerda Lerner, ed., *Black Women in White America: A Documentary History* (New York: Pantheon Books 1972). Kali Nicole Gross, "African American Women, Mass Incarceration, and the Politics of Protection," *The Journal of American History* 102, no. 1 (June 2015): 25–33; Monica White, "'A Pig and a Garden': Fannie Lou Hamer and the Freedom Farms Cooperative," *Food and Foodways* 25, no. 1 (February 2017): 20–39. Erin Ryan, "Telling it from the Mountain: A Rhetorical Analysis of Fannie Lou Hamer's Speech before the Democratic National Convention," *Young Scholars in Writing* 11 (September 2014): 80–85.

10 Matteo Forgiarini, Marcello Gallucci, and Angelo Maravita, "Racism and the Empathy for Pain on Our Skin," *Frontiers in Psychology* 2, no. 108 (May 2011): 1–7.

11 Nancy Gertner, "Women and Sentencing," *American Criminal Law Review* 57, no. 4 (Fall 2020); Sophie Trawalter, Kelly M. Hoffman, and Adam Waytz, "Racial Bias in Perceptions of Others' Pain," *PLOS ONE* 7, no. 11 (November 2012): e48546, https://doi.org/10.1371/journal.pone.0048546; James D. Johnson et al., "Rodney King and OJ Revisited: The Impact of Race and Defendant Empathy Induction on Judicial Decisions," *Journal of Applied Social Psychology* 32, no. 6 (2002): 1208–23; Aneeta Rattan et al., "Race and the Fragility of the Legal Distinction between Juveniles and Adults," *PLOS ONE* 7, no. 5 (May 2012): e36680, https://doi.org/10.1371/journal.pone.0036680; Joshua H. Tamayo-Sarver et al., "Racial and Ethnic Disparities in Emergency Department Analgesic Prescription," *American Journal of Public Health* 93, no. 12 (December 2003): 2067–73.

16

WRONGFUL CONVICTIONS OF QUEER PEOPLE

Where Bias Meets Faulty Forensic Evidence

Valena Elizabeth Beety

When Kim arrived at King's Daughters Medical Center in Brookhaven, Mississippi, in March 2000, she was in a coma and in respiratory arrest. She had suffered a massive drug overdose.

Kim's Aunt Penny was in the hospital waiting room when a phone call was passed to her.

"Hi, how is Kim doing?" a husky female voice asked.

"Who is this?" asked Penny. But she had a suspicion. "Did you leave the rehab center with Kim?"

"Yes." It was Tami Vance, Kim's friend.

"Well, you should have stayed there, shouldn't you?"

"Can I come up to the hospital?"

"No."

"I'm not a user," said Tami. "I loved Kim."

Penny hung up.

Tami's girlfriend, Leigh, had also been at the rehab center. She had called the ambulance for Kim, and she too called the hospital because she was worried about Kim. Penny ended this phone call just as abruptly.

Penny was angry as well as scared. Her niece had been in a rehab program in hopes of leaving behind her history of drug dependence. But the previous day, she had left the program in the company of Leigh and Tami. Now her life was in danger. Even worse, a criminal investigation was beginning; the police thought Kim had been assaulted. To Penny, Leigh and Tami were criminals, the people who had harmed her niece.

Before long, Leigh and Tami would be pulled into an investigation that would result in long prison sentences for both of them—then, ten years later, exonerations. I am a professor and innocence litigator, and I represented Leigh after she was convicted of assaulting Kim. We proved that she and Tami were wrongfully

DOI: 10.4324/9781003169468-21

convicted, and they were freed. They had each received a 44-year sentence in prison.

How does an innocent person like Leigh become an incarcerated "criminal"? One way is false evidence presented to a jury, like bite mark evidence. Another has to do with bias, like homophobia. Leigh and Tami were the victims of both.

First Signs of Sexual Assault

Once Kim was stable, the medical center prepared to transfer her by ambulance to the hospital in Jackson. That's when emergency room doctor Joe Moak and the respiratory therapist noticed bruises on Kim. Dr. Moak categorized them as marks from physical abuse: bruises around the nipples, scrapes to her buttocks "as if she had been hit by a board or a belt," as well as swelling and redness that Dr. Moak said was "like she had been sexually abused in the vagina area and the rectal area."

Dr. Moak called the Brookhaven Police Department and spoke with Detective Nolan Jones. Detective Jones turned to the two people who had called 911 and saved Kim's life: Leigh and Tami. After Detective Jones called the hotel and talked with them, Leigh started to have an idea that suspicions were gathering around her.

The day after Kim's overdose, Detective Jones asked to speak to Leigh and Tami again, this time in person. He told them that the nursing aide had seen injuries to Kim the night before when she was bathing her. This was the first time that Leigh and Tami had any clue that authorities suspected something more than an overdose had occurred—that the police were investigating an assault in addition to the overdose. They were shocked. They had stopped at Kim's boyfriend's house on the drive from the rehab center. Had he done this? Or could it have happened at the rehab center?

Perhaps surprisingly, not many violent crimes result in jail time. Over the past 30 years, law enforcement has only found and arrested a suspect in 10% of major crimes. In only 2% of major crimes have these suspects been convicted.[1] The vast majority of *reported* crimes of violence go unsolved (and most crimes of violence go unreported).

But the case of Kim, Leigh, and Tami came with a narrative that made prosecution and conviction much more likely. The story read like this: Kim overdosed and arrived at the hospital with signs of a possible sexual assault, and she had been in the company overnight of two lesbians. These two lesbians were right down the street and willing to voluntarily talk to police. Plus, they had given police their actual home addresses and phone numbers.

This was one sexual assault the county was going to solve and prosecute.

Detective Jones Interviews Leigh

On March 14, just over a week after Kim was admitted to the hospital, Detective Jones wanted to interview Leigh and Tami again. They drove the 55 miles to meet him with Sheila, Leigh's mother. They arrived at the police station around 1 p.m. Detective Jones greeted them and suggested that Sheila go get something to eat. "This could take a while," he said.

"Thank you, Detective, I'm not hungry," Sheila replied.

"Sheila, no need to worry. I'll be treating Leigh like my own daughter."

"Do we need a lawyer?" Sheila asked.

"This is just routine questioning," Jones replied.

Sheila stayed in the waiting room, separated from Leigh and Tami, who were taken to the back of the station. When she heard a man yelling, she didn't realize it was Detective Jones—and that he was yelling at Leigh. Sheila eventually went out to Leigh's truck and took a nap. When she awoke it was five p.m. She was shocked that she had been there for so long.

"Sheila, please, come into my office," Detective Nolan told her when she re-entered the police station.

"I know Leigh didn't do this," he said. "But we're going to need her teeth impressions. Leigh has told me she's eager to give them over. In fact, she joked with me that I could have her teeth if I needed them."

"Okay," Sheila said.

"Now what about a polygraph?"

"Why, Detective, that should be no problem," Sheila said.

"You know, Sheila, Kim's family has asked me to find out who did this to Kim. I have to look into this."

"I understand, Detective Nolan."

"Did you know that Tami and Leigh were . . ." He paused. ". . . an item?"

"What?"

"That they're in a relationship?"

"Who told you that?" Sheila asked. "Did they tell you that themselves?"

"It's well known," Jones said.

He noted that Leigh's latest drug test had come back clean. "I think Tami is the one who really did this, and that Leigh knows it," he said.

"I hate drug users' code of ethics," Sheila responded.

Drug use and lesbian relationships were important to the narrative of the case that Jones was developing; it relied on the implication that such people were likely to commit sexual assault. But his story had some holes in it. By the times Jones spoke to Dr. Joe Moak a second time, Dr. Moak had become more adamant in his opinion. At this point, he said the "sexual assault injuries" that he noticed "indicated that the sexual battery was very forceful and was not a consensual act." He also said "the injuries looked like something a man would do." Dr. Moak dated the injuries "from the coloring" to two to four days before Kim arrived at the hospital. The injuries "were a few days old and were not immediate"—well before Kim overdosed. They would have had to be acquired at the rehab facility.

The doctor's statement did not fit Nolan Jones's timeline or his theory. But he would soon bring in a different kind of evidence.

Dr. Michael West Finds Bite Marks

On March 10, Dr. Michael West travelled to Jackson at the request of Detective Jones and Assistant District Attorney Jerry Rushing. Dr. West was a well-known local dentist. Jones and Rushing asked Dr. West to examine and photograph Kim's body at Baptist Memorial Hospital in Jackson, where she had been transferred from Brookhaven.

Dr. West took photos and videos of Kim, who was unconscious, after Kim's mother gave permission. These were not just any photos. Dr. West videotaped Kim's naked body with digital video and took photos with a Polaroid. He asked the nurses to spread Kim's legs, and then to spread the lips of Kim's vulva. He took photos of what he said was trauma to the vulva, bruising and redness, and "injuries to lateral aspect of right thigh."

Michael West was a forensic odontologist, meaning he studied bite marks. No medical personnel at either hospital, including intensive care unit doctors, reported seeing any bite marks on Kim. Dr. West immediately said he found a human bite mark on Kim's thigh.

Dr. West went home and drafted his report. According to his analysis, part of Kim's vulva had been chewed off. In language that suggests expertise but is in fact pseudoscientific, he wrote: "the injuries to Kim's vagina appear to be masticatory to the left labium majus and avulsion of the right labium majus, due to biting. Hematoma of the glans of clitoris is consistent with severe negative pressure. All of which is consistent with severe oral sex." In other words, according to West an assailant had chewed Kim's left labia, bitten and torn off her right labia, and then sucked on her clitoris to cause swelling.

The scenario faced by authorities was this: A 23-year-old woman, who had spiraled into substance use disorder after a traumatic event the previous year, went into treatment. At some point, either at the treatment center or afterward, she had a physically aggressive sexual encounter. There was no evidence to suggest whether it was consensual or not. Kim's memory was damaged by the overdose. An older male dentist examined her naked body without her consent. She was unconscious while this complete stranger looked over her entire body, rolled part of her body over to see "bite marks" more clearly, and thoroughly scrutinized her vulva. He did it on videotape so viewers could later see her naked body and injuries for themselves.

That night, Dr. West called one of the prosecutors, Jerry Rushing, and requested teeth impressions. Within five days, he had the dental models of Leigh and Tami.

On March 15, West examined Kim's body anew. He turned to the sets of dental molds he had brought with him: those of Tami Vance and Leigh Stubbs. However, five days later, the strawberry bruise had faded, and with it the alleged bite mark. Nevertheless, on the videorecording he created during his second visit, Dr. West pressed Leigh's dental mold into Kim's naked hip. He then took a photo of the "match"—the visual that he had just created.

As a follow-up, Dr. West decided to perform his analysis comparing the teeth molds to photos he had taken of the alleged injury five days earlier. Dr. West again found a match: Leigh Stubbs. In his words, Leigh's teeth were consistent with the bite mark. He excluded Tami as the biter.

The prosecution paid Michael West over $3,000 for his video and bite mark expertise. Later, another bill of nearly $6,000 would be charged directly to Leigh and Tami.

Charges in September

Kim was discharged from the hospital. While she continued to recover, Lincoln County prosecutors went before a grand jury to obtain an indictment against Leigh and Tami. Dr. West was their key witness. When the grand jury approved, a charge of aggravated assault was filed on September 20, 2000 against Tami Vance and Leigh Stubbs.

Neither the indictment nor the prosecution case at trial would specifically clarify what the serious bodily injury was. But the state would give the jury multiple possibilities, including chewing off Kim's vulva and biting Kim on the hip.

At trial, Dr. West testified about bite marks. His words make plain that assumptions about lesbians were at work in the case—and also that the evidence he was presenting relied on his own opinion.

Dr. West told the jury that markings may not appear to be bite marks except to an expert. "When the teeth drag over the skin, often times it leaves a mark that a lay person would not see as a bite mark," he said. Referring to the photograph of Kim's hip, he told the jury, "I must admit that to a novice, this may not appear to be a bite mark by any means."

"Are bite marks any more or less prevalent in a homosexual assault than a heterosexual rape case?" Prosecutor Lampton asked.

"In male homosexuality, in those cases of violence, there seems to be a much greater propensity of bite marks," Dr. West said. "In female homosexual activity, I haven't had enough experience or read anything in the literature, but it's documented that male homosexual activity is much greater in bite marks."

Everything Dr. West said—from matching points on Leigh's teeth model to the splotchy raspberry injury on Kim's hip, to the "propensity" of homosexuals to bite people—was unreliable and unverified. His forensic odontology, his "wound pattern analysis," were speculation dressed up in scientific names and descriptors.

But on the stand, Dr. West was the king of his dominion, the only expert the prosecution needed to call. To reaffirm his credentials, Prosecutor Lampton asked, "When you lecture in China or to Scotland Yard or to the FBI or to other dentists, are you telling them basically just what you've told this jury, showing them the way you compare bite marks and the techniques that are used?"

"Well, of course, we go into a lot greater detail, but yes, it's the same protocol," Dr. West said.

Lampton continued. "So, in a rape case or a homosexual rape case, you would expect to find bite marks? It would not be unusual at all to find bite marks on the skin?"

"No, it wouldn't be unusual," Dr. West answered.

"In fact," Lampton asked, "it would almost be expected?"

"Almost."

Dr. Galvez, A Forensic Pathology Expert for the Defense

Leigh's attorney called Dr. Rodrigo Galvez, an expert in pathology who would testify to forensic odontology. After medical school, Dr. Galvez had taken additional training to become a board-certified forensic pathologist. Then he went back to school and became a board-certified psychiatrist. He was non-controversial.

Dr. Galvez began his testimony by noting that he did not see any vaginal trauma. "It's important not to make mistakes," he told the jury. "And when I read the first report of Dr. West and then I saw the movies, there was a big mistake. . . . There was no trauma to the vagina."

It was seemingly an "Aha!" moment—but was quickly deflated.

"The trauma was to the vulva, V-U-L-V-A," he continued.

"So, I proceed to look at the videotapes, and sure enough, the labia majora, and it was torn more so on the right side than on the left side. There were pieces missing," Galvez concluded.

Significantly, he said that there was no evidence of chewing.

Dr. Galvez testified that he did not see the swelling of the clitoris, didn't see signs of sucking or "severe negative pressure." Dr. Galvez added, "What I can tell you, and I am under oath, with absolute degree of certainty, there is nothing that can prove there was chewing."

But then his testimony—and the defense case itself—went off the rails. Even Leigh's defense was infected by bias against people like her.

"Could be done by hands, by instrument, sometimes sadistic people get pliers, or those nail pullers," Dr. Galvez speculated. "I know that to you, that is very violent. I've seen it. And when they pull it, clamp and mutilate the nipple, not necessarily chewing. Did I answer your question?"

"Yes, sir," Defense Attorney Barnett responded. "Why don't we move on to—why don't we move on to the trauma on her hip. . . . What you're saying is on the hip it would be very hard to get somebody's entire mouth with every tooth in their mouth to make a bite there?"

"Not to leave so many teeth," Dr. Galvez responded. "You can leave so many teeth marks because you can squeeze and literally take a good bite, but there would be another change, there would be superficial cuts or abrasions or tears on the skin that were not there."

But then Galvez returned to the vulva.

"That in the vulva could be a bite, could be," he suggested. "Although I am telling you [it] can be done by many other ways, too, because [a] bite like this chews up a piece of tissue."

Dr. Galvez's primary contribution to the defense was that animal bites are U-shaped, like the mark on Kim's hip, while human bites are round or oval. (However, 14 years later, members of the American Board of Forensic Odontology were asked to examine a bite mark and determine first, whether it was human or animal, and second, whether it matched the human dentition provided. They couldn't even agree on whether it was an animal or human bite mark.[2])

Ultimately, Dr. Galvez testified that he didn't believe the marks on the hip were the result of a bite, by either an animal or a human.

Prosecutor Lampton began his cross-examination by greeting Dr. Galvez.

"Dr. Galvez, good to see you again," Lampton said. "You've testified in this court; you've sat in that chair before."

"Mr. Lampton, I am under oath, and I have to tell you the truth: I already had the honor and pleasure to work with you," Dr. Galvez said.

"Thank you," Lampton responded.

"And I take you as a dear friend of mine," Dr. Galvez added.

"We've known each other for several years to say the least," Lampton confirmed. "Twenty-five years. Your hair was dark, so was mine," he chuckled.

This verbal hug-fest did not bode well for the defense.

Dr. Galvez revealed that this was his first-ever testimony on bite marks. He had testified as a pathologist and as a psychiatrist, but not on the subject of bite marks. He was not a dentist, let alone a forensic odontologist. He said he did not even know any forensic odontologists.

Lampton asked, "Would you say that the bite mark to the vulva—or you said the mark to the vulva where it was excised or cut off, that that could be a bite?"

"That could be a bite, could be done with another instrument, including the hands," Dr. Galvez conceded. "But in the heat of the moment, sometimes they proceed to tear out pieces of tissue with hands."

"Would you expect to find biting, or would biting be consistent with a lesbian rape-type situation? In a homosexual rape?" Lampton asked.

"Yes," Dr. Galvez confirmed. "In homosexual crimes, all, they are very sadistic. Most violent times I've seen in my experience are homosexual to homosexual. They do what we call overkill. They do tremendous damage, tremendous damage."

"They are brutal assaults?" Lampton suggested.

"Yes, sir," Dr. Gonzalez declared. "They're more gory. The more repulsive crimes I've ever seen were homosexual to homosexual."

Dr. Galvez's testimony capped—or perhaps sunk—the defense case. Tami's attorney didn't call a single witness. Both women were convicted and sentenced to 44 years in prison.

Forensic Evidence Problem: Faulty Scientific Evidence

In its 2009 report *Strengthening Forensic Science in the United States: A Path Forward*, the National Academy of Sciences (NAS) criticized forensic evidence, particularly hair matching, bloodstain patterns, and bite mark analysis. For decades, this forensic evidence has been regularly admitted in criminal trials, in part due to a lack of robust pretrial discovery of evidence by prosecutors.[3]

The NAS report implored judges to re-examine any thoughtless admission of forensic evidence at trial and issued recommendations to ensure that criminal courts only admitted scientifically valid and reliable evidence. The report reserved particularly harsh criticism for the forensic odontology subdiscipline of bite mark comparison analysis.

The use of bite mark analysis in North America dates back to the infamous Salem witch trials. A Massachusetts colony "witch hunter" alleged that a local minister was recruiting young girls to practice witchcraft. As his only proof, he argued that the minister's teeth matched purported bite marks on the girls, and the prosecution forced open the minister's mouth at trial to present his teeth. Reverend Burroughs was convicted and executed. He was posthumously exonerated.

Bite mark analysis relies on a belief that each human has unique dentition, and that human skin accurately records those unique dentition features. Neither of these beliefs has been scientifically proven. Instead, the NAS found that bite marks on skin change over time and can be distorted by swelling, healing, and natural changes in the skin. Bite mark analysts also lack a standard for indicating bite marks, and their findings vary wildly.

The NAS Report concluded that there is no scientific evidence that bite mark comparison analysis can match a bite mark to a biter. Analysts cannot correctly and reliably identify a bite mark as made by a human instead of an animal. Analysts cannot accurately identify a bite mark at all, as shown by their own internal studies.

But bite mark evidence—like other pseudoscientific "forensic evidence"—is responsible for dozens of wrongful convictions, including Leigh and Tami's. Even when false evidence or false testimony is revealed, courts won't necessarily free the person they sent to prison.

Cases are frozen at the time of the conviction. Our laws discourage judges from revisiting the evidence and convictions. The premise of science is that hypotheses are tested and re-tested; the premise of our criminal legal system is that there are winners and losers. The finality of a conviction trumps other considerations. Courts refuse to change a trial's outcome even when the facts change, even when scientific evidence is proven wrong. Science is an evolving story, while criminal procedure strains to control or banish alternative narratives once a conviction is final.

We need two solutions. We must prevent faulty forensic evidence and testimony from entering at trial, and address faulty forensic evidence and testimony discovered post-conviction.

Criminalizing and Pathologizing Queer People

Pseudoscientific evidence played an important part in the wrongful conviction of Leigh and Tami; so did their identity. As lesbians, they faced bias that made police, prosecutors, jury, and judge more likely to believe that they had committed a grisly assault.

As Joey Mogul, Andrea Ritchie, and Kay Whitlock write in *Queer (In)Justice: The Criminalization of LGBT People in the United States*, LGBTQ+ identity has long been associated "with concepts of *danger, degeneracy, disorder, deception, disease, contagion, sexual predation, depravity, subversion, encroachment, treachery*, and *violence*."[4] As a result, queer people live with a constant "specter of criminality." What scholars call queer criminal archetypes directly influence policing and punishment of people who are queer or not acceptably gendered.

Gender and sexual nonconformity has often been pathologized. Psychiatrists historically labeled LGBTQ+ people as mentally ill. Around World War II, criminologists labeled lesbians as "menacing social types," extrapolating from incarcerated lesbians to the broader population.[5] Race influenced these portrayals; criminologists often described White incarcerated lesbians as victims or as only "temporary" lesbians. By the 1960s, criminologists labeled all incarcerated lesbians as "sexual aggressors," and had a particular disdain for White, working-class lesbians.

Queer people have not only been pathologized; their identities have also been outlawed. A longstanding historical example of the criminalization of queerness can be found in sumptuary laws, which allowed people to be arrested because of what they were wearing. In the US, laws against cross-dressing date back to 1845, but some were enforced until the 1980s. Some laws required people to wear three articles of clothing that matched the gender they were assigned at birth. Such laws and prohibitions signaled that everyone must conform to particular ideas about what to wear and how to act—not just queer people.

Other laws addressed sex that falls outside a very narrow heterosexual norm. Oral sex was made a felony by the state of California in 1915. By the 1950s, all states criminalized sodomy—anal and oral sex—in some form. In the 1960s, punishment for sodomy included prison sentences of two to ten years. Until the late twentieth century, prosecutors and police erratically punished people who appeared queer and had queer sex. Although the laws applied to straight people as well, it was almost exclusively gay men who were prosecuted for violations.

In many places "lewd conduct" laws are still on the books; they tend to be used against trans people and queer people of color. Individual officers can decide what counts as "lewd" and whom to arrest. LGBTQ+ identities are criminalized, medicalized, and pathologized, despite decades of research proving that LGBTQ+ people are not intrinsically predatory, pathological, or deviant.

These abstract associations have had dire consequences for queer people. For example, lesbians have been overrepresented on death row. In 1993, case studies found that women sentenced to death were frequently characterized as "manly" and "man-hating." They went to trial and were punished, both for breaking the law and for defying gender roles and femininity. Even if they were not confirmed lesbians, the media had described these women as possibly lesbian or portrayed them as masculine. The media rarely discussed how most of the women on death row were survivors of abuse. Instead, narratives justified male violence against women by alleging the survivor was a lesbian.[6]

Laws and norms about gender identity and sexuality have certainly come a long way since the 1950s. In 1961, Illinois became the first state to legalize consensual sodomy. This marked a wave of decriminalization, particularly when states adopted the Model Penal Code, which did not criminalize consensual adult sodomy. Gay and lesbian activists used empirical research by Alfred Kinsey and Evelyn Hooker to openly advocate that the psychiatric profession drop its diagnosis of homosexuality as a mental disease. In 1973, homosexuality was dropped from the Diagnostic and Statistical Manual of Mental Disorders (the DSM).

By 2003, 40 states had decriminalized sodomy. (Mississippi, where Leigh and Tami were convicted, was one of the ten that hadn't.) That year, the US Supreme Court decision *Lawrence v. Texas* finally legalized private sexual conduct between consenting adults. The Court found that anti-sodomy laws were unconstitutional because they violated an individual's right to privacy. So, since 2003, private sexual conduct between consenting adults has been legal across the United States. In other words, it's not a crime to be gay.

Lawrence v. Texas was not a unanimous decision, however. Justice Antonin Scalia's stinging dissent reads like a summary of stereotypes against queer people: "Many Americans do not want persons who openly engage in homosexual conduct as partners in their business, as scoutmasters for their children, as teachers in their children's schools, or as boarders in their home. They view this as protecting themselves and their families from a lifestyle that they believe to be immoral and destructive." The Mississippi statute criminalizing consensual oral and anal sex, Mississippi Code §97–29–59, is still on the books, even though *Lawrence v. Texas* makes such laws unconstitutional. Fourteen states still have laws against consensual sodomy; Kansas criminalizes sodomy between "members of the same sex," and Texas outlaws "homosexual conduct."

While these laws can't be enforced, they can give police cover to arrest gay people. When a sheriff in Baton Rouge, Louisiana enforced "sting" operations to entrap and arrest gay men under the state anti-sodomy statute, he told the press, "This is a law that is currently on the Louisiana books, and the sheriff is charged with enforcing the laws passed by our Louisiana Legislature. . . . Whether the law is valid is something for the courts to determine, but the sheriff will enforce the laws that are enacted."[7]

The prosecutor later dropped the charges. Stories, narratives, can change. And people in power can make different decisions.

Bias and Wrongful Convictions

Leigh and Tami weren't charged with being gay. But perhaps they were arrested and imprisoned because they were. The "expert" forensic testimony that put them behind bars matched up with biases that told those judging them that lesbians were more likely to commit violent, deviant acts. When I took the case, I didn't think these biases could lead to wrongful convictions. Now I worry they lead to far more than we know about.

The carceral state relies on creating binaries: innocent or guilty, law-abiding or deviant, good or bad. Laws codify norms of acceptable conduct alongside existing prejudices in order to control behavior. Then the criminal legal system ostracizes and punishes people for violating these laws.

Laws can only maintain their legitimacy if we accept the criminal system's own story that laws, and punishment, are impartial. They are not.

Fortunately for Leigh and Tami, we uncovered crucial evidence from the FBI relevant to their case. The prosecution had failed to disclose the FBI evidence at the time of trial—evidence that exonerated the two women. Dr. West recanted his bite mark testimony against Leigh and Tami. "Throw the bite marks out," he said. "When I testified in this case, I believed in the uniqueness of human bite marks. I no longer believe in that."

After ten years in prison, Leigh and Tami were exonerated. Their story has a happy ending. But I hope their case will teach us to take bias seriously, and recognize its impact on who is arrested, prosecuted, and convicted in our criminal legal system.

Valena Elizabeth Beety is Professor of Law at Arizona State University's Sandra Day O'Connor College of Law and the Deputy Director of the Academy for Justice, a criminal justice center connecting research with policy reform. Previously, Professor Beety served as a law professor and the founding director of the West Virginia Innocence Project at the West Virginia University College of Law. Her experiences as a federal prosecutor in Washington, DC and as an innocence litigator in Mississippi and West Virginia, shape her research and writing on wrongful convictions, forensic evidence, the opioid crisis, and incarceration. Professor Beety has successfully exonerated wrongfully convicted clients, obtained presidential grants of clemency for drug offenses, and served as an elected board member of the national Innocence Network and an appointed commissioner on the West Virginia Governor's Indigent Defense Commission. She is the coeditor of the *Wrongful Convictions Reader* (Carolina Academic Press, 2008, 2022), and the author of *Manifesting Justice: Wrongly Convicted Women Reclaim Their Rights* (Citadel Press, 2022).

Notes

1 Shima Baradaran Baughman, "How Effective Are Police? The Problem of Clearance Rates and Criminal Accountability," *Alabama Law Review* 72, no. 1 (November 2020): 94.
2 Adam Freedman and Iain Pretty, *Construct Validity of Bitemark Assessments Using the ABFO Decision Tree* (American Board of Forensic Odontology, 2015), https://online.wsj.com/public/resources/documents/ConstructValidBMdecisiontreePRETTYFREEMAN.pdf.
3 National Research Council of the National Academies, *Strengthening Forensic Science in the United States: A Path Forward* (Washington, DC: National Academies Press, 2009), 175–76.
4 Joey Mogul, Andrea Ritchie, and Kay Whitlock, *Queer (In)Justice: The Criminalization of LGBT People in the United States*, 1st ed. (Boston: Beacon Press, 2012), 23.

5 Kathryn Ann Farr, "Defeminizing and Dehumanizing Female Murderers: Depictions of Lesbians on Death Row," *Women & Criminal Justice* 11, no. 1 (2000): 54.
6 Ruthann Robson, *Lesbian (Out) Law: Survival Under the Rule of Law* (Ithaca, NY: Firebrand Books, 1992); Farr, "Defeminizing and Dehumanizing Female Murderers."
7 Meredith Bennett-Smith, "Louisiana Police Sting Targets, Arrests Gay Men for Sex Using Unconstitutional Anti-Sodomy Law," *HuffPost*, July 29, 2013.

17

DISABILITY, AESTHETICS, AND THE MAKING OF A "CRIMINAL"

Jasmine E. Harris

In recent years, the public has grown to recognize how the burdens of criminality fall disproportionately on people of color. Far less known or discussed is that these burdens also fall on people with disabilities.[1] In this chapter, I will first discuss how (and at what points) people with disabilities become involved with the criminal justice system. This discussion will illustrate how disability itself is criminalized. Then, I will argue that the disproportionate burden placed on people with disabilities by the justice system is rooted in what I call the *aesthetics of disability*. When people perceive disability, they are responding to a set of markers that trigger negative affective responses and ultimately lead a mind or body to receive a label of deviance and criminality. This claim has broad ramifications. It shows how structural ideals of beauty affect moral judgments about behavior and construct certain bodies and minds as "criminal." It asks how society "sees" and subsequently identifies disability in everyday interactions. Using a critical disability lens to examine the question "What Is a criminal?" gives new insight into the ways in which society perceives, surveils, judges, and punishes deviance.

As a preliminary matter, I use the term "disability" in its broadest sense; that is, beyond its legal, medical, or technical definitions or restrictions. Despite its popular portrayal as a narrow group of people with extreme functional impairments (often physical and often "visible" to the onlooker), disability exists along a very organic, broad continuum of functional capabilities of the body and mind that may be more or less "visible" depending on society's values and resource distribution. The Centers for Disease Control estimates that approximately 61 million (one in four) adults in the United States have one or more disabilities.[2] When you include the number of young people ages three to 21 receiving special education services, the absolute number of people with disabilities increases by an estimated 7.3 million.[3] Furthermore, most (if not all) people will experience disability directly through temporary or long-term impairments (for example, those associated with aging).

DOI: 10.4324/9781003169468-22

Disability and the Criminal Justice System

People with disabilities experience disproportionate contacts with all aspects of the criminal justice system,[4] from surveillance and arrests to jails and prisons.[5] They represent roughly 50% of those killed by law enforcement in the United States.[6] Notably, disability does not exist in a vacuum, but interacts with other axes of marginalization, including race, national origin, immigration status, gender, sexuality, class, and geographic location. A recent empirical study, for example, estimates that more than 50% of Black people with disabilities have been arrested at least once by age 28, relatively twice the finding for White people with disabilities.[7]

Disability plays an important role in stages of the criminal justice process like law enforcement interrogation and the plea-bargaining process. This can lead to wrongful convictions and, in states with capital punishment, even death. One study surveyed more than 1200 people with psychiatric disabilities about their experience in the plea-bargaining process and concluded that 37% of them reported having falsely pled guilty at one point in their lives, in part motivated by a desire to end interrogations.[8] Another study researching false confessions found that 43% of them were made by people with disabilities, far outstripping the proportion of people with disabilities in the general population.[9]

One reason for this is that textbook methods of police interrogations may lead to false confessions because some individuals with intellectual and developmental disabilities (IDD) may be unable to understand the adversarial nature of interrogations. "Good cop" tactics may mislead the individual into a false sense of security pre- and post-Miranda warnings.[10] Furthermore, the individual with IDD may have a desire for affirmation and connection and, consequently, misunderstand the "good cop" behavior, particularly when coupled with their negative experience under interrogation by the "bad cop." While police interrogations, by design, focus on this "good cop/bad cop" strategy, the difference in the case of intellectual and developmental disabilities, for example, is that the person with IDD lacks the capacity (through experience, education, or cognitive impairment) to identify and respond to this coercive strategy. Similarly, the use of leading questions that build on each other presents a danger of confusion for some with cognitive impairments in processing speed. Furthermore, when these questions are asked by the "good cop," they may present an opportunity to bond or please from the perspective of the person with IDD. Although coercive interrogation practices and false confessions affect nondisabled people in the criminal justice system as well, given the high percentage of people with mental disabilities among those who falsely confess, the negative effects of false confessions fall disproportionally on those with disability.

Legal remediation of the disparate treatment of people with disabilities in the criminal justice system, while possible, raises certain practical challenges. First, remediation, by definition, occurs after a disabled individual has experienced the trauma and violence of the criminal justice system. Release from prison or other carceral institutions may remedy the improper confinement, expungement may allow for future employment, but law cannot make the individual whole in terms of lost opportunities, experiences, relationships, education, employment, and, in capital cases, the life itself. Second, remediation requires an institutional actor to become aware of disability (to "see" it) and recognize, ex post, the effects of disability on the individual enough to retroactively review prior stages in the criminal justice pipeline (arrest, interrogation, confession, etc.). Third, the law itself creates hurdles to remediation. In death penalty cases, for example, the Supreme Court has ruled that executing people with intellectual disabilities violates the Eighth Amendment's prohibition on cruel and unusual punishment. However, legal doctrine is highly localized and medicalized in this area. State statutes define the legal contours of capacity to be put to death, yet the actual nuances of functional capacity are reduced to medical testimony regarding performance on IQ tests and standard deviations and rates of error rather than a more holistic examination that would consider structural conditions that may weigh on the individual's IQ, access to special education services, and accommodations as a child.

In addition to its disproportionate effects on people with disabilities, the criminal justice system *creates* new disabilities. Once incarcerated, close to two in five, or 38%, of all state and federal prisoners report at least one disability. That rate is more than twice that of the general population's self-reporting, which suggests that many of those disabilities are acquired after incarceration.[11] The exercise of state violence creates disability (and possible death) at all stages, including violence in the arrest process and the creation of psychological trauma through contacts with law enforcement, prosecutors, defense counsel, judges, courts, corrections officers, and other state actors. For some people who enter the system without a disability, the conditions of carceral experience—including poor prison conditions and poor available health care—can produce physical and mental disabilities including anxiety, depression, or post-traumatic stress disorder.[12] To give one example: after his three-year detention in the Rikers Island jail, awaiting trial for allegedly stealing a backpack when he was 16 years old (with two of those years spent in solitary confinement), Kalief Browder died by suicide.[13] An example of a person who became physically disabled in custody is Cheryl Weimar. While incarcerated in a Florida prison, she was assigned to clean toilets, but was unable to complete the task. This triggered an altercation with and beating by prison officers. Weimar endured serious physical injuries, including permanent paralysis of the legs.[14]

Intersections of Disability with Other Identities

People with disabilities also hold other, intersecting identities. A person with a disability who is Black, for example, is more likely to become justice-involved than one who is White; women with disabilities encounter different treatment than men. The following examples show some of the complex interactions of disability with race and gender. These few instances barely scratch the surface of representing a much larger population of people: those with intersecting identities that "make a criminal" in different ways. Consider how disability (and other marginalized identities) operates in each one of the examples below to construct "criminality."

Reginald "Neli" Latson, an 18-year-old teenager with autism, was sitting on the lawn outside of his local public library waiting for the doors to open when a police officer approached him asking for his identification. The officer was responding to a call about a "suspicious" Black male, possibly with a gun. Latson, who had committed no crime, experienced a "fight or flight" response when the officer attempted to restrain him. In the process, the officer sustained an injury leading him to arrest Latson and agree to press charges; the court sentenced Latson to ten years in a state prison. Once incarcerated, Latson experienced long periods in solitary confinement and, at one point, was placed on suicide watch.[15] Latson ultimately received an official pardon from the governor of Virginia, but his life is forever altered.

Reporting on his pardon, a *Washington Post* writer explained: "On the day of his arrest, Latson was not just a Black teenager. He was a Black, autistic teenager. And both parts of his identity matter when talking about his case."[16] This quote aptly captures the intersectionality required to understand how blackness and disability come together to create a criminal profile for Latson and, in the process, became a self-fulfilling prophecy. The 911 caller and the officer "saw" blackness as deviance; Latson's behavioral response—a highly sensitive "fight or flight" response associated with autism—became the evidence of his criminality in the eyes of the officer and the criminal justice system.

Atypical communication, like behavior or appearance, similarly constructs criminality. Magdiel Sánchez, a 35-year-old deaf Latino, was sitting on his porch in Oklahoma City when a police unit, responding to a hit-and-run accident, approached his address based on information from a witness to the accident.[17] He was holding a two-foot metal pipe with a leather strap. Neighbors later reported that was not out of the ordinary; he often carried a stick to ward off the stray dogs. As the police approached Sánchez, neighbors yelled to the police that Sánchez was deaf and could not understand the commands they were shouting at him. One officer opened fire on Sánchez, while the other used a taser when Sánchez was within 15 feet of them. Sánchez died of his wounds. Police statements noted that the officers' use of deadly force was in response to Sánchez's weapon (the two-foot metal pipe) and the fact that Sánchez was approaching them despite their instructions to stop. Sánchez was not involved in the hit-and-run accident. The police officers saw Sánchez as a threat, and, like Neli Latson, his disability made him unable to comply with their commands and served as a justification for greater use of force.

Disabled women of color also experience the compounding effects of race and disability with the added effects of gender, particularly in the case of mental, psychiatric, and psychosocial disabilities. In 2016, a New York City Police Department sergeant fatally shot Deborah Danner, a 66-year-old Black woman with schizophrenia. Officers responded to a call that Danner was shouting and tearing down posters in her room. While attempting to convince her to leave her room, one of the officers reached for Danner, who then picked up a nearby baseball bat; the officer alleged that he shot Danner in self-defense.[18] Her case is unusual in one way: she left behind a written account of what it was like to live under the dangers of law enforcement officers' perceptions of disability as a disabled Black woman. In a 2012 essay, Danner captured the experience of police interactions for many disabled people: "We are all aware of the all too frequent news stories about the mentally ill who come up against law enforcement instead of mental health professionals and end up dead."[19] She illustrates her point by sharing the story of another disabled woman called Gompers "who was killed by police by shotgun because she was perceived as a 'threat to the safety' of several grown men who were also police officers. They used deadly force to subdue her because **they were not trained sufficiently in how to engage the mentally ill in crisis**."[20] Tragically, her own death would result from the same cause.

As Danner noted of Gompers's shooting, "[T]his is not an isolated event." In 2008, San Francisco police officers responding to a call from a group home manager about a resident in crisis shot but did not kill Theresa Sheehan, a 56-year-old White woman with psychiatric disabilities. The police officers alleged they acted in self-defense as Sheehan threatened them with a knife. Notably, the group home manager called for assistance to take Sheehan to the hospital for evaluation and potential short-term civil commitment to facilitate her treatment. The officers knew of her disability and the concerns of the group home manager. Sheehan survived 14 shots from the officers' guns and sustained serious injuries. She later sued the City of San Francisco under Title II of the Americans with Disabilities Act for failing to accommodate her disability and the responding officers in their personal capacities for use of excessive force under the Fourth Amendment.[21] The City argued in its merits brief to the Court that the ADA analysis was inapplicable because Sheehan posed a "direct threat" to the officers which defeated her "qualification" as a person with a disability entitled to reasonable modifications in the arrest process.[22] Sheehan's disabilities, like those of the other disabled individuals discussed here, offered justified grounds for surveillance, control, arrest, and the use of force precisely because of how they were understood (or not) by law enforcement and the public more broadly. Perceptions of threatening and deviant behavior rely on ableist expectations, as the following section explains.

The Aesthetics of Disability and Criminality

People with disabilities have disproportionate contacts with the criminal justice system from policing to incarceration. As suggested above, one reason for this may be the lack of training and understanding about disability and mental health. However, I argue that there are deeper reasons that have to do with how we see the world and each other. What role do perception and aesthetics play in the criminalization of people with disabilities?

The word *aesthetics* refers to an area of study that seeks to understand human experiences rooted in beauty and pleasure. In present practice, aesthetics includes not only esoteric study of certain works of art, but also applies to contemporary (and less extraordinary) objects such as food, fashion, events, activities, and the bodies of ordinary people.[23] In this section, I discuss how the perception and aesthetic valuing of people's bodies through the lens of disability can cause the unjust treatment of disabled people shown in the previous section.

When we perceive another person, we do not simply see what they look like. Perception is a socio-political act, the product of individual and collective history and experiences. Those experiences give meaning to differences in physical appearance—skin tone, facial symmetry, body shapes. The images we see trigger emotional, sensory, bodily reactions. For much of history, these reactions have been understood as involuntary, predetermined, and hardwired in the brain. As the theory goes, hardwired reactions prompt predetermined emotions about the person bearing the physical differences; these emotions, in turn, may cause individuals to act in certain ways. We see; we feel; we act. More recent neuroscience research complicates this theory. While reactions to people's appearance may appear automatic, new evidence suggests that emotions are constructed through an interaction between the brain and experiential learning.[24] In other words, what we have learned from our society affects how we perceive others' appearance and behavior. For example, imagine a person who is eating with their feet rather than their hands. A viewer might react with disgust, which may be popularly understood as a fear of disease or contagion. But the latest research suggests that this response, instead, may reflect human conditioning to ableist norms of eating with one's hands and utensils. If we understand certain behaviors as indicating deviation from able-bodied norms, we react to those behaviors negatively.

As discussed above, perceptions of disability intersect with other categories. For example, policing at the intersection of race, disability, and gender draws upon popular tropes of Black women as "angry," "loud," "crazy" "welfare queens" to construct their perceived deviance. Dr. Celeste Henery paints a vivid picture of how aesthetics produce criminality in the case of Black women with disabilities: "Magnified by black skin, their bodies and actions are suspect of irrational states of mind: their movements unpredictable and threatening, their laughter possibly a sign of madness, their dissent or anger, aggressive."[25]

The object of aesthetic admiration, what we perceive to be "beautiful," is highly normative—in other words, it reflects what society tells us we *should* admire. Consider, for example, children's fairytales in which wicked, ugly witches scheme to steal eternal beauty from fair-skinned and -haired princesses, who embody kindness and all that is good. What we like or dislike, find pleasurable or distasteful, depends on a set of collective norms shaped by perceptions of race, color, national origin, class, sexuality, gender, age, and disability. While beauty standards change slightly with fashions and trends, beauty norms have consistent structural elements over time: whiteness, thinness, facial symmetry, tall stature, and, importantly, able bodies.[26] In the past, beauty standards varied somewhat by geographic region, but increasing global connectivity through technology has reduced the variation in what little difference existed, making the structural roots of beauty much clearer.[27] If we say beauty is in the eye of the beholder, we're using an individualist lens that masks the structural dimensions of beauty, and may fail to see how these structures underwrite resource allocation and social organization.

While beauty standards might seem of little relevance to the criminal justice system, they are entwined with conceptions of morality, worthiness, and deviance—all of which can have both direct and indirect effects on how people are policed, sentenced, and so on. From fairy tales to novels and movies, cultural texts tell us that beauty is linked to goodness, and even as adults, people are prone to this fallacy.[28] This is particularly important to how we think about the next piece of the puzzle: action and conduct. If we perceive a person as being outside an aesthetic norm, we might treat them differently. Aesthetics trigger emotional responses, which we understand to be visceral but instead are conditioned by social structures and privileges; then people act based on those emotions. The fearful, suspicious conduct of people in the justice system toward people with disabilities, based on such responses, has more to do with existing norms than objective knowledge of deviance or danger. Consider "thinness" and how this intersects with race and perceptions of criminality captured in police reports. Sophia King, a Black disabled woman, was fatally shot by law enforcement officers at her home (like Sheehan). The police report described King as "big," "large," and "tall" (she was 5'7").[29]

There is no biological set of visible markers of disability; what "looks like" disability is aesthetic, not objective. Particular physical features and atypical behaviors have come to be associated with disability, including facial tics, the absence of eye contact, repetitive behaviors, and drooling.[30] In my prior research, I refer to these socially constructed physical or behavioral "markers" collectively as the *aesthetics of disability*.[31] Although society treats these markers as biologically determined, obvious, and non-contentious, they are highly normative and reflect social values and fears. As I write elsewhere, the aesthetics of disability "reflect a collective preference that emphatically denies vulnerability, mortality, and uncertainty."[32] Said differently, aesthetics shape who is perceived as deviant and dangerous, giving public and private actors (police, community members) permission to surveil and regulate them.

Attention to aesthetics helps us understand the construction of criminality, what physical features and behaviors are considered socially undesirable, and, by extension, grounds for suppression, restraint, or behavioral management. Aesthetic affective theories such as the one discussed in this chapter show us how perception itself, the result of deeply rooted associations between images and emotions, can transform disability and neurodivergence into criminality. This chapter introduced the concept of *the aesthetics of disability* as one critical lens to better understand the construction of the criminal. Criminality, like disability, reflects society's values and choices about how to organize itself, which bodies to privilege and which to police, surveil, and punish.[33]

Is it possible to change the aesthetic responses that lead to the criminalization of people with disabilities? The research on aesthetic "reeducation" cautions us to proceed intentionally but realistically, as the roots of aesthetic discrimination run deep across other axes of subordination such as race, gender, immigration status, sexuality, age, religion, class, geography, and on and on. It might seem that the aesthetics of disability are so deeply rooted that there's little to be done about them. But on the contrary, our ability to see the social constructedness of our aesthetic responses means that there is room to generate new norms of beauty, behavior, and interconnectedness. These efforts will require an interdisciplinary response (drawing on law, neuroscience, media, sociology, and psychology) to change public representations of disability. Law has a role to play, but activism and advocacy that center those most impacted by these issues will be the key to long term change.

Jasmine E. Harris, Professor of Law in the University of Pennsylvania's Carey Law School, is a law and inequality legal scholar with expertise in disability law, antidiscrimination law, and evidence. Professor Harris's work seeks to address the relationship between law and equality with a focus on law's capacity to advance social norms of inclusion in the context of disability. Her recent academic articles appear in such publications as the *Columbia Law Review*, *New York University Law Review*, *University of Pennsylvania Law Review*, *Yale Law Journal Forum*, and *Cornell Law Review*, as well as peer-reviewed journals. Professor Harris recently joined leading evidence law experts as a coeditor of the preeminent evidence treatise, *McCormick on Evidence*. Professor Harris also writes frequently about disability and equality law for popular audiences. Her essays have appeared in the *New York Times*, *San Francisco Chronicle*, *Ms. Magazine*, and *Tribune Wire*. She is regularly interviewed and has been widely quoted in publications and media outlets such as the *New York Times*, *Washington Post*, *TIME Magazine*, *Forbes*, CNBC, National Public Radio, *PBS NewsHour*, *Chronicle of Higher Education*, *Guardian*, *Harper's BAZAAR*, and *USA Today*. Professor Harris graduated magna cum laude from Dartmouth College and earned her juris doctorate from Yale Law School. She has extensive work experience in both private and public interest law.

Notes

1 See generally Jasmine E. Harris, "Reckoning with Race and Disability," *Yale Law Journal* 130, Forum 916 (June 2021), www.yalelawjournal.org/forum/reckoning-with-race-and-disability.

2 Centers for Disease Control and Prevention, "CDC: 1 in 4 US Adults Live with a Disability," press release, August 16, 2018, www.cdc.gov/media/releases/2018/p0816-disability.html.

3 National Center for Education Statistics, "Students with Disabilities," *Condition of Education*, US Department of Education: Institute of Education Sciences (updated May 2021), https://nces.ed.gov/programs/coe/indicator/cgg. Notably, the 7.3 million students receiving services does not reflect the entirety of school-aged children with disabilities in the United States. Not all students with disabilities in public schools, for example, receive special education services by choice or eligibility. In order to receive special education services under the Individuals with Disabilities Education Act, for example, students must have a disability that negatively affects their ability to access a "free appropriate public education." 20 U.S.C. §1401 (3) (A) ("The term "child with a disability" means a child—(i) with intellectual disabilities, hearing impairments (including deafness), speech or language impairments, visual impairments (including blindness),

serious emotional disturbance (referred to in this chapter as "emotional disturbance"), orthopedic impairments, autism, traumatic brain injury, other health impairments, or specific learning disabilities; and (ii) who, by reason thereof, needs special education and related services.")

4 I use the phrase "criminal justice system" broadly to encompass everything from surveillance to short-term detention in jails or prisons as well as psychiatric hospitals or forensic units.

5 This includes the overrepresentation of students with disabilities, many of whom also share other marginalized identity axes, in the "school to prison pipeline." For example, Black students with disabilities receiving special education services represented 2.3% of total student enrollment, but 8.4% of students disciplined and referred to law enforcement and 9.1% of students arrested. "Student Arrests in Allegheny County Public Schools: The Need for Transparency and Accountability," *ACLU of Pennsylvania* (January 2022), https://aclupa.org/sites/default/files/field_documents/student_arrests_allegheny_co_jan2022.pdf.

6 See, e.g., Vilissa Thompson, "Understanding the Policing of Black, Disabled Bodies," *Center for American Progress*, February 10, 2021, www.americanprogress.org/article/understanding-policing-black-disabled-bodies/. As Thompson notes, "Freddie Gray, Laquan MacDonald, Kevin Matthews, Tamir Rice, Eric Garner, Charleena Lyles, Sandra Bland, Quintonio LeGrier, Stephon Watts, Korryn Gaines, Natasha McKenna, Eric Smith, and Daniel Prude are all Black, disabled victims of state violence."

7 Thompson, "Policing of Black, Disabled Bodies." See also Erin J. McCauley, "The Cumulative Probability of Arrest by Age 28 Years in the United States by Disability Status, Race/Ethnicity, and Gender," *American Journal of Public Health* 107, no. 12 (December 2017): 1977.

8 Ram Subramanian et al., *In the Shadows: A Review of the Research on Plea Bargaining* (New York: The Vera Institute of Justice, September 2020), 45, www.vera.org/downloads/publications/in-the-shadows-plea-bargaining.pdf. See also Samson J. Schatz, "Interrogated with Intellectual Disabilities: The Risks of False Confession," *Stanford Law Review* 70, no. 2 (February 2018): 643–47, which discusses the literature on false confessions in the context of intellectual disability.

9 See, e.g., Brandon Garrett, "The Substance of False Confessions," *Stanford Law Review* 62, no. 4 (April 2010): 1051, 1094–95, which discusses a study of the content of a sample of false confessions, showing that 43 percent of those who falsely confessed were people with mental disabilities.

10 I do not imply that law enforcement is always aware of intellectual or other disability and intentionally misleads or traps individuals with disabilities; there can be cases where law enforcement officers are not aware of the manifestations of certain disabilities. Structurally, the methods of law enforcement create a flawed process that works against those with certain disabilities. However, these structural flaws are problematic and, given the weight of the stakes and the existence of legal protections and availability of research on disability and law enforcement practices, failure to account for and remedy these structural issues may rise to the level of legal liability.

11 Laura M. Maruschak, Jennifer Bronson, and Mariel Alper, *Survey of Prison Inmates, 2016: Disabilities Reported by Prisoners* (US Department of Justice: Bureau of Justice Statistics, March 2021), https://bjs.ojp.gov/content/pub/pdf/drpspi16st.pdf. This is also supported by the number of formal and informal complaints filed by incarcerated individuals against correctional officers and prisons for negligence, intentional torts (assault and battery), false imprisonment, or, in some limited cases of recklessness, emotional distress. Examples of legal authorities here are the Civil Rights Act of 1871, codified in 42 U.S.C. § 1983 (claims against state prisons and officers) and the Federal Torts Claims Act, 28 U.S.C. Part VI, Chapter 171 (claims against federal actors).

12 Rebecca Vallas, "Disabled Behind Bars," *Center for American Progress*, July 18, 2016, www.americanprogress.org/article/disabled-behind-bars/. See also Rabia Belt, "The

Fat Prisoners' Dilemma: Slow Violence, Intersectionality, and a Disability Rights Framework for the Future," *Georgetown Law Journal* 110, no. 3 (June 16, 2022): 785, which discusses how the conditions of confinement create and exacerbate obesity.

13 Benjamin Weiser, "Kalief Browder's Suicide Brought Changes to Rikers. Now It Has Led to a $3 Million Settlement," *New York Times*, January 24, 2019, www.nytimes.com/2019/01/24/nyregion/kalief-browder-settlement-lawsuit.html.

14 Adam Walser, "Officers Accused of Inmate Beating Which Left Woman Paralyzed Not Charged Nearly 3 Years Later," *ABC Action News*, April 14, 2022, www.abcactionnews.com/news/local-news/i-team-investigates/officers-accused-of-inmate-beating-which-left-woman-paralyzed-not-charged-nearly-3-years-later.

15 Latson v. Clarke, 794 Fed. Appx. 266, 268 (4th Cir. 2019). "While in solitary confinement, MCTC kept Latson alone in a cell between 22 and 24 hours each day, with limited access to recreation, phone calls, personal items, television, music, books, and magazines. Experts believe that incarceration in solitary confinement is counter-productive and increases aggressive responses for many prisoners, including those with Autism Spectrum Disorder and for Latson himself."

16 Theresa Vargas, "Neli Latson Is—Finally—Free. It Only Took 11 Years, Two Governors and a National Conversation about Race and Disability," *Washington Post*, June 23, 2021, www.washingtonpost.com/local/neli-latson-black-autistic-free/2021/06/23/1024d4e4-d446-11eb-a53a-3b5450fdca7a_story.html. See also "Neli Latson Pardon," *The Arc*, June 30, 2021, https://thearc.org/resource/neli-latson-pardon/.

17 James Doubek, "Oklahoma City Police Fatally Shoot Deaf Man Despite Yells of 'He Can't Hear,'" *National Public Radio*, September 21, 2017, www.npr.org/sections/thetwo-way/2017/09/21/552527929/oklahoma-city-police-fatally-shoot-deaf-man-despite-yells-of-he-cant-hear-you.

18 Ashley Southall, "Officer Faces Discipline 5 Years after Killing Mentally Ill Woman," *New York Times*, October 4, 2021, www.nytimes.com/2021/10/04/nyregion/nypd-killing-mental-illness.html.

19 Deborah Danner, "Living with Schizophrenia," *New York Times*, October 19, 2016, www.nytimes.com/interactive/2016/10/19/nyregion/document-Living-With-Schizophrenia-by-Deborah-Danner.html.

20 Ibid. (emphasis in original).

21 For a discussion of disability and Fourth Amendment jurisprudence, see Jamelia Morgan, "Disability's Fourth Amendment," *Columbia Law Review 122*, no. 2 (2022): 489.

22 City & County of San Francisco v. Sheehan, 575 U.S. 600 (2015); see also amicus brief in support of Respondent Theresa Sheehan, at www.apa.org/about/offices/ogc/amicus/sheehan.pdf. The district court granted summary judgment for the City of San Francisco, held that police officers are not required to consider reasonable accommodations before they act in self-defense, and dismissed the Fourth Amendment claims against the officers. The Ninth Circuit Court of Appeals reversed the district court's decision on the ADA question, holding that a jury had to decide whether the City of San Francisco should have accommodated Sheehan's psychiatric disabilities. The US Supreme Court granted certiorari on the question of reasonable accommodations when officers attempted to arrest "an armed, violent, and mentally ill suspect." Ultimately, the Court dismissed the ADA question as "improvidently granted" after the City of San Francisco reframed the issue from whether Title II applies to arrests to how it applies.

23 See, e.g., Yuriko Saito, *Everyday Aesthetics* (Oxford, UK: Oxford University Press, 2007); Thomas Leddy, *The Extraordinary in the Ordinary: The Aesthetics of Everyday Life* (Peterborough, Ontario: Broadview Press, 2013).

24 See, e.g., Lisa Feldman Barrett, *How Emotions Are Made: The Secret Life of the Brain* (New York: Houghton Mifflin Harcourt, 2017).

25 Celeste Henery, "Black Women, Police Violence, and Mental Illness," *African American Intellectual History Society: Black Perspectives*, June 28, 2017, www.aaihs.org/black-women-police-violence-and-mental-illness/.

26 See Jasmine E. Harris, "The Aesthetics of Disability," *Columbia Law Review* 119, no. 4 (May 2019): 895.
27 See, e.g., Michelle Lelwica, Emma Hoglund, and Jenna McNallie, "Spreading the Religion of Thinness from California to Calcutta: A Critical Feminist Postcolonial Analysis," *Journal of Feminist Studies in Religion* 25, no. 1 (April 2009): 19, 35–36, which discusses converging ideals of "thinness" across countries.
28 Debates about the relationship and its degree of rationality date back to early philosophers, but more contemporary research suggests that casting moral judgment on another has strong aesthetic and affective dimensions. See, e.g., Xuan Cui et al., "Different Influences of Facial Attractiveness on Judgments of Moral Beauty and Moral Goodness," *Scientific Reports* 9, no. 1 (August 2019): 1–2, and accompanying notes; and Barrett, *How Emotions Are Made,* 19, 35–36, which uses the concept of degeneracy to refute the notion that emotions have discernable, unique "fingerprints" in the brain.
29 Henery, "Black Women, Police Violence, and Mental Illness."
30 A rare physical manifestation of a biological impairment is Down's Syndrome; while the physical difference may be shared across individuals with this disability, the aesthetic marker says nothing about actual functional capabilities.
31 Harris, "The Aesthetics of Disability," 953–57, on typology of aesthetics.
32 Harris, "The Aesthetics of Disability," 957.
33 For a further discussion of the role of the disabled body in the criminal justice system, see, e.g., Jamelia N. Morgan, "Policing under Disability Law," *Stanford Law Review* 73, no. 6 (June 2021): 1401; "Rethinking Disorderly Conduct," *California Law Review* 109, no. 5 (October 2021): 1637.

BIBLIOGRAPHY

"25,000 Years Lost to Wrongful Convictions." *National Registry of Exonerations*, June 2021. www.law.umich.edu/special/exoneration/Documents/25000%20Years.pdf.

ACLU. *A Tale of Two Countries: Racially Targeted Arrests in the Era of Marijuana Reform*. New York: American Civil Liberties Union, April 2020.

Alexander, Michelle. *The New Jim Crow: Mass Incarceration in the Age of Colorblindness*. New York: The New Press, 2010.

Anderson, James F. *Criminological Theories: Understanding Crime in America*. 2nd ed. Burlington, MA: Jones & Bartlett Learning, 2015.

Archer, John. "Testosterone and Human Aggression: An Evaluation of the Challenge Hypothesis." *British Journal of Psychology* 82, pt. 1 (February 1991): 1–28. https://doi.org/10.1111/j.2044-8295.1991.tb02379.x.

Arnold, David, Will Dobbie, and Crystal S. Yang. "Racial Bias in Bail Decisions." *Quarterly Journal of Economics* 133, no. 4 (May 2018): 1885–932. https://doi.org/10.1093/qje/qjy012.

Austermuhle, Martin. "District of Corrections: Does D.C. Really Have the Highest Incarceration Rate in the Country?" *WAMU 88.5: American University Radio Local News*, September 10, 2019. https://wamu.org/story/19/09/10/district-of-corrections-does-d-c-really-have-the-highest-incarceration-rate-in-the-country/.

Austin, James, and Garry Coventry. *Emerging Issues on Privatized Prisons*. US Department of Justice, Office of Justice Programs, February 2001.

Baca, Alex, and Nick Finio. "Gentrification in DC Isn't Just a Black and White Issue." *Greater Washington*, May 25, 2020. https://ggwash.org/view/77621/gentrification-in-dc-is-not-just-a-black-and-white-issue_1.

Baguley, Ian J., Joanne Cooper, and Kim Felmingham. "Aggressive Behavior Following Traumatic Brain Injury: How Common Is Common?" *Journal of Head Trauma Rehabilitation* 21, no. 1 (January 2006): 45–56. https://doi.org/10.1097/00001199-200601000-00005.

Barrett, Lisa Feldman. *How Emotions Are Made: The Secret Life of the Brain*. New York: Houghton Mifflin Harcourt, 2017.

Bartollas, Clemens, and Frank Schmalleger. *Juvenile Delinquency*. 2nd ed. New York: Pearson Education, 2015.

Baughman, Shima Baradaran. "How Effective Are Police? The Problem of Clearance Rates and Criminal Accountability." *Alabama Law Review* 72, no. 1 (November 2020): 47–130. https://dx.doi.org/10.2139/ssrn.3566383.

Bayer, Ronald. "Crime, Punishment, and the Decline of Liberal Optimism." *Crime and Delinquency* 27, no. 2 (April 1981): 169–90. https://doi.org/10.1177%2F001112878102700201.

Beaver, Kevin M. *Biosocial Criminology: A Primer*. 1st ed. Dubuque, IA: Kendall Hunt Publishing Company, 2009.

———. "The Familial Concentration and Transmission of Crime." *Criminal Justice and Behavior* 40, no. 2 (February 2013): 139–55. https://doi.org/10.1177/0093854812449405.

Belt, Rabia. "The Fat Prisoners' Dilemma: Slow Violence, Intersectionality, and a Disability Rights Framework for the Future." *Georgetown Law Journal* 110, no. 3 (June 16, 2022): 785–833. https://ssrn.com/abstract=4138574.

Bennett-Smith, Meredith. "Louisiana Police Sting Targets, Arrests Gay Men for Sex Using Unconstitutional Anti-Sodomy Law." *HuffPost*, July 29, 2013. www.huffpost.com/entry/louisiana-police-sting-gay-men-anti-sodomy-law_n_3668116.

Benson, David Frank, and Dietrich Blumer. "Personality Changes with Frontal and Temporal Lobe Lesions." In *Psychiatric Aspects of Neurologic Disease*, edited by David Frank Benson and Dietrich Blumer. New York: Grune and Stratton, 1975.

Berdejó, Carlos. "Criminalizing Race: Racial Disparities in Plea-Bargaining." *Boston College Law Review* 59, no. 4 (2018): 1187–249. https://learning.hccs.edu/faculty/eva.foster/engl1301/final-exam-readings-nov-dec-readings/criminalizing-race-racial-disparities-in-plea-bargaining-carlos-berdejo/at_download/file.

Birzer, Michael L., and Paul F. Cromwell. *In Their Own Words: Criminals on Crime*. 7th ed. New York: Oxford University Press, 2017.

Book, Angela S., Katherine B. Starzyk, and Vernon L. Quinsey. "The Relationship Between Testosterone and Aggression: A Meta-Analysis." *Aggression and Violent Behavior* 6, no. 6 (November 2001): 579–99. http://dx.doi.org/10.1016/S1359-1789(00)00032-X.

Bostic, Bobby. *Life Goes on Inside Prison*. Self-published, 2021.

———. *Time: Endless Moments in Prison*. Self-published, 2021.

Brooks, Cornell William, Roslyn M. Brock, and Barbara Bolling-Williams. *Born Suspect: Stop-and-Frisk Abuse and the Continued Fight to End Racial Profiling in America*. Baltimore: The National Association for the Advancement of Colored People, September 2014.

Brooks-Gunn, Jeanne, and Greg J. Duncan. "The Effects of Poverty on Children." *The Future of Children* 7, no. 2 (1997): 55–71. https://doi.org/10.2307/1602387.

Bursik, Robert J. Jr. "Social Disorganization and Theories of Crime and Delinquency: Problems and Prospects." *Criminology* 26, no. 4 (November 1988): 519–52. https://doi.org/10.1111/J.1745-9125.1988.TB00854.X.

Centers for Disease Control and Prevention. "CDC: 1 in 4 US Adults Live with a Disability." Press release. August 16, 2018. www.cdc.gov/media/releases/2018/p0816-disability.html.

Chambliss, William J. "The Saints and the Roughnecks." *Society* 11, no. 1 (November 1973): 24–31. https://doi.org/10.1007/BF03181016.

Choy, Olivia, Adrian Raine, Peter H. Venables, and David P. Farrington. "Explaining the Gender Gap in Crime: The Role of Heart Rate." *Criminology* 55, no. 2 (April 2017): 465–87. http://dx.doi.org/10.1111/1745-9125.12138.

Cooke, Willard R. "The Different Psychology of the American Woman." *American Journal of Obstetrics and Gynecology* 49, no. 4 (April 1945): 457–72. https://doi.org/10.1016/S0002-9378(45)90002-0.

Cui, Xuan, Cheng Quiping, Wuji Lin, and Lei Mo. "Different Influences of Facial Attractiveness on Judgments of Moral Beauty and Moral Goodness." *Scientific Reports* 9, no. 1 (August 2019). https://doi.org/10.1038/s41598-019-48649-5.

Danner, Deborah. "Living with Schizophrenia." *New York Times*, October 19, 2016. www.nytimes.com/interactive/2016/10/19/nyregion/document-Living-With-Schizophrenia-by-Deborah-Danner.html.

d'Orban, P. T., and J. Dalton. "Violent Crime and the Menstrual Cycle." *Psychological Medicine* 10, no. 2 (May 1980): 353–59. https://doi.org/10.1017/S0033291700044123.

Doubek, James. "Oklahoma City Police Fatally Shoot Deaf Man Despite Yells of 'He Can't Hear.'" *National Public Radio*, September 21, 2017. www.npr.org/sections/thetwo-way/2017/09/21/552527929/oklahoma-city-police-fatally-shoot-deaf-man-despite-yells-of-he-cant-hear-you.

"DrugFacts: Treatment Approaches for Drug Addiction." National Institute on Drug Abuse, National Institutes of Health, January 17, 2019. https://nida.nih.gov/publications/drugfacts/treatment-approaches-drug-addiction.

DuRant, Robert H., David Altman, Mark Wolfson, Shari Barkin, Shelley Kreiter, and Daniel Krowchuk. "Exposure to Violence and Victimization, Depression, Substance Use, and the Use of Violence by Young Adolescents." *Journal of Pediatrics* 137, no. 5 (November 2000): 707–13. https://doi.org/10.1067/mpd.2000.109146.

Durlauf, Steven N., and Daniel S. Nagin. "Imprisonment and Crime: Can Both be Reduced?" *Criminology & Public Policy* 10, no. 1 (February 2011): 13–54. https://doi-org.unh.idm.oclc.org/10.1111/j.1745-9133.2010.00680.x.

Elliott, Delbert S., and Suzanne S. Agetan. "Reconciling Race and Class Differences in Self-Reported and Official Estimates of Delinquency." *American Sociological Review* 45, no. 1 (February 1980): 95–110. https://psycnet.apa.org/doi/10.2307/2095245.

Eslinger, Paul J., and Antonio R. Damasio. "Severe Disturbance of Higher Cognition After Bilateral Frontal Lobe Ablation: Patient EVR." *Neurology* 35, no. 12 (December 1985): 1731–41. https://doi.org/10.1212/wnl.35.12.1731.

Falcone, David N. *Prentice Hall's Dictionary of American Criminal Justice, Criminology, and Criminal Law*. 2nd ed. Upper Saddle River, NJ: Pearson Education, 2010.

Farr, Kathryn Ann. "Defeminizing and Dehumanizing Female Murderers: Depictions of Lesbians on Death Row." *Women & Criminal Justice* 11, no. 1 (2000): 49–66. https://doi.org/10.1300/J012v11n01_03.

Farrington, David P. "The Relationship Between Low Resting Heart Rate and Violence." In *Biosocial Bases of Violence*, edited by Adrian Raine, Patricia A. Brennan, David P. Farrington, and Sarnoff A. Mednick, 89–105. New York: Springer Science+Business Media, 1997.

Ferkenhoff, Eric. "After 43 Years in Prison on a Wrongful Conviction, Kevin Strickland Is Getting No Restitution. He's Not Alone." *USA Today*, December 9, 2021. www.usatoday.com/story/news/nation/2021/12/09/kevin-strickland-case-exposes-gaps-state-restitution-laws-wrongly-convicted-exonerated/8834538002/.

Forgiarini, Matteo, Marcello Gallucci, and Angelo Maravita. "Racism and the Empathy for Pain on Our Skin." *Frontiers in Psychology* 2, no. 108 (May 2011): 1–7. https://doi.org/10.3389%2Ffpsyg.2011.00108.

Fox, James Alan, Jack Levin, and Kenna Quinet. *The Will to Kill: Making Sense of Senseless Murder*. 5th ed. Thousand Oaks, CA: SAGE Publications, 2018.

Freedman, Adam, and Iain Pretty. "Construct Validity of Bitemark Assessments Using the ABFO Decision Tree." Presentation to the American Board of Forensic Odontology, 2015. https://online.wsj.com/public/resources/documents/ConstructValidBMdecisiontreePRETTYFREEMAN.pdf.

Friedman, Matthew. "Just Fact: As Many Americans Have Criminal Records as College Diplomas." Brennan Center for Justice, November 17, 2015. www.brennancenter.org/our-work/analysis-opinion/just-facts-many-americans-have-criminal-records-college-diplomas.

Garrett, Brandon. "The Substance of False Confessions." *Stanford Law Review* 62, no. 4 (April 2010): 1051–118. www.jstor.org/stable/40649624.

Gertner, Nancy. "Women and Sentencing." *American Criminal Law Review* 57, no. 4 (Fall 2020): 1401–10.

Grimley, Nadine. "Liberty Mom Deflects Haters, Gets $100K in Support Following Child Endangering Charge." *WKBN First News*, February 18, 2021. www.wkbn.com/news/local-news/liberty-mom-deflects-haters-gets-100k-in-support-following-child-endangering-charge/.

Gross, Alexandra. "Ernest Ray Willis." National Registry of Exonerations, last modified October 21, 2021. www.law.umich.edu/special/exoneration/Pages/casedetail.aspx?caseid=3755.

Gross, Kali Nicole. "African American Women, Mass Incarceration, and the Politics of Protection." *The Journal of American History* 102, no. 1 (June 2015): 25–33. https://doi.org/10.1093/jahist/jav226.

Gross, Samuel, Barbara O'Brien, Chen Hu, and Edward H. Kennedy. "Rate of False Conviction of Criminal Defendants Who Are Sentenced to Death." *Proceedings of the National Academy of Sciences* 111, no. 20 (April 2014): 7230–35. https://doi.org/10.1073/pnas.1306417111.

Hall, Michael. "Death Isn't Fair." *Texas Monthly*, December 2002. www.texasmonthly.com/articles/death-isnt-fair/.

———. "The State of Texas Tried to Kill Ernest Willis. But He Still Had a Lot of Living to Do." *Texas Monthly*, October 2021. www.texasmonthly.com/news-politics/texas-tried-kill-ernest-willis-still-had-living-to-do/.

Hamilton, Ramon, dir. *The wHOLE*. Castaic, CA: Think Ten Media Group, 2016.

Hare, Robert D. *The Hare Psychopathy Checklist—Revised*. 2nd ed. Toronto, ON: Multi-Health Systems, 2003.

Harris, Jasmine E. "The Aesthetics of Disability." *Columbia Law Review* 119, no. 4 (May 2019): 895–972. www.jstor.org/stable/26632274.

———. "Reckoning with Race and Disability." *Yale Law Journal* 130, Forum 916 (June 2021). www.yalelawjournal.org/forum/reckoning-with-race-and-disability

Henery, Celeste. "Black Women, Police Violence, and Mental Illness." *African American Intellectual History Society: Black Perspectives*, June 28, 2017. www.aaihs.org/black-women-police-violence-and-mental-illness/.

Henry, Jessica. *Smoke but No Fire: Convicting the Innocent of Crimes that Never Happened*. Berkeley, CA: University of California Press, 2020.

Hinton, Elizabeth, and DeAnza Cook. "The Mass Criminalization of Black Americans: A Historical Overview." *Annual Review of Criminology* 4, no. 1 (June 2020): 261–86. http://dx.doi.org/10.1146/annurev-criminol-060520-033306.

Hinton, Elizabeth, LeShae Henderson, and Cindy Reed. *An Unjust Burden: The Disparate Treatment of Black Americans in the Criminal Justice System*. New York: The Vera Institute of Justice. May 2018.

Hirschi, Travis, and Michael J. Hindelang. "Intelligence and Delinquency: A Revisionist Review." *American Sociological Review* 42, no. 4 (August 1977): 571–87. https://doi.org/10.2307/2094556.

Johnson, James D., Carolyn H. Simmons, Amanda Jordan, Leslie MacLean, Jeffrey Taddei, Duane Thomas, John F. Dovidio, and William Reed. "Rodney King and OJ Revisited:

The Impact of Race and Defendant Empathy Induction on Judicial Decisions." *Journal of Applied Social Psychology* 32, no. 6 (2002): 1208–23. https://psycnet.apa.org/doi/10.1111/j.1559-1816.2002.tb01432.x.

Kansal, Tushar. *Racial Disparities in Sentencing: A Review of the Literature*. Washington, DC: The Sentencing Project, 2005.

Kiehl, Kent A. *The Psychopath Whisperer: The Science of Those Without Conscience*. New York: Crown Publishing, 2014.

Lagerberg, Tyra, Seena Fazel, Yasmina Molero, Mikael Andersson Franko, Qi Chen, Clara Hellner, Paul Lichtenstein, and Zheng Chang. "Association Between Selective Serotonin Reuptake Inhibitors and Violent Crime in Adolescents, Young, and Older Adults—A Swedish Register-Based Study." *European Neuropsychopharmacology* 36 (July 2020): 1–9. https://doi.org/10.1016/j.euroneuro.2020.03.024.

Leddy, Thomas. *The Extraordinary in the Ordinary: The Aesthetics of Everyday Life*. Peterborough, Ontario: Broadview Press, 2013.

Lee, Matthew R., Michael O. Maume, and Graham C. Ousey. "Social Isolation and Lethal Violence across the Metro/Nonmetro Divide: The Effects of Socioeconomic Disadvantage and Poverty Concentration on Homicide." *Rural Sociology* 68, no. 1 (March 2003): 107–31. https://doi.org/10.1111/j.1549-0831.2003.tb00131.x.

Lelwica, Michelle, Emma Hoglund, and Jenna McNallie. "Spreading the Religion of Thinness from California to Calcutta: A Critical Feminist Postcolonial Analysis." *Journal of Feminist Studies in Religion* 25, no. 1 (April 2009): 19–41. http://dx.doi.org/10.1353/jfs.0.0065.

Lerner, Gerda, ed. *Black Women in White America: A Documentary History*. New York: Pantheon Books, 1972.

Lewis, Oscar. "The Culture of Poverty." *Scientific American*, October 1966: 19–25.

Martin, Eric. "Hidden Consequences: The Impact of Incarceration on Dependent Children." *National Institute of Justice Journal* 278 (May 2017). https://nij.ojp.gov/topics/articles/hidden-consequences-impact-incarceration-dependent-children.

Maruschak, Laura M., Jennifer Bronson, and Mariel Alper. *Survey of Prison Inmates, 2016: Disabilities Reported by Prisoners*. US Department of Justice: Bureau of Justice Statistics, March 2021. https://bjs.ojp.gov/content/pub/pdf/drpspi16st.pdf.

McCaghy, Charles H. *Deviant Behavior: Crime, Conflict, and Interest Groups*. New York: MacMillan, 1976.

McCauley, Erin J. "The Cumulative Probability of Arrest by Age 28 Years in the United States by Disability Status, Race/Ethnicity, and Gender." *American Journal of Public Health* 107, no. 12 (December 2017): 1977–81.

Mednick, Sarnoff A., and Karl O. Christiansen. *Biosocial Bases of Criminal Behavior*. New York: Gardner Press, 1977.

Mednick, Sarnoff A., William F. Gabrielli Jr., and Barry Hutchings. "Genetic Influences in Criminal Convictions: Evidence from an Adoption Cohort." *Science* 224, no. 4651 (May 1984): 891–94. https://doi.org/10.1126/science.6719119.

Melamed, Samantha. "Generations of Philly Families Are Incarcerated Together." *The Philadelphia Inquirer*, January 25, 2018. www.inquirer.com/crime/inq/generations-philadelphia-families-are-incarcerated-together-20180125.html.

Moffitt, Terrie E., Gary L. Brammer, Avshalom Caspi, J. Paul Fawcett, Michael Raleigh, Arthur Yuwiler, and Phil Silva. "Whole Blood Serotonin Relates to Violence in an Epidemiological Study." *Biological Psychiatry* 43, no. 6 (March 1998): 446–57. https://doi.org/10.1016/S0006-3223(97)00340-5.

Mogul, Joey, Andrea Ritchie, and Kay Whitlock. *Queer (In)Justice: The Criminalization of LGBT People in the United States*. 1st ed. Boston: Beacon Press, 2012.

Moore, Megan. "Psychological Theories of Crime and Delinquency." *Journal of Human Behavior in the Social Environment* 21, no. 3 (April 2011): 226–39. https://doi.org/10.1080/10911359.2011.564552.

Morgan, Jamelia N. "Policing Under Disability Law." *Stanford Law Review* 73, no. 6 (June 2021): 1401–69. https://ssrn.com/abstract=3689161.

———. "Rethinking Disorderly Conduct." *California Law Review* 109, no. 5 (October 2021): 1637–702. https://dx.doi.org/10.2139/ssrn.3552620.

———. "Disability's Fourth Amendment." *Columbia Law Review* 122, no. 2 (2022): 489–580. https://dx.doi.org/10.2139/ssrn.3820117.

Morse, Malcom B. "True Justice: The Disturbing Truth About Incarceration in D.C." *Georgetown Journal of Law & Modern Critical Race Perspectives*, February 17, 2020. www.law.georgetown.edu/mcrp-journal/blog/true-justice-the-disturbing-truth-about-incarceration-in-d-c/.

Natapoff, Alexandra. *Punishment without Crime: How Our Massive Misdemeanor System Traps the Innocent and Makes America More Unequal*. New York: Basic Books, 2018.

National Center for Education Statistics. "Students with Disabilities." *Condition of Education*, US Department of Education: Institute of Education Sciences (updated May 2021). https://nces.ed.gov/programs/coe/indicator/cgg

National Research Council of the National Academies. *Strengthening Forensic Science in the United States: A Path Forward*. Washington, DC: National Academies Press, 2009.

"Neli Latson Pardon." *The Arc*, June 30, 2021. https://thearc.org/resource/neli-latson-pardon/.

Ng, Shelley. "'F—all of You!': Ohio Teen Psycho T.J. Lane Gives the Finger and Smirks as He Is Sentenced to Life for Shooting Rampage that Left Three Chardon High School Students Dead." *New York Daily News*, September 11, 2014. www.nydailynews.com/news/national/ohio-teen-faces-life-prison-shooting-rampage-left-high-school-students-dead-article-1.1292702.

Overly, Steven, Delece Smith-Barrow, Katy O'Donnell, and Ming Li. "Washington Was an Icon of Black Political Power. Then Came Gentrification." *Politico Magazine*, April 15, 2022. www.politico.com/news/magazine/2022/04/15/washington-dc-gentrification-black-political-power-00024515.

Park, Robert E., and Ernest W. Burgess. *The City: Heritage of Sociology Series*. Chicago: University of Chicago Press, 2019 (1925).

Pfaff, John. *Locked In: The True Causes of Mass Incarceration and How to Achieve Real Reform*. New York: Basic Books, 2017.

Pfeiffer, Sacha. "A Terrible Thing to Waste." *The Boston Globe*, October 18, 2018. https://apps.bostonglobe.com/spotlight/gladiator/cte/.

Rabuy, Bernadette, and Daniel Kopf. "Prisons of Poverty: Uncovering the Pre-Incarceration Incomes of the Imprisoned." *Prison Policy Initiative*, July 9, 2015. www.prisonpolicy.org/reports/income.html.

"Racial and Ethnic Disparities in Correctional Facilities." Infographic, *Prison Policy Initiative*. Accessed April 18, 2022. www.prisonpolicy.org/profiles/US.html#disparities.

Raine, Adrian, Peter H. Venables, and Sarnoff A. Mednick. "Low Resting Heart Rate at Age 3 Years Predisposes to Aggression at Age 11 Years: Evidence from the Mauritius Child Health Project." *Journal of the American Academy of Child & Adolescent Psychiatry* 36, no. 10 (October 1997): 1457–64. https://psycnet.apa.org/doi/10.1097/00004583-199710000-00029.

Rattan, Aneeta, Cynthia S. Levine, Carol S. Dweck, and Jennifer L. Eberhardt. "Race and the Fragility of the Legal Distinction between Juveniles and Adults." *PLOS One* 7, no. 5 (May 2012). https://doi.org/10.1371/journal.pone.0036680.

Read, Tracey. "Chardon High School Shooter T.J. Lane Sentenced to Life Without Parole in Ohio Courtroom." *The Times Herald*, March 19, 2013. www.timesherald.com/2013/03/19/chardon-high-school-shooter-tj-lane-sentenced-to-life-without-parole-in-ohio-courtroom/.

Regoli, Robert M., John D. Hewitt, and Matt DeLisi. *Delinquency in Society: The Essentials*. 5th ed. Boston: McGraw-Hill, 2003.

Roberts, Dorothy. "Race." In *The 1619 Project: A New Origin Story*, edited by Nikole Hannah-Jones, Caitlin Rober, Ilena Silverman, and Jake Silverstein, 45–61. New York: One World, 2021.

Robson, Ruthann. *Lesbian (Out) Law: Survival Under the Rule of Law*. Ithaca, NY: Firebrand Books, 1992.

Rowe, David C. *Biology and Crime*. 2nd ed. Los Angeles: Roxbury Publishing Company, 2002.

Ryan, Erin. "Telling it from the Mountain: A Rhetorical Analysis of Fannie Lou Hamer's Speech before the Democratic National Convention." *Young Scholars in Writing* 11 (September 2014): 80–85. https://youngscholarsinwriting.org/index.php/ysiw/article/view/173.

Saito, Yuriko. *Everyday Aesthetics*. Oxford, UK: Oxford University Press, 2007.

Sbardone, Robert J. "The Executive Functions of the Brain." In *Neuropsychological Assessment in Clinical Practice: A Guide to Test Interpretation and Integration*, edited by Gary Groth-Marnat, 437–56. New York: John Wiley & Sons, 2000.

Schatz, Samson J. "Interrogated with Intellectual Disabilities: The Risks of False Confession." *Stanford Law Review* 70, no. 2 (February 2018): 643–90. https://ssrn.com/abstract=3056103.

Schram, Pamela J., and Stephen G. Tibbetts. *Introduction to Criminology: Why Do they Do It?* 3rd ed. Thousand Oaks, CA: SAGE Publications, 2021.

Scommegna, Paola. "Parents' Imprisonment Linked to Children's Health, Behavioral Problems." *Population Reference Bureau* (December 2014). https://www.prb.org/resources/parents-imprisonment-linked-to-childrens-health-behavioral-problems/

Sealock, Mirriam D., and Sally S. Simpson. "Unraveling Bias in Arrest Decisions: The Role of Juvenile Offender Type-Scripts." *Justice Quarterly* 15 (September 1998): 427–57. https://doi.org/10.1080/07418829800093831.

Shannon, Sarah K. S., Christopher Uggen, Jason Schnittker, Melissa Thompson, Sara Wakefield, and Michael Massoglia. "The Growth, Scope, and Spatial Distribution of People with Felony Records in the United States, 1948–2010." *Demography* 54 (2017): 1795–818. https://doi.org/10.1007/s13524-017-0611-1.

Shaver, Katherine. "D.C. Has the Highest 'Intensity' of Gentrification of Any U.S. City, Study Says." *The Washington Post*, March 19, 2019. www.washingtonpost.com/transportation/2019/03/19/study-dc-has-had-highest-intensity-gentrification-any-us-city/.

Shaw, Clifford R., and Henry D. McKay. "Juvenile Delinquency and Urban Areas." In *Understanding Deviance: Connecting Classical and Contemporary Perspectives*, edited by Tammy L. Anderson, 106–27. New York: Routledge, 2014.

Shlafer, Rebecca J., Tyler Reedy, and Laurel Davis. "School-Based Outcomes Among Youth with Incarcerated Parents: Differences by School Setting." *Journal of School Health* 87, no. 9 (September 2017): 687–95. https://doi.org/10.1111/josh.12539.

Shover, Neal. *Aging Criminals*. Beverly Hills: Sage Publications, 1985.

Siegel, Larry J. *Criminology: Theories, Patterns, and Typologies*. 12th ed. Boston: Cengage Learning, 2016.

"Solitary Confinement in New Hampshire: A Report of the New Hampshire Advisory Committee to the US Commission on Civil Rights." April 2021. www.usccr.gov/files/2021/04-26-New-Hampshire-Advisory-Committee-Report-Solitary-Confinement.pdf.

Solomon, Akiba, ed. "The Language Project." *The Marshall Project*. www.themarshallproject.org/2021/04/12/the-language-project.

Southall, Ashley. "Officer Faces Discipline 5 Years After Killing Mentally Ill Woman." *New York Times*, October 4, 2021. www.nytimes.com/2021/10/04/nyregion/nypd-killing-mental-illness.html.

"Student Arrests in Allegheny County Public Schools: The Need for Transparency and Accountability." *ACLU of Pennsylvania* (January 2022). www.aclupa.org/en/publications/student-arrests-allegheny-county-schools-need-transparency-and-accountability.

Subramanian, Ram, Léon Digard, Melvin Washington II, and Stephanie Sorage. *In the Shadows: A Review of the Research on Plea Bargaining*. New York: The Vera Institute of Justice, September 2020. www.vera.org/downloads/publications/in-the-shadows-plea-bargaining.pdf.

Sung, Hung-En, and Linda Richter. "Rational Choice and Environmental Deterrence in the Retention of Mandated Drug Abuse Treatment Clients." *International Journal of Offender Therapy and Comparative Criminology* 51, no. 6 (January 2008): 686–702. http://dx.doi.org/10.1177/0306624X07299226.

Tamayo-Sarver, Joshua H., Susan W. Hinze, Rita K. Cydulka, and David W. Baker. "Racial and Ethnic Disparities in Emergency Department Analgesic Prescription." *American Journal of Public Health* 93, no. 12 (December 2003): 2067–73. https://doi.org/10.2105/ajph.93.12.2067.

Tang, Michael H., Kristen S. Hill, Alexy Arauz Boudreau, Recai Yucel, James Perrin, and Karen A. Kuhlthau. "Medicaid Managed Care and the Unmet Need for Mental Health Care among Children with Special Health Care Needs." *Health Services Research* 43, no. 3 (July 2008): 882–900. http://dx.doi.org/10.1111/j.1475-6773.2007.00811.x.

Thompson, Vilissa. "Understanding the Policing of Black, Disabled Bodies." *Center for American Progress*, February 10, 2021. www.americanprogress.org/article/understanding-policing-black-disabled-bodies/.

Tiihonen, Jari, Pirjo Halonen, Laura Tiihonen, Hannu Kautiainen, Markus Storvik, and James Callaway. "The Association of Ambient Temperature and Violent Crime." *Scientific Reports* 7, no. 1 (December 2017): 1–7. http://dx.doi.org/10.1038/s41598-017-06720-z.

Tomas, Jan. "Pecos County Jury Gives Death Sentence in Arson-Murder Case." *San Angelo Standard Times*, August 6, 1987.

Trawalter, Sophie, Kelly M. Hoffman, and Adam Waytz. "Racial Bias in Perceptions of Others' Pain." *PLOS ONE* 7, no. 11 (November 2012). https://doi.org/10.1371/journal.pone.0048546.

Tunnell, Kenneth D. *Living Off Crime*. 2nd ed. Lanham, MD: Rowman & Littlefield Publishers, 2006.

Vallas, Rebecca. "Disabled Behind Bars." Center for American Progress, July 18, 2016. www.americanprogress.org/article/disabled-behind-bars/.

Vargas, Theresa. "Neli Latson Is—Finally—Free. It Only Took 11 Years, Two Governors and a National Conversation about Race and Disability." *Washington Post*, June 23, 2021. www.washingtonpost.com/local/neli-latson-black-autistic-free/2021/06/23/1024d4e4-d446-11eb-a53a-3b5450fdca7a_story.html.

Wake Forest University Baptist Medical Center. "Violence Is a Learned Behavior, Say Researchers at Wake Forest University." *Science Daily*, November 9, 2000. www.sciencedaily.com/releases/2000/11/001106061128.htm.

Wallace, Rodrick. "Expanding Coupled Shock Fronts of Urban Decay and Criminal Behavior: How U.S. Cities are Becoming 'Hollowed Out.'" *Journal of Quantitative Criminology* 7, no. 4 (December 1991): 333–56. www.jstor.org/stable/23365772.

Walser, Adam. "Officers Accused of Inmate Beating Which Left Woman Paralyzed Not Charged Nearly 3 Years Later." *ABC Action News*, April 14, 2022. www.abcactionnews.com/news/local-news/i-team-investigates/officers-accused-of-inmate-beating-which-left-woman-paralyzed-not-charged-nearly-3-years-later.

Walsh, Anthony. *Biosocial Criminology: Introduction and Integration*. Cincinnati, OH: Anderson Publishing Company, 2002.

Ward, David A., Mark C. Stafford, and Louis N. Gray. "Rational Choice, Deterrence, and Theoretical Integration." *Journal of Applied Social Psychology* 36, no. 3 (March 2006): 571–85. http://dx.doi.org/10.1111/j.0021-9029.2006.00061.x.

Warren, Jared S., Philip L. Nelson, Sasha A. Mondragon, Scott A. Baldwin, and Gary M. Burlingame. "Youth Psychotherapy Change Trajectories and Outcomes in Usual Care: Community Mental Health Versus Managed Care Settings." *Journal of Consulting and Clinical Psychology* 78, no. 2 (April 2010): 144–55. https://doi.org/10.1037/a0018544.

Webster, Cheryl Marie, Anthony N. Doob, and Franklin E. Zimring. "Proposition 8 and Crime Rates in California: The Case of the Disappearing Deterrent." *Criminology & Public Policy* 5, no. 3 (August 2006): 417–48. http://dx.doi.org/10.1111/j.1745-9133.2006.00401.x.

Weiser, Benjamin. "Kalief Browder's Suicide Brought Changes to Rikers. Now It Has Led to a $3 Million Settlement." *New York Times*, January 24, 2019. www.nytimes.com/2019/01/24/nyregion/kalief-browder-settlement-lawsuit.html.

"When Cops Rape: Daniel Holtzclaw & the Vulnerability of Black Women to Police Abuse." *Democracy Now!* December 15, 2015. www.democracynow.org/2015/12/15/daniel_holtzclaw_convicted_of_serial_rape.

White, Monica. "'A Pig and a Garden': Fannie Lou Hamer and the Freedom Farms Cooperative." *Food and Foodways* 25, no. 1 (February 2017): 20–39. https://doi.org/10.1080/07409710.2017.1270647.

Widom, Cathy Spatz. "Long-Term Impact of Childhood Abuse and Neglect on Crime and Violence." *Clinical Psychology: Science and Practice* 24, no. 2 (April 2017): 186–202. https://psycnet.apa.org/doi/10.1037/h0101743.

Wilson, James Q., and Richard J. Herrnstein. *Crime and Human Nature*. New York: Simon and Schuster, 1985.

Worrall, John L. "Reconsidering the Relationship Between Welfare Spending and Serious Crime: A Panel Data Analysis with Implications for Social Support Theory." *Justice Quarterly* 22, no. 3 (September 2005): 364–91. https://doi.org/10.1080/07418820500219094.

Wright, John Paul, and Danielle Boisvert. "What Biosocial Criminology Offers Criminology." *Criminal Justice and Behavior* 36, no. 11 (2009): 1228–40.

INDEX

Note: Page numbers followed by 'n' indicate a note.